How to Start a Business in New York

Third Edition

Paul W. Barnard

Mark Warda

Attorneys at Law

SPHINX® PUBLISHING
AN IMPRINT OF SOURCEBOOKS, INC.®
NAPERVILLE, ILLINOIS
www.SphinxLegal.com

Third Edition, 2005

Published by: Sphinx® Publishing, A Division of Sourcebooks, Inc.®

Naperville Office
P.O. Box 4410
Naperville, Illinois 60567-4410
630-961-3900
Fax: 630-961-2168
www.sourcebooks.com
www.SphinxLegal.com

This publication is designed to provide accurate and authoritative information in regard to the subject matter covered. It is sold with the understanding that the publisher is not engaged in rendering legal, accounting, or other professional service. If legal advice or other expert assistance is required, the services of a competent professional person should be sought.

From a Declaration of Principles Jointly Adopted by a Committee of the
American Bar Association and a Committee of Publishers and Associations

This product is not a substitute for legal advice.

Disclaimer required by Texas statutes.

Library of Congress Cataloging-in-Publication Data
Barnard, Paul W., 1954-
   How to start a business in New York / by Paul W. Bernard and Mark Warda.--
3rd ed.
      p. cm.
   Includes index.
   ISBN 1-57248-469-1 (alk. paper)
   1. Business law--New York (State) 2. Business enterprises--Law and
legislation--New York (State)--Popular works. I. Warda, Mark. II. Title.
KFN5084.B87B37 2004
346.747'065--dc22
                                    2005004761

Printed and Bound in the United States of America
DR — 10 9 8 7 6 5 4 3 2 1

CONTENTS

USING SELF-HELP LAW BOOKS

Before using a self-help law book, you should realize the advantages and disadvantages of doing your own legal work and understand the challenges and diligence that this requires.

The Growing Trend

Rest assured that you won't be the first or only person handling your own legal matter. For example, in some states, more than seventy-five percent of the people in divorces and other cases represent themselves. Because of the high cost of legal services, this is a major trend and many courts are struggling to make it easier for people to represent themselves. However, some courts are not happy with people who do not use attorneys and refuse to help them in any way. For some, the attitude is, "Go to the law library and figure it out for yourself."

We write and publish self-help law books to give people an alternative to the often complicated and confusing legal books found in most law libraries. We have made the explanations of the law as simple and easy to understand as possible. Of course, unlike an attorney advising an individual client, we cannot cover every conceivable possibility.

Cost/Value Analysis

Whenever you shop for a product or service, you are faced with various levels of quality and price. In deciding what product or service to buy, you make a cost/value analysis on the basis of your willingness to pay and the quality you desire.

When buying a car, you decide whether you want transportation, comfort, status, or sex appeal. Accordingly, you decide among such choices as a Neon, a Lincoln, a Rolls Royce, or a Porsche. Before making a decision, you usually weigh the merits of each option against the cost.

When you get a headache, you can take a pain reliever (such as aspirin) or visit a medical specialist for a neurological examination. Given this choice, most people, of course, take a pain reliever, since it costs only pennies; whereas a medical examination costs hundreds of dollars and takes a lot of time. This is usually a logical choice because it is rare to need anything more than a pain reliever for a headache. But in some cases, a headache may indicate a brain tumor and failing to see a specialist right away can result in complications. Should everyone with a headache go to a specialist? Of course not, but people treating their own illnesses must realize that they are betting on the basis of their cost/value analysis of the situation. They are taking the most logical option.

The same cost/value analysis must be made when deciding to do one's own legal work. Many legal situations are very straight forward, requiring a simple form and no complicated analysis. Anyone with a little intelligence and a book of instructions can handle the matter without outside help.

But there is always the chance that complications are involved that only an attorney would notice. To simplify the law into a book like this, several legal cases often must be condensed into a single sentence or paragraph. Otherwise, the book would be several hundred pages long and too complicated for most people. However, this simplification necessarily leaves out many details and nuances that would apply to special or unusual situations. Also, there are many ways to interpret most legal questions. Your case may come before a judge who disagrees with the analysis of our authors.

Therefore, in deciding to use a self-help law book and to do your own legal work, you must realize that you are making a cost/value analysis. You have decided that the money you will save in doing it yourself outweighs the chance that your case will not turn out to your satisfaction. Most people handling their own simple legal matters never have a problem, but occasionally people find that it ended up costing them more to have an attorney straighten out the situation than it would have if they had hired an attorney in the beginning. Keep this in mind while handling your case, and be sure to consult an attorney if you feel you might need further guidance.

Local Rules   The next thing to remember is that a book which covers the law for the entire nation, or even for an entire state, cannot possibly include every procedural difference of every jurisdiction. Whenever possible, we provide the exact form needed; however, in some areas, each county, or even each judge, may require unique forms and procedures. In our state books, our forms usually cover the majority of counties in the state, or provide examples of the type of form which will be required. In our national books, our forms are sometimes even more general in nature but are designed to give a good idea of the type of form that will be needed in most locations. Nonetheless, keep in mind that your state, county, or judge may have a requirement, or use a form, that is not included in this book.

You should not necessarily expect to be able to get all of the information and resources you need solely from within the pages of this book. This book will serve as your guide, giving you specific information whenever possible and helping you to find out what else you will need to know. This is just like if you decided to build your own backyard deck. You might purchase a book on how to build decks. However, such a book would not include the building codes and permit requirements of every city, town, county, and township in the nation; nor would it include the lumber, nails, saws, hammers, and other materials and tools you would need to actually build the deck. You would use the book as your guide, and then do some work and research involving such matters as whether you need a permit of some kind, what type and grade of wood are available in your area, whether to use hand tools or power tools, and how to use those tools.

Before using the forms in a book like this, you should check with your court clerk to see if there are any local rules of which you should be aware, or local forms you will need to use. Often, such forms will require the same information as the forms in the book but are merely laid out differently or use slightly different language. They will sometimes require additional information.

Changes in the Law   Besides being subject to local rules and practices, the law is subject to change at any time. The courts and the legislatures of all fifty states are constantly revising the laws. It is possible that while you are reading this book, some aspect of the law is being changed.

In most cases, the change will be of minimal significance. A form will be redesigned, additional information will be required, or a waiting period will be extended. As a result, you might need to revise a form, file an extra form, or wait out a longer time period; these types of changes will not usually affect the outcome of your case. On the other hand, sometimes a major part of the law is changed, the entire law in a particular area is rewritten, or a case that was the basis of a central legal point is overruled. In such instances, your entire ability to pursue your case may be impaired.

INTRODUCTION

Each year in New York State tens of thousands of new corporations are established and thousands more partnerships and proprietorships open for business. New York has always been a place of great opportunity. New York City, with its millions of citizens, is a thriving, trend-setting center of activity where little shops can bloom into expansive enterprises. New York's other cities and towns, large and small, also offer many opportunities.

The best way to take advantage of these opportunities is to run your own business, be your own boss, and be as successful as you dare to be. However, if you do not follow New York's laws dealing with setting up a business your progress can be slowed—or stopped—by government fines, civil judgments, or even criminal penalties.

This book is intended to give you the framework for legally starting a business in New York State. It also includes information on where to find special rules for each type of business. If you have problems that are not covered by this book, you should seek out an attorney.

You should read through this entire book, rather than skipping to the parts that look most important, in order to cover all of the aspects of any business you are thinking of starting. There are many laws that may not sound like they apply to you, but which have provisions that will affect your business.

In recent years, the government bureaucracies have been amending and lengthening their forms regularly. The forms included in this book are the most recent available at the time of publication. It is possible that some may have been revised by the time you read this book, but in most cases they will be similar and require the same information. Up-to-date forms are always available on the Internet, at a local legal stationary store, the Internal Revenue Service office, or from the New York Secretary of State's office in Albany.

I DECIDING TO START A BUSINESS

If you are reading this book, then you have probably made a serious decision to take the plunge and start your own business. You need to know why some succeed while others fail. Knowledge can only help your chances of success. Some of what follows may seem obvious, but to someone wrapped up in a new business idea, some of this information is occasionally overlooked.

Know Your Strengths

You should consider all the skills and knowledge that running a successful business needs and decide if you have what it takes. If you do not, it does not necessarily mean you are doomed to be an employee all your life. Perhaps you just need a partner who has the skills you lack. You can also hire the skills you need or structure your business to avoid areas where you are weak. If those suggestions do not work, maybe you can learn the skills you are lacking.

For example, if you are not good at dealing with employees (either you are too passive and get taken advantage of or too tough and scare them off), you can:

✪ handle product development yourself and have a partner or manager deal with employees;

✪ take seminars in employee management; or,

✪ structure your business so that you do not need employees. Either use independent contractors or set yourself up as an independent contractor.

Here are some of the factors to consider when planning your business.

✪ If it takes months or years before your business turns a profit, do you have the resources to hold out? (Businesses have gone under or been sold just before they were about to take off.)

✪ Are you willing to put in a lot of overtime to make your business a success? (Owners of businesses do not set their own hours, the businesses set the hours for the owners. Many business owners work long hours seven days a week, but they enjoy running their business more than family picnics or fishing.)

✪ Are you willing to do the dirtiest or most unpleasant work of the business? (Emergencies come up and employees are not always dependable. You might need to mop up a flooded room, spend a weekend stuffing ten thousand envelopes, or work Christmas if someone calls in sick.)

✪ Do you know enough about the product or service? Are you aware of the trends in the industry and what changes new technology might bring?

✪ Do you know enough about accounting and inventory to manage the business? Do you have a good *head for business*? (Some people naturally know how to save money and do things profitably, while others are in the habit of buying the best and the most expensive of everything. The latter can be fatal to a struggling new business.)

✪ Are you good at managing employees?

✪ Do you know how to sell your product or service? (You can have the best product on the market but people *do not* beat a path to your door. If you are a wholesaler, shelf space in major stores is hard to get—especially for a new company without a track record, a large line of products, or a large advertising budget.)

✪ Do you know enough about getting publicity? (The media receive thousands of press releases and announcements each day and most are thrown away. Do not count on free publicity to put your name in front of the public.)

Know Your Business

You need the experience of working in a business as well as the concept of a business. Maybe you always dreamed of running a bed and breakfast or having your own pizza place. Have you ever worked in such a business? If not, you may have no idea of the day-to-day headaches and problems of the business. Do you really know how much to allow for theft, spoilage, and unhappy customers?

You might feel silly taking an entry level job at a pizza place when you would rather start your own, but it might be the most valuable preparation you could have. A few weeks of seeing how a business operates could mean the difference between success and failure in your new business.

Working in a business as an employee is one of the best ways to be a success at running such a business. New people with new ideas who work in older industries have been known to revolutionize them with obvious improvements that no one before dared to try.

Do the Math

Conventional wisdom says you need a business plan before committing yourself to a new venture, but many businesses are started successfully without one. The owner has a great concept, puts it on the market, and it takes off. But you at least need to do some basic calculations to see if the business can make a profit. The following are some examples.

✪ If you want to start a retail shop, figure out how many people are close enough to become customers and how many other stores will be competing for those customers. Visit some of those other shops and see how busy they are. Without giving away your plans to compete, ask some general questions like *How is business?* Maybe they will share their frustrations or successes.

✪ Whether you sell a good or a service, find out how much profit is possible. For example, if you plan to start a house painting company, find out what you will have to pay to hire painters; what it will cost you for all of the insurance, bonding, and licensing you will need; and, what the advertising will cost. Figure out how many jobs you can do per month and what other painters are charging.

✪ Find out if there is a demand for your product or service. Suppose you have designed a beautiful new kind of candle and your friends all say you should open a shop because *everyone will want them.* Before making a hundred of them and renting a store, bring a few to craft shows or flea markets and see what happens.

✪ Figure out what the income and expenses would be for a typical month of your new business. List monthly expenses such as rent, salaries, utilities, insurance, taxes, supplies, advertising, services, and other overhead. Then figure out how much profit you will average from each sale. Next, figure out how many sales you will need to cover your overhead and then divide by the number of business days in the month. Can you reasonably expect that many sales? How will you get those sales?

Most types of businesses have trade associations, which often have figures on the profitability of its members. Some even have start-up kits for people wanting to start businesses. One good source of information on such organizations is the *Encyclopedia of Associations* published by Gale Research Co. It is available in many library reference sections. Producers of products to the trade often give assistance to small companies getting started to win their loyalty. Contact the largest suppliers of the products your business will be using and see if they can be of help.

Sources of Further Guidance

The following offices offer free or low-cost guidance to new businesses.

Service Corps of Retired Executives is a nonprofit group of retired people who volunteer to give guidance to businesses. Its website, **www.score.org**, offers multiple resources for a new business. You can also contact a local chapter at one of the following locations.

Auburn SCORE
c/o Chamber of Commerce
30 South Street
Auburn, NY 13021
315-252-7291

Bay Shore SCORE Office
c/o Astoria Federal Savings
300 East Main Street
Bay Shore, NY 11706
631-666-4642

Brookhaven SCORE Chapter
1 Independence Hill, 3rd Floor
Farmingville, New York 11738
631-451-6563

Brooklyn Public Library
280 Cadman Plaza West
Brooklyn, NY 11201
718-722-3325

Buffalo Niagara SCORE
Federal Building
111 West Huron Street, Room 1311
Buffalo, NY 14202
716-551-4301

Carmel SCORE Office
Putnam County Economic
  Development
34 Gleneida Avenue
Carmel, NY 10512
914-628-5553

Chautauqua Region SCORE
c/o Jamestown Chamber
  of Commerce
101 West Fifth Street
Jamestown, NY 14701
716-484-1101

Chemung SCORE
c/o SBA
333 East Water Street, 4th Floor
Elmira, NY 14901
607-734-3358

Clinton, Franklin, Essex
7061 Route 9
Plattsburgh, NY 12901
518-563-1000

Dover Plains SCORE Office
First National Bank, Mill Street
Dover Plains, NY 12522
914-454-1700

Dutchess SCORE
c/o Chamber of Commerce
1 Civic Center Plaza
Poughkeepsie, NY 12601
845-454-1700

Dutchess SCORE Chapter
c/o Chamber of Commerce
110 Main Street
Poughkeepsie, NY 12601
914-454-1700

East Meadow SCORE Office
East Meadow Public Library
1886 Front Street
East Meadow, NY 11554
516-571-3303

Fishkill SCORE Office
Southern Dutchess Chamber
300 Westgate Business Center
Fishkill, NY 12524
914-897-2067

Glen Cove SCORE Office
Glen Cove City Hall
9 Glen Street
Glen Cove, NY 11542
516-676-2004

Harlem SCORE Office
BRISC, 290 Lenox Avenue
New York, NY 10027
212-876-2246

Hempstead SCORE Office
Hempstead Public Library
115 Nichols Ct.
Hempstead, NY 11550
516-571-3303

Huntington SCORE Chapter
c/o Chamber of Commerce
151 W. Carver Street
Huntington, NY 11743
631-423-6100

Kingston SCORE Office
Business Resource Center
One Development Court
Kingston, NY 12401
914-687-5035

Long Beach SCORE Office
Long Beach Chamber of Commerce
350 National Blvd.
Long Beach, NY 11561
516-432-6100

Mahopac SCORE Office
Chamber of Commerce
925 South Lake Boulevard
Mahopac, NY 10541
914-628-5553

Melville SCORE Office
35 Pinelawn Road
Suite 207W
Melville, NY 11747
631-454-0771

Monroe SCORE Office
Chamber of Commerce
562 Route 17M
Monroe, NY 10950
914-782-2007

Monticello SCORE Office
Sullivan County Chamber
198 Bridgeville Road
Monticello, NY 12701
914-794-2212

Mount Vernon SCORE Office
Chamber of Commerce
4 North 7th Avenue
Mount Vernon, NY 10550
914-667-7500

Nassau County SCORE Chapter
Department of Commerce &
  Industry
400 County Seat Drive, Room 140
Mineola, NY 11501
516-571-3303

New Paltz SCORE Office
Chamber of Commerce
257½ Main Street
New Paltz, NY 12561
914-255-0253

New Rochelle SCORE Office
Chamber of Commerce
557 Main Street
New Rochelle, NY 10801
914-632-5700

New York Public Library SBIL
188 Madison Avenue
New York, NY 10016
212-592-7033

New York SCORE Chapter
26 Federal Plaza, Room 3100
New York, NY 10278
212-264-4507

Newburgh SCORE Office
Chamber of Commerce
47 Grand Street
Newburgh, NY 12550
914-562-5100

Northeast SCORE
Albany Col. Chamber of Commerce
1 Computer Drive South
Albany, NY 12205
518-446-1118

Orange County SCORE Chapter
c/o Chamber of Commerce
40 Matthews Street, Suite 103
Goshen, NY 10924
914-294-8080

Peekskill SCORE Office
Chamber of Commerce
South Division Street
Peekskill, NY 10566
914-737-3600

Port Jervis SCORE Office
Tri-State Chamber of Commerce
10 Sussex Street
Port Jervis, NY 12771
914-856-6694

Poughkeepsie SCORE Office
Business Development Center
3 Neptune Road
Poughkeepsie, NY 12601
914-454-1700

Queens County SCORE Chapter
120-55 Queens Blvd
Room 333
Queens Borough Hall
Kew Gardens, NY 11424
718-263-8961

Red Hook SCORE Office
Pawling Savings Bank
137 South Broadway
Red Hook, NY 12571
914-454-1700

Rochester SCORE
601 Keating Federal Building
100 State Street
Room 410
Rochester, NY 14614
585-263-6473

S Tier Binghamton SCORE
49 Court Street,
  Metro Center/2nd Floor
Binghamton, NY 13902
607-772-8860

Smithtown SCORE Office
Smithtown Chamber of Commerce
1 W. Main Street
Suite 5
Smithtown, NY 11787
631-979-8069

Staten Island SCORE Office
Independence Bank
1550 Richmond Road
Staten Island, NY 10306
718-351-4500, ext. 47

Suffolk County SCORE Chapter
Riverhead Town Hall
Main Conference Center
200 Howell Avenue
Riverhead, NY 11901
631-727-3200, ext. 200

Syracuse SCORE
401 S. Salina Street, 5th Floor
Syracuse, NY 13202
315-471-9393, ext. 221

Ulster County SCORE Chapter
Ulster County Community College
Clinton Building
Room 102
Stone Ridge, NY 12484
914-687-5035

Ulster SCORE
Business Resource Center
One Development Court
Room 101
Kingston, NY 12401
845-339-0468

Utica SCORE
SUNY Institute of Technology
Route 12
Utica, NY 13504
315-792-7553

Watertown SCORE
518 Davidson Street
Watertown, NY 13601
315-788-1200

West Nyack SCORE Office
Chamber of Commerce
180 West Nyack Road
West Nyack, NY 10994
914-353-2936

Westchester SCORE Chapter
350 Main Street
White Plains, NY 10601
914-948-3907

Yonkers SCORE Office
Chamber of Commerce
20 South Broadway, #1207
Yonkers, NY 110701
914-963-0332

2

CHOOSING THE FORM OF YOUR BUSINESS

An important decision that needs to be made at the outset is the choice of legal structure for your business. There are numerous factors that will need to be considered to make the correct decision for your particular business. The most important consideration is that the corporate form will limit your liability for business debts and adverse judgments solely to the corporate assets as opposed to your own personal assets.

Basic Forms of Doing Business

The five most popular forms for a business in New York State are sole proprietorship, partnership, corporation, limited partnership, and limited liability company. The characteristics, advantages, and disadvantages of each are as follows.

Sole Proprietorship

Characteristics. A sole proprietorship is one person doing business in his or her own name or under a *fictitious* name.

Advantages. A sole proprietorship has simplicity. Plus, there is no organizational expense and no extra tax forms or reports.

Disadvantages. The proprietor is personally liable for all debts and obligations. Also, there is no continuation of the business after death. All profits are directly taxable, certainly a disadvantage for the proprietor, and business affairs are easily mixed with personal affairs.

Partnership   *Characteristics.* A general partnership involves two or more people carrying on a business together—normally pursuant to a partnership agreement—and sharing the profits and losses.

Advantages. Partners can combine expertise and assets. A general partnership also allows liability to be spread among more people. The business can be continued after the death of a partner if bought out by the surviving partner.

Disadvantages. Each partner is liable for acts of other partners within the scope of the business. This means that if your partner harms a customer or signs a million-dollar credit line in the partnership name, you can be held personally liable. Even if left in the business, all profits are taxable. Control is shared by all parties and the death of a partner may result in liquidation. In a general partnership, it is often difficult to get rid of a bad partner.

Corporation   *Characteristics:* A corporation is an artificial, legal *person* that carries on business through its officers for its shareholders. (In New York State one person may form a corporation and be the sole shareholder and officer.) Laws covering corporations are contained in the *New York Business Corporation Law* and the *New York Not-for-Profit Corporation Law.*

An *S corporation* is a corporation that has filed IRS Form 2553, choosing to have all its profits taxed to the shareholders, rather than to the corporation. An S corporation files a tax return but pays no federal or state tax. The profit shown on the S corporation tax return is reported on the owners' tax returns.

A *C corporation* is any corporation that has not elected to be taxed as an S corporation. A C corporation pays income tax on its profits. As a result, when dividends are paid to shareholders, they are taxed twice—once by the corporation and once on the income of the shareholders. In New York, a C corporation must also pay corporate franchise taxes.

A *professional service corporation* is a corporation formed by a professional such as a doctor or accountant. New York has special rules for professional service corporations that differ slightly from those of other corporations. These are included in Article 15 of the *Business Corporation Law*. There are also special tax rules for professional service corporations.

A *nonprofit corporation* is usually used for charitable organizations, churches, and condominium associations. However, with careful planning some types of businesses can be set up as nonprofit corporations and save a fortune in taxes. While a nonprofit corporation cannot pay dividends, it can pay its officers and employees fair salaries. Some of the major American nonprofit organizations pay their officers well over $100,000 a year. New York's rules for nonprofit corporations are included in a special statute known as the *Not-for-Profit Corporation Law*.

Advantages: If properly organized, a corporation has a number of advantages over other forms of business, including:

- ✪ shareholders have no liability for corporate debts and lawsuits;

- ✪ officers usually have no personal liability for their corporate acts;

- ✪ the existence of a corporation may be perpetual;

- ✪ there is prestige in owning a corporation; and,

- ✪ capital may be raised by issuing stock. It is easy to transfer ownership upon death.

There are tax advantages allowed only to corporations. For example, a small corporation can be set up as an S corporation to avoid corporate taxes but still retain corporate advantages. Some types of businesses can be set up as nonprofit corporations, which provide significant tax savings.

Disadvantages:

- ✪ There are start-up costs for forming a corporation.

- ✪ There are certain formalities such as annual meetings, separate bank accounts, and tax forms.

- ✪ Unless a corporation registers as an S corporation it must pay federal income tax separate from the tax paid by the owners, and must pay New York income and franchise taxes.

Limited Partnership

Characteristics. A limited partnership has characteristics similar to both a corporation and a partnership. There are *general partners* who have the control and liability and there are *limited partners* who only put up money and whose liability is limited to what they paid for their share of the partnership (like corporate stock).

Advantages. Capital can be contributed by limited partners who have no control of the business or liability for its debts.

Disadvantages. High start-up costs are a great disadvantage. Also, an extensive partnership agreement is required because general partners are personally liable for partnership debts and for each other's acts. (One solution to this problem is to use a corporation as the general partner.)

Limited Liability Company

Characteristics: A limited liability company is like a limited partnership without general partners. It has characteristics of both a corporation and a partnership. None of the partners have personal liability and all can have some control. New York also provides for professional service limited liability companies.

Advantages: The limited liability company offers the tax benefits of a partnership with the protection from liability of a corporation. It offers more tax benefits than an S corporation because it may pass through more depreciation and deductions. It may have different classes of ownership, an unlimited number of members, and may have aliens as members. It is similar to a Latin-American *Limitada* or a German *GmbH & Co. K.G.* Additional rules apply if the limited liability company derives any income from New York City.

Disadvantages: There are start-up costs and limited liability companies must pay New York corporate franchise taxes. Because the limited liability company is a fairly new way of doing business, there may not be a lot of answers to legal questions that may come up. (However, the courts will probably rely on corporation and limited partnership law.)

Choosing the Right Form of Business

The selection of a form of doing business is best made with the advice of an accountant and an attorney. If your business is selling harmless objects by mail, a proprietorship would be the easiest way to get started. However, if you own a taxi service, it would be important to incorporate to avoid losing your personal assets if one of your drivers were to injure someone in an accident and the damages exceeded your insurance.

If you can expect a high cash buildup the first year, a corporation may be the best way to keep taxes low. If you expect the usual start-up losses, then a , partnership, or S corporation would probably be best.

Start-Up Procedures

Each form of business has its own start-up procedures.

Proprietorship   All accounts and licenses are taken in the name of the owner. See Chapter 3 for information about using a fictitious name.

Partnership   A written agreement should be prepared to spell out the rights and obligations of the parties. You can have this drawn up by a lawyer or can write it up yourself. There are a number of books on the market that can help you write a partnership agreement. Check your bookstore or library. See Chapter 3 for information about using a fictitious name for your partnership.

Corporation   Articles of Incorporation must be filed with the Secretary of State in Albany along with $170 in filing fees and taxes on shares of stock being issued. A formal organizational meeting is then held. At the organizational meeting, officers are elected, stock is issued, and other formalities are complied with to avoid the corporate entity being set aside later as a *shell*. Licenses and accounts are titled in the name of the corporation.

Limited Partnership   A written limited partnership certificate must be drawn up and filed with the county clerk in the county in which the principal office of the partnership is located. Also, notice of this filing must be published in two local newspapers. Because of the complexity of securities laws and the criminal penalties for violation, you may want to have an attorney organize a limited partnership.

Limited Liability Company   Two or more persons may form a limited liability company by filing Articles of Organization and a limited liability company certificate with the Secretary of State in Albany. Licenses and accounts are titled in the name of the company.

Business Start-Up Checklist

☐ Make your plan
  ☐ Obtain and read all relevant publications on your type of business
  ☐ Obtain and read all laws and regulations affecting your business
  ☐ Calculate whether your plan will produce a profit
  ☐ Plan your sources of capital
  ☐ Plan your sources of goods or services
  ☐ Plan your marketing efforts
☐ Choose your business name
  ☐ Check other business names and trademarks
  ☐ Register your name, trademark, etc.
☐ Choose the business form
  ☐ Prepare and file organizational papers
  ☐ Prepare and file fictitious name if necessary
☐ Choose the location
  ☐ Check competitors
  ☐ Check zoning
☐ Obtain necessary licenses
  ☐ City   ☐ State
  ☐ County   ☐ Federal
☐ Choose a bank
  ☐ Checking
  ☐ Credit card processing
  ☐ Loans
☐ Obtain necessary insurance
  ☐ Workers' Comp   ☐ Automobile
  ☐ Liability   ☐ Health
  ☐ Hazard   ☐ Life/disability
☐ File necessary federal tax registrations
☐ File necessary state tax registrations
☐ Set up a bookkeeping system
☐ Plan your hiring
  ☐ Obtain required posters
  ☐ Obtain or prepare employment application
  ☐ Obtain new hire tax forms
  ☐ Prepare employment policies
  ☐ Determine compliance with health and safety laws
☐ Plan your opening
  ☐ Obtain all necessary equipment and supplies
  ☐ Obtain all necessary inventory
  ☐ Do all necessary marketing and publicity
  ☐ Obtain all necessary forms and agreements
  ☐ Prepare your company policies on refunds, exchanges, returns

Business Comparison Chart

	Sole Proprietorship	General Partnership	Limited Partnership	Limited Liability Co.	Corporation C or S	Nonprofit Corporation
Liability Protection	No	No	For limited partners	For all members	For all shareholders	For all members
Taxes	Pass through	Pass through	Pass through	Pass through	S corps. pass through C corps. pay tax	None on income—Employees pay on wages
Minimum # of members	1	2	2	1	1	3
Startup fee	None	$100	$125	$285	$145	$75
Annual fee	None	None	None	None	None	None
Diff. classes of ownership	No	Yes	Yes	Yes	S corps. No C corps. Yes	No ownership Diff. classes of membership
Survives after Death	No	No	Yes	Yes	Yes	Yes
Best for	1 person low-risk business or no assets	low-risk business	low-risk business with silent partners	All types of businesses	All types of businesses	Educational

3 REGISTERING THE NAME OF YOUR BUSINESS

The name of a business can be very important. For some businesses, the single greatest asset that the business has may be its name. Companies spend billions of dollars each year on advertising in an effort to enhance the public's awareness of their names. Often, as a business matures, the name will attract business because it is associated with quality and good practices.

Preliminary Considerations

Before deciding on a name for your business, be sure that it is not already being used by someone else. Many business owners have spent thousands of dollars on publicity and printing only to throw it all away because another company owned the name. A company that owns a name can take you to court and force you to stop using that name. It can also sue you for damages if it thinks your use of the name caused it a financial loss.

Even if you will be running a small local shop with no plans for expansion, check if the name has been trademarked. If someone else is using the same name anywhere in the country and has registered it as a federal trademark, they can sue you. If you plan to expand or to deal nationally, do a thorough search of the name.

The first places to look are the local phone books and official records of your county. Next, you should check with the Secretary of State's office in Albany to see if someone has registered a fictitious name or corporate name the same as, or confusingly similar to, the one you have chosen. There is a $30 search fee.

To do a national search, you should check trade directories and phone books of major cities. These can be found at many libraries and are usually reference books which cannot be checked out. The *Trade Names Directory,* published by Gale Research Co., is a two volume set of names compiled from many sources.

Using the Internet, you can search all of the Yellow Page listings in the U.S. at a number of sites for no charge. One website, **www.yellowpages.com**, offers free searches of Yellow Pages for all states at once.

To be sure that your use of the name does not violate someone else's trademark rights, have a trademark search done in the United States Patent and Trademark Office. In the past, this required a visit to their offices or the hiring of a search, which can cost over a hundred dollars. Now, the USPTO trademark records can be searched online at:

www.uspto.gov

If you do not have access to the Internet you might be able to perform a search at a public library or to have one of its employees order an online search for you for a small fee. If this is not available to you, you can have the search done through a firm. One such firm is:

Government Liaison Services, Inc.
200 N. Glebe Road, Suite 321
Arlington, VA 22203

The firm can be reached at 800-642-6564. It also offers searches of hundreds of sources.

No matter how thorough your search is, there is no guarantee that there is not a local user somewhere with rights to the mark. If, for example, you register a name for a new chain of restaurants and later find out that someone in Tucumcari, New Mexico has been using the name longer than you, that person will still have the right to use the name, but just in his or her local area. If you do not want his or her restaurant to cause confusion with your chain, you can try to buy him or her out. Similarly, if you are operating a small business under a unique name and a law firm in New York writes and offers to buy the right to your name, you can assume that some large corporation wants to start a major expansion under that name.

The best way to make sure a name you are using is not already owned by someone else is to make up a name. Such names as Xerox, Kodak, and Exxon were made up and didn't have any meaning prior to their use. Remember that there are millions of businesses and even something you make up may already be in use. It is safer to do a search anyway.

Assumed Names

In New York, as in most states, unless you do business in your own legal name or operate as a corporation, you must register the name you are using. The name must be registered with the county clerk in the county of the principal office of the business. Assumed corporate names that are different from the actual corporate name must also be filed, but these must be with the Secretary of State in Albany.

It is a misdemeanor to fail to register an assumed name. If you fail to register, you may not sue anyone as your business will not be recognized. If someone sues you and you are not registered, they may be entitled to attorney's fees and court costs, in addition to any other remedies they may seek.

If your name is *John Doe* and you are operating a masonry business, you may operate your business as *John Doe, Mason* without registering it. But any other use of a name should be registered, such as:

Doe Masonry	Doe Masonry Company
Doe Company	Empire State Masonry

If you are forming a partnership you must register your fictitious name and the fact that you are a partnership.

You cannot use the words, *corporation, incorporated, corp.,* or *Inc.* unless you are forming a corporation. Corporations do not have to register the name they are using unless it is different from their registered corporate name. (*New York General Business Law*, Sec. 130(1) & (1-a).)

When you use a fictitious name, you are *doing business as* (d/b/a) whatever fictitious name you are using. Legally, you would use the name *John Doe d/b/a Doe Masonry*.

To carry on a business under an assumed name, a person must file a certificate that states the name of the business and the names and addresses of its people involved. (see form 2, p.197.)

As discussed previously, you should do some research to see whether the name you intend to use is already being used by anyone else. Even if the name you wish to use is not registered, someone else may have legal rights to the name through use.

Some businesses and professions have special requirements for registration of their fictitious names. See Chapter 3 for a list of state regulated professions with references to the laws that apply to them.

Corporate Names

A corporation has a legal name and does not have to register a fictitious name unless it is different from the legal corporate name. The name of a corporation must contain one of the following words.

Incorporated	Corp.
Inc.	Limited
Corporation	Ltd.

It is not advisable for a corporation to use only the word *Company* or *Co.* because unincorporated businesses also use these words, and a person dealing with the corporation might not realize it is incorporated. If this happens, the corporate officers might end up with personal liability for corporate debts. You can use a combination of two of the words, such as *ABC Co., Inc.*

If the name of the corporation does not contain one of the above words, it will be rejected by the Secretary of State. It will also be rejected if the name is already taken or is too similar to the name of another corporation. This is why a name search should be conducted as the first step in incorporating.

If a name you pick is taken by another company, you may be able to change it slightly and have it accepted. For example, if there is already a Tri-City Upholstery, Inc., and it is in a different county, you may be allowed to use Tri-City Upholstery of Albany County, Inc.

Warning: If your name is similar to another corporation's name, even if this is approved by the Secretary of State, you might get sued by the other company under trademark law if your business is close to theirs or there is a likelihood of confusion in the use of the name.

To find out if the name you want is available, call the Secretary of State at 518-474-0050. As previously mentioned, there are companies you may employ to deal with the Secretary of State for a name search.

Once you have chosen a corporate name and know it is available, you should immediately complete all the papers that are needed in order to incorporate. There are companies that complete the incorporation process for you, which can be very helpful at this stage. They provide you with a corporate kit and guide you through the procedure. These services generally start around $300, plus filing fees, depending upon the number and kind of shares you want to issue. A name can be reserved for only a limited time, so it is important to file your papers promptly.

Do not order any printing of corporate stationary, business cards, and so on until your corporate papers are returned to you. Sometimes a name is approved over the phone and rejected when sent in.

If a corporation wants to do business under a name other than its corporate name, it can register a fictitious name such as *Doe Corporation d/b/a Doe Industries.* (see form 1, p.195.) But if the fictitious name leads people to believe that the business is not a corporation, the right to limited liability may be lost. If such a name is used it should always be accompanied by the corporate name.

Professional Service Corporations

Professional service corporations are corporations formed by professionals such as attorneys, doctors, dentists, and architects. Under New York law, a professional service corporation must use the words *professional corporation* or the abbreviation *P.C.*

Domain Names

With the Internet being so new and changing so rapidly, all of the rules for Internet names have not yet been worked out. Originally, the first person to reserve a name owned it, and enterprising souls bought up the names of most of the *Fortune 500* corporations and held them for ransom. Then a few of the corporations went to court and the rule was developed that if a company had a trademark for a name, that company could stop someone else from using it as a domain name.

You cannot yet get a trademark merely for using a domain name. Trademarks are granted for the use of a name in commerce. Once you have a valid trademark, you will be safe in using it for your domain name.

In the next few years there will probably be several changes to the domain name system to make it more flexible and useful throughout the world. One proposed change is the addition of more *top level domains* (TLDs), which are the last parts of the names, like *com* and *gov*.

The following TLDs are either available now or will be soon:

aero	coop	llc	school
agent	family	llp	scifi
arts	free	love	shop
auction	game	ltd	soc
biz	golf	med	sport
bz	inc	mp3	tech
cc	info	museum	travel
chat	kids	names	tv
church	kids.us	nu	us
club	law	pro	video
			xxx

If you wish to protect your domain name the best thing to do at this point is to get a trademark for it. To do this you would have to use it on your goods or services. (See Chapter 9 for more information on domain names and the Internet.)

Trademarks

As your business builds goodwill, its name will become more valuable and you will want to protect it from others who may wish to copy it. To protect a name used to describe your goods or services you can register it as a trademark (for goods) or a service mark (for services), with either the Secretary of State of the State of New York or with the United States Patent and Trademark Office.

You cannot obtain a trademark for the name of a business, but you can trademark the name you use on goods and services. In most cases a company name is used on its goods as a trademark, so it, in effect, protects the company name. Another way to protect the company name is to incorporate. A particular corporate name can only be registered by one company in New York.

State registration would be useful if you only expect to use your trademark within the state of New York. Federal registration protects a mark anywhere in the country. The registration of a mark gives you exclusive use of the mark for the types of goods for which you register it. The only exception is persons who have already been using the mark. You cannot stop people who have been using the mark prior to your registration.

State Registration

The procedure for state registration is simple and the cost is $50. Call the New York Department of State at 518-473-2492 to ask them to search the name you would like to use and to request that they send you a registration form for filing the trademark. This is similar to what you did for your business name, but could include any name you are trying to trademark. After receipt of the form and the fee, a name search is conducted. For questions about filing the application, call the New York Department of State at the number listed above.

Before a mark can be registered, it must be used in New York. For goods this means it must be used on the goods themselves, or on containers, tags, labels, or displays of the goods. For services, it must be used in the sale or advertising of the services. The use must be in an actual transaction with a customer.

The registration is good for ten years. Six months prior to its expiration, it must be renewed. The renewal fee is $50 for each class of goods.

A sample filled-in form for a New York trademark can be found in Appendix B A blank application to register a trademark is in Appendix C. (see form 3, p.199.) (A blank application to register a service mark is in Appendix C. (see form 4, p.205.))

Federal Registration

For federal registration, the procedure is a little more complicated. There are two types of applications, depending on whether you have already made *actual use* of the mark or whether you merely have an *intention to use* the mark in the future.

For a trademark that has been in use, you must file an application form along with specimens showing actual use and a drawing of the mark that complies with all of the rules of the United States Patent and Trademark Office.

For an intent to use application, you must file two separate forms: one when you make the initial application and the other after you have made actual use of the mark, along with the specimens and drawing.

Before a mark can be entitled to federal registration, the use of the mark must be in *interstate commerce*, or in commerce with another country. The fee for registration is $335, but if you file an *intent to use* application, there is a second fee of $100 for the filing after actual use.

4 FINANCING YOUR BUSINESS

The way to finance your business is determined by how quickly you would like your business to grow and how much risk of failure you are willing to handle. Letting the business grow with its own income is the slowest but safest way to grow. Taking out a personal loan against your house to expand quickly is the fastest but riskiest way to grow.

Growing with Profits

Many successful businesses have started out with little money and used the profits to grow larger. If you have another source of income to live on (such as a job or a spouse) you can plow all the income of your fledgling business into growth.

Some businesses start as hobbies or part-time ventures on the weekend while the entrepreneur holds down a full-time job. Many types of goods or service businesses start this way. Even some multi-million dollar corporations, such as *Apple Computer*, started out this way.

This allows you to test your idea with little risk. If you find you are not good at running that type of business, or the time or location was not right for your idea, all you are out is the time you spent and your start-up capital.

However, a business can only grow so big from its own income. In many cases, as a business grows, it gets to a point in which the orders are so big that money must be borrowed to produce the product to fill them. With this kind of order, there is the risk that if the customer cannot pay or goes bankrupt, the business will also go under. At such a point, a business owner should investigate the credit worthiness of the customer and weigh the risks. Some businesses have grown rapidly, some have gone under, and others have decided not to take the risk and stayed small. You can worry about that down the road.

Using Your Savings

One of the best sources of money to fund the start of your business is often your personal savings. You will not have to pay high interest rates and you will not have to worry about paying someone back.

Home Equity   If you have owned your home for several years, it is possible that the equity has grown substantially and you can get a second mortgage to finance your business. If you have been in the home for many years and have a good record of paying your bills, some lenders will make second mortgages that exceed the equity. Just remember—if your business fails, you may lose your house.

Retirement Accounts   Be careful about borrowing from your retirement savings. There are tax penalties for borrowing from or against certain types of retirement accounts. Also, your future financial security may be lost if your business does not succeed.

Having too much Money   It probably does not seem possible to have too much money with which to start a business, but many businesses have failed for that reason. With plenty of start-up capital available, a business owner does not need to watch expenses and can become wasteful. Employees get used to lavish spending. Once the money runs out and the business must run on its own earnings, it fails. Many *dot.com* start-ups recently faced this problem and failed.

Starting with the bare minimum forces a business to watch its expenses and be frugal. It necessitates finding the least expensive solutions to problems that arise and creative ways to be productive.

Borrowing Money

It is extremely tempting to look to others to get the money to start a business. The risk of failure is less worrisome and the pressure is lower, but that is a problem with borrowing. If it is others' money, you may not have the same incentive to succeed as you would if everything you own is on the line.

You should be even more concerned when using the money of others. Your reputation should be more valuable than the money, which can always be replaced. Yet that is not always the case. Many people borrow again and again from their parents for failed business ventures.

Family Depending on how much money your family can spare, it may be the most comfortable or most uncomfortable source of funds. If you have been assured a large inheritance and your parents have more funds than they need to live on, you may be able to borrow against your inheritance without worry. It will be your money anyway, and you need it much more now than you will ten or twenty or more years from now. If you lose it all, it is your own loss.

However, if you are borrowing your widowed mother's only source of income or asking her to cash in a CD she lives on to finance your get-rich-quick scheme, you should have second thoughts about it. Stop and consider all the real reasons your business might not take off and what your mother would do without the income.

Friends Borrowing from friends is like borrowing from family members. If you know they have the funds available and could survive a loss, you may want to risk it. If they would be loaning you their only resources, do not chance it.

Financial problems can be the worst thing for a relationship, whether it is a casual friendship or a long-term romantic involvement. Before you borrow from a friend, try to imagine what would happen if you could not pay it back and how you would feel if it caused the end of your relationship.

The ideal situation is if your friend were a co-venturer in your business and the burden would not be totally on you to see how the funds were spent. Still, realize that such a venture will put extra strain on the relationship.

Banks　　A bank may be a more comfortable party from which to borrow money, because you do not have a personal relationship with it like you do with a friend or family member. If you fail, the bank will write your loan off rather than disown you. But a bank can also be the least comfortable party to borrow from because it will demand realistic projections and be on top of you to perform. If you do not meet the bank's expectations, it may call your loan just when you need it most.

The best thing about a bank loan is that it will require you to do your homework. You must have plans that make sense to a banker. If your loan is approved, you know that your plans are at least reasonable.

Bank loans are not cheap or easy. You will be paying interest and you will have to put up collateral. If your business does not have equipment or receivables, the bank may require you to put up your house and other personal property to guarantee the loan.

Banks are a little easier to deal with when you get a *Small Business Administration* (SBA) loan. That is because the SBA guarantees that it will pay the bank if you default on the loan. SBA loans are obtained through local bank branches.

Credit Cards　　Borrowing against a credit card is one of the fastest growing ways of financing a business, but it can be one of the most expensive ways. The rates can go higher than twenty percent. However, some cards offer lower rates and many people are able to get numerous cards. Some successful businesses have used the partners' credit cards to get off the ground or to weather through a cash crunch, but if the business does not begin to generate the cash to make the payments, you could soon end up in bankruptcy. A good strategy is to use credit cards only for a long-term asset, like a computer, or for something that will quickly generate cash, like buying inventory to fill an order. Do not use credit cards to pay expenses that are not generating revenue.

Getting a Rich Partner

One of the best business combinations is a young entrepreneur with ideas and ambition and a retired investor with business experience and money. Together they can supply everything the business needs.

How can you find such a partner? Be creative. You should have investigated the business you are starting and know others who have been in such businesses. Have any of them had partners retire over the last few years? Are any of them planning to phase out of the business?

Selling Shares of Your Business

Silent investors are one of the the best sources of capital for your business. You retain full control of the business, and if it happens to fail, you have no obligation to them. Unfortunately, few silent investors are interested in a new business. It is only after you have proven your concept to be successful and built up a rather large enterprise that you will be able to attract such investors.

The most common way to obtain money from investors is to issue stock to them. For this, the best type of business entity is the corporation. It gives you almost unlimited flexibility in the number and kinds of shares of stock you can issue.

Understanding Securities Laws

There is one major problem with selling stock, partnership, or membership interests in your business—there are many federal and state regulations with which you must comply. Both the state and federal governments have long and complicated laws dealing with the sales of *securities*. There are also hundreds of court cases attempting to explain what these laws mean. A thorough explanation of this area of law is obviously beyond the scope of this book.

Basically, securities have been held to exist in any case in which a person provides money to someone with the expectation that he or she will get a profit through the efforts of that person. This can apply to any situation where someone buys stock in or makes a loan to your business. What the laws require is disclosure of the risks involved and in some cases, registration of the securities with the government. There are some exemptions, such as for small amounts of money and for limited numbers of investors.

Penalties for violation of securities laws are severe, including triple damages and prison terms. Consult a specialist in securities laws before issuing any security. You can often get an introductory consultation at a reasonable rate to learn your options.

Using the Internet to Find Capital

The Internet does have some sources of capital listed. The following sites may be helpful.

America's Business Funding Directory
www.businessfinance.com

U.S. Small Business Administration (SBA)
www.sba.gov/financing

NVST
www.nvst.com

The Capital Network
www.thecapitalnetwork.com

Before attempting to market your company's shares on the Internet, be sure to get an opinion from a securities lawyer.

5 | LOCATING YOUR BUSINESS

The right location for your business will be determined by what type of business it is and how fast you expect to grow. For some types of businesses, the location will not be important to your success or failure. In others it will be crucial.

Working Out of Your Home

Many small businesses get started out of the home. Chapter 6 discusses the legalities of home businesses. This section discusses the practicalities.

Starting a business out of your home can save you the rent, electricity, insurance, and other costs of setting up at another location. For some people this is ideal. They can combine their home and work duties easily and efficiently. For other people it is a disaster. Spouses, children, neighbors, television, and household chores can be so distracting that no other work gets done.

Since residential telephone rates are usually lower than business lines, many people use their residential telephone line to conduct business or add a second residential line. However, if you wish to be listed in the Yellow Pages, you will need to have a business line in your home. If you are running two or more types of businesses, you can probably add their names as additional listings on the original number and avoid paying for another business line.

You also should consider whether the type of business you are starting is compatible with a home office. For example, if your business mostly consists of making phone calls or calling clients, then the home may be an ideal place to run it. If your clients need to visit you or you will need daily pickups and deliveries by truck, then the home may not be a good location. (This is discussed in more detail in Chapter 6.)

Choosing a Retail Site

For most types of retail stores, the location is of prime importance. Such things to consider are how close it is to your potential customers, how visible it is to the public, and how easily accessible it is to both autos and pedestrians. The attractiveness and safety should also be considered.

Location would be less important for a business that was the only one of its kind in the area. For example, if there was only one moped parts dealer or Armenian restaurant in a metropolitan area, people would have to come to wherever you are if they want your products or services. However, even with such businesses, keep in mind that there is competition. People who want moped parts can order them by mail and restaurant customers can choose another type of cuisine.

Look up all the businesses similar to the one you plan to run in the phone book and mark them on a map. For some businesses, such as a cleaners, you would want to be far from the others. For other businesses, such as antique stores, you would want to be near the others that are similar. (Antique stores usually do not carry the same things, therefore they do not compete, and people like to go to an *antique district* and visit all the shops.)

Choosing Office, Manufacturing, or Warehouse Space

If your business will be the type in which customers will not come to you, then locating it near customers is not as much of a concern. You can probably save money by locating away from the high traffic central business districts. However, you should consider the convenience for employees and not locate in an area that would be unattractive to them or too far from where they would likely live.

For manufacturing or warehouse operations, consider your proximity to a post office, trucking company, or rail line. Where several sites are available, you might consider which one has the earliest or most convenient pick-up schedule for the carriers you plan to use.

Leasing a Site

A lease of space can be one of the biggest expenses of a small business, so do a lot of homework before signing one. There are a lot of terms in a commercial lease that can make or break your business. These are the most critical.

Zoning Before signing a lease, be sure that everything your business will need to do is allowed by the zoning of the property. Your county zoning board can explain what is and is not allowed for how your property is zoned.

Restrictions In some shopping centers, existing tenants have guarantees that other tenants do not compete with them. For example, if you plan to open a restaurant and bakery, you may be forbidden to sell carry out baked goods if the supermarket next door has a bakery and a noncompete clause.

Signs Business signs are regulated by zoning laws, sign laws, and property restrictions. If you rent a hidden location with no possibility for adequate signage, your business will have a lot smaller chance of success than with a more visible site or much larger sign.

ADA Compliance   The *Americans with Disabilities Act* (ADA) requires that reasonable accommodations be made to make businesses accessible to the handicapped. When a business is remodeled, many more changes are required than if no remodeling is done. When renting space you should be sure that it complies with the law or that the landlord will be responsible for compliance. Be aware of the full costs you will bear.

Expansion   As your business grows, you may need to expand your space. The time to find out about your options is before you sign the lease. Perhaps you can take over adjoining units when those leases expire.

Renewal   Location is a key to success for some businesses. If you spend five years building up a clientele, you do not want someone to take over your locale at the end of your lease. Therefore, you should have a renewal clause on your lease. This usually allows an increase in rent based on inflation.

Guaranty   Most landlords of commercial space will not rent to a small corporation without a personal guaranty of the lease. This is a very risky thing for a new business owner to do. The lifetime rent on a long-term commercial lease can be hundreds of thousands of dollars. If your business fails, the last thing you want to do is be personally responsible for five years of rent.

Where space is scarce or a location is hot, a landlord can get the guaranties he or she demands and there is nothing you can do about it (except perhaps set up an asset protection plan ahead of time). But where several units are vacant or the commercial rental market is soft, you can often negotiate out of the personal guaranty. If the lease is five years, maybe you can get away with a guaranty of just the first year.

Duty to Open   Some shopping centers have rules requiring all shops to be open certain hours. If you cannot afford to staff it the whole time required or if you have religious or other reasons that make this a problem, negotiate it out of the lease or find another location.

Sublease   At some point you may decide to sell your business, and in many cases the location is the most valuable aspect of it. For this reason you should be sure that you have the right to either assign your lease or to sublease the property. If this is impossible, one way around a prohibition is to incorporate your business before signing the lease, and then when you sell the business, sell the stock. Some lease clauses prohibit transfer of *any interest* in the business, so read the lease carefully.

Buying a Site

If you are experienced with owning rental property, you will probably be more inclined to buy a site for your business. If you have no experience with real estate, you should probably rent and not take on the extra cost and responsibility of property ownership.

One reason to buy your site is that you can build up equity. Rather than pay rent to a landlord, you can pay off a mortgage and eventually own the property.

Separating the Ownership

One risk in buying a business site is that if the business gets into financial trouble, the creditors may go after the building as well. For this reason most people who buy a site for their business keep the ownership out of the business.

> **Example:** The business will be a corporation and the real estate will be owned personally by the owner or by a trust unrelated to the business.

Expansion

Before buying a site, consider the growth potential of your business. If it grows quickly, will you be able to expand at that site or will you have to move? Might the property next door be available for sale in the future if you need it? Can you get an option on it?

If the site is a good investment whether or not you have your business, then by all means, buy it. But if its main use is for your business, think twice.

Zoning

Some of the concerns when buying a site are the same as when renting. You will want to make sure that the zoning permits the type of business you wish to start or that you can get a variance without a large expense or delay. Be aware that just because a business is now using the site does not mean that you can expand or remodel the business at that site. Check with the zoning department and find out exactly what is allowed.

Signs

Signs are another concern. Some cities have regulated signs and do not allow new or larger ones. Some businesses have used these laws to get publicity. A car dealer who was told to take down a large number of American flags on his lot filed a federal lawsuit and the community rallied behind him.

ADA Compliance ADA compliance is another concern when buying a commercial building. Find out from the building department if the building is in compliance or what needs to be done to put it in compliance. If you remodel, the requirements may be more strict.

NOTE: *When dealing with public officials, keep in mind that they do not always know what the law is or do not accurately explain it. They occasionally try to intimidate people into doing things that are not required by law. Read the requirements yourself and question the officials if they seem to be interpreting it wrong. Seek legal advice if officials refuse to reexamine the law or move away from an erroneous position.*

Also consider that keeping them happy may be worth the price. If you are already doing something they have overlooked, do not make a big deal over a little thing they want changed or they may subject you to a full inspection or audit.

Checking Government Regulations

When looking for a site for your business, investigate the different government regulations in your area. For example, a location just outside the city or county limits might have a lower licensing fee, a lower sales tax rate, and less strict sign requirements.

6 | LICENSING YOUR BUSINESS

The federal and state legislatures and local governments have an interest in protecting consumers from bad business practices. Therefore, in order to ensure that consumers are protected from unscrupulous business people and to require a minimum level of service to the public, the federal, state, and local governments have developed hundreds of licensing requirements that cover occupations and services ranging from attorneys to barbers to day care providers and hundreds of others.

Occupational Licenses and Zoning

After deciding the form of business (corporation, partnership, etc.) and after all necessary filings and other formalities, you must next find out, before actually beginning operations, what other special requirements exist within the particular village, town, or city in which you wish to operate. There may also be county requirements. For example, all municipalities require a *Certificate of Occupancy* for the building in which you are doing business.

The *Certificate of Occupancy* may contain restrictions on what activities may be done in the building. Some may have other requirements, such as a sign permit or some form of occupational license. Contact the local village, town, or city hall, and the county clerk's office to find out what other licenses, permits, etc., will be needed.

Also, you will have to make sure that the local zoning ordinance permits the type of business you want to run. It is not enough to say that you are in a commercial zone. Many commercial zones specify the particular type of business permitted. Again, you must check with the local municipal office. Businesses that do work in several municipalities, such as builders, must obtain a license from each municipality in which they do work.

Whatever licenses or permits are necessary can be obtained from the local municipal office. For example, city licenses are usually available at city hall. Be sure to find out whether zoning allows your type of business before buying or leasing property. The licensing departments will check the zoning before issuing your license.

If you will be preparing or serving food, you will need to check with the local health department to be sure that the premises comply with the health code. This will involve a detailed inspection by the local health authorities.

Home Business   Problems occasionally arise when someone attempts to start a business in their home. New small businesses cannot always afford to pay rent for commercial space and cities often try to forbid business in residential areas. Getting a county occupational license or advertising a fictitious name often gives notice to the city that a business is being conducted in a residential area.

Some people avoid the problem by starting their businesses without occupational licenses, figuring that the penalties are less expensive than the cost of office space. Others get the county license and ignore the city rules. If a person has commercial trucks and equipment all over his or her property, there will probably be complaints from neighbors and the city will probably take legal action. But if a person's business consists merely of making phone calls out of the home and keeping supplies there, the problem may never come up.

If a problem does arise regarding a home business that does not disturb the neighbors, a good argument can be made that the zoning law that prohibits the business is unconstitutional. But court battles with a city are expensive and probably not worth the effort for a small business. The best course of action is to keep a low profile. Using a post office box is sometimes helpful in diverting attention away from the residence.

State Regulated Professions

Many professionals require special state licenses and/or special exams. You will probably be called upon to produce such a license when applying for a license to do business.

If you are in a regulated profession you should be aware of the laws that apply to your profession. The following pages contain a list of professions and the state laws covering them. You can make copies of these laws at your local public library or county law library. If you do not think your profession is regulated, you should read through the list anyway. Some of those included may surprise you.

Regulated Professions in New York and the Governing Statutes

Citations are to McKinney's Consolidated Laws of New York.

Accountancy	Education Law Art. 149
Acupuncture	Education Law Art. 160
Aircraft, Pilots, and Airports	General Business Law Art. 14
Architecture and Landscape Architecture	Education Law Art. 147
Athletic Trainers	Education Law Art. 162
Attorneys (including mandatory continued legal education)	Judiciary Law Sec. 460
Auctioneers	Town Law Sec. 136, 137
Barbering	General Business Law Art. 28
Cable TV companies	Public Service Law Art. 11
Cemeteries	Various Laws in Town Law & Village Law
Chiropractic	Education Law Art. 132

Clinical Social Workers	Education Law Art. 154
Cosmetology and Hair Styling	General Business Law Art. 27
Counseling and Psychotherapy	Education Law Art. 153
Dentistry (including mandatory continued education)	Education Law Art. 133
Dieticians and Nutritionists	Education Law Art. 157
Driving Schools	Education Law Art. 17
Electrical Contracting	Public Service Law Art. 4
Engineering	Education Law Art. 145
Funeral Directing, Embalmery and Direct Disp.	Public Health Law Art. 34
Geologists and Gas Stations	Environmental Conservation Law Art. 23
Hearing Aid Sales	General Business Law Art. 37-A
Interior Design	Education Law Art. 161
Land Surveying	Education Law Art. 145
Landscape Architects	Education Law Art. 148
Massage Practice	Education Law Art. 155
Medical Doctors	Education Law Art. 131
Midwifery	Education Law Art. 140
Mortgage Brokers	Banking Law Art. 12D
Motion Picture Operators	General City Law Sec. 18
Nursing	Education Law Art. 139
Nursing Homes	Public Health Law Art. 28-D
Occupational Therapists	Education Law Art. 156
Opthamology	Education Law Art. 144
Opticians	Education Law Art. 143
Optometry	Education Law Art. 143
Osteopathy	Education Law Sec. 6524
Pest Control	Environmental Conservation Law Art. 33
Pharmacy	Education Law Art. 137
Plumbing	General City Law Art. 4
Podiatry	Education Law Art. 141
Physical Therapy	Education Law Art. 136
Physician Assistants	Education Law Art. 131-B
Private Investigative Services	General Business Law Art. 7
Psychological Services	Education Law Art. 153
Radiologic Technologists	Public Health Law Sec. 3503
Real Estate Brokerage, Sales and Schools	Real Property Law Art. 12-A
Respiratory Therapists	Education Law Part 164

Restaurants	Town Law Sec. 136, 137
Sanitariums	General City Sec. 20
Second-hand watches	General Business Law Sec. 392
Septic Tank Contracting	General Environmental
	Conservation Law Art. 40
Speech Pathology and Audiology	Education Law Art. 159
Telegraph & Telephone companies	Public Service Law Art. 5
Telemarketing	General Business Law Sec. 399-P
Veterinary Medicine	Education Law Art. 135

Federal Licenses

There are few businesses that require federal registration. If you are in any of the types of businesses listed below, you should check with the federal agency below it.

Radio or television stations or manufacturers of equipment emitting radio waves:

Federal Communications Commission
445 12th Street, SW
Washington, DC 20554
www.fcc.gov

Manufacturers of alcohol, tobacco, firearms, or explosives:

Bureau of Alcohol, Tobacco, Firearms and Explosives
Office of Liaison and Public Information
650 Massachusetts Avenue, NW Room 8290
Washington, DC 20226
www.atf.treas.gov

Securities brokers and providers of investment advice:

Securities and Exchange Commission
Fort Worth District Office
801 Cherry Street, 19th Floor
Fort Worth, TX 76102
www.sec.gov

Manufacturers of drugs and processors of meat:

Food and Drug Administration
5600 Fishers Lane
Rockville, MD 20857
www.fda.gov

Interstate carriers:

Surface Transportation Board
1925 K Street, NW
Washington, DC 20423
www.stb.dot.gov

Exporting:

Bureau of Industry and Security
Department of Commerce
14th Street and Constitution Avenue, NW
Washington, DC 20230
www.bxa.doc.gov

7 CONTRACT LAWS

As a business owner, you will need to know the basics of forming a simple contract for your transactions with both customers and vendors. There is a lot of misunderstanding about what the law is and people may give you erroneous information. Relying on it can cost you money. This chapter gives you a quick overview of the principles that apply to your transactions and the pitfalls to avoid. If you face more complicated contract questions, consult a law library or an attorney familiar with small business law.

Traditional Contract Law

One of the first things taught in law school is that a contract is not legal unless three elements are present: *offer*, *acceptance*, and *consideration*. The rest of the semester dissects exactly what may be a valid offer, acceptance, and consideration. For your purposes, the important things to remember are as follows.

✪   If you make an offer to someone, it may result in a binding contract, even if you change your mind or find out it was a bad deal for you.

✪   Unless an offer is accepted and both parties agree to the same terms, there is no contract.

✪ A contract does not always have to be in writing. Some laws require certain contracts to be in writing, but as a general rule an oral contract is legal. The problem is in proving that the contract existed.

✪ Without consideration (the exchange of something of value or mutual promises), there is not a valid contract.

The most important rules for the business owner are as follows.

✪ An advertisement is not an offer. Suppose you put an ad in the newspaper offering *New IBM computers only $1995!* but there is a typo in the ad and it says $19.95? Can people come in and say, *I accept, here's my $19.95*, creating a legal contract? Fortunately, no. Courts have ruled that the ad is not an offer that a person can accept. It is an invitation to come in and make offers, which the business can accept or reject.

✪ The same rule applies to the price tag on an item. If someone switches price tags on your merchandise or if you accidentally put the wrong price on it, you are not required by law to sell it at that price. If you intentionally put the wrong price, you may be liable under the *bait and switch* law. Many merchants honor a mistaken price just because refusing to would constitute bad will and a lost customer.

✪ When a person makes an offer, several things may happen. It may be accepted, creating a legal contract. It may be rejected. It may expire before it has been accepted. Or, it may be withdrawn before acceptance. A contract may expire either by a date made in the offer (*This offer remains open until noon on January 29, 2005*) or after a reasonable amount of time. What is *reasonable* is a legal question that a court must decide. If someone makes you an offer to sell goods, clearly you cannot come back five years later and accept. Can you accept a week later or a month later and create a legal contract? That depends on the type of goods and the circumstances.

✪ A person accepting an offer cannot add any terms to it. If you offer to sell a car for $1,000 and the other party says they accept as long as you put new tires on it, there is no contract. An acceptance with changed terms is considered a rejection and a counteroffer.

✪ When someone rejects your offer and makes a counteroffer, a contract can be created by your acceptance of the counteroffer.

These rules can affect your business on a daily basis. Suppose you offer to sell something to one customer over the phone and five minutes later another customer walks in and offers you more for it. To protect yourself, you should call the first customer and withdraw your offer before accepting the offer of the second customer. If the first customer accepts before you have withdrawn your offer, you may be sued if you sell the item to the second customer.

There are a few exceptions to the basic rules of contracts. They are as follows.

✪ *Consent* to a contract must be voluntary. If it is made under a threat, the contract is not valid. If a business refuses to give a person's car back unless they pay $200 for changing the oil, the customer could probably sue and get the $200 back.

✪ Contracts to do *illegal acts* or acts *against public policy* are not enforceable. If an electrician signs a contract to put some wiring in a house that is not legal, the customer could probably not force him or her to do it because the court would refuse to require an illegal act.

✪ If either party to an offer *dies*, then the offer expires and cannot be accepted by the heirs. If a painter is hired to paint a portrait and dies before completing it, his wife cannot finish it and require payment. However, a corporation does not die, even if its owners die. If a corporation is hired to build a house and the owner dies, his or her heirs may take over the corporation and finish the job and require payment.

✪ Contracts made under *misrepresentation* are not enforceable. For example, if someone tells you a car has 35,000 miles on it and you later discover it has 135,000 miles, you may be able to rescind the contract for fraud and misrepresentation.

✪ If there was a *mutual mistake*, a contract may be rescinded. For example, if both you and the seller thought the car had 35,000 miles on it and both relied on that assumption, the contract could be rescinded. However, if the seller knew the car had 135,000 miles on it, but you assumed it had 35,000 and did not ask, you probably could not rescind the contract.

Statutory Contract Law

The previous section discussed the basics of contract law. These are not stated in the statutes, but are the principles decided by judges hundreds of years ago. In recent times, the legislatures have made numerous exceptions to these principles, and in most cases, these laws have been passed when the legislature felt that traditional law was not fair. The important laws that affect contracts follow.

Statutes of Fraud

The *statutes of fraud* state when a contract must be in writing to be valid. Some people believe a contract is not valid unless it is in writing, but that is not true. Only those types of contracts mentioned in the statutes of fraud must be in writing. Of course, an oral contract is much harder to prove in court than one in writing. In New York, the contracts that must be in writing are found in the *General Obligations Law* (Gen. Oblig. Law). Some of the contracts that must be in writing are:

- ✪ agreements that take over one year to complete (*Gen. Oblig. Law, Sec.5-701*);

- ✪ sales of any interest in real estate (*Gen. Oblig. Law, Sec.5-703*);

- ✪ leases of real estate over one year (*Gen. Oblig. Law, Sec.5-703*);

- ✪ guarantees of debts of another person (*Gen. Oblig. Law, Sec.5-701*);

- ✪ sales of goods of over $500 (*Uniform Commercial Code Secs.1-206 and 2-201*); and,

- ✪ brokerage agreements to obtain a loan or buy or sell real property (*Gen. Oblig. Law, Sec.5-707*).

Plain Language Statute

Every residential lease signed after November 1, 1978 must be written in common, everyday language that is clearly divided and captioned into various logical sections. (*Gen. Oblig. Law, Sec. 5-702.*)

Consumer Protection Laws

Due to the alleged unfair practices by some types of businesses, laws have been passed controlling the types of contracts they may use. Most notable among these are health clubs and door-to-door solicitations. The laws covering these businesses usually give the consumer a certain time to cancel the contract. These laws are described in Chapter 12.

Preparing Your Contracts

Before you open your business, you should obtain or prepare the contracts or policies you will use in your business. In some businesses, such as a restaurant, you will not need much. Perhaps you will want a sign near the entrance stating *shirt and shoes required* or *diners must be seated by 10:30 p.m.*

However, if you are a building contractor or a similar business, you will need detailed contracts to use with your customers. If you do not clearly spell out your rights and obligations, you may end up in court and lose thousands of dollars in profits.

The best way to have an effective contract is to have one prepared by an attorney who is experienced in the subject. However, since this may be too expensive for your new operation, you may want to go elsewhere. Three sources for the contracts you will need are other businesses like yours, trade associations, and legal form books. Obtain as many different contracts as possible, compare them, and decide which terms are most comfortable for you.

8 | INSURANCE LAWS

There are not many laws requiring you to have insurance. However, if you do not have insurance, you may face liability that could ruin your business. You should be aware of the types of insurance available and weigh the risks of a loss against the cost of a policy.

Be aware that there can be a wide range of prices and amounts of coverage in insurance policies. You should get at least three quotes from different insurance agents and ask each one to explain the benefits of his or her policy.

Workers' Compensation

The one form of insurance that is required, if you have any employees, is *workers' compensation insurance*. The term *employee* is specifically defined in Article 1, Section 2 of New York's *Workers' Compensation Law*. You should read this law *carefully* if you think you need to comply with it. For example, part time employees, students, aliens, and illegal workers count as employees. However, under certain conditions, volunteers doing charitable work, real estate agents, officers of a corporation, casual workers, babysitters, and nonprofit amateur athletes are not considered employees. Independent contractors as defined in Section 2 are also not considered employees.

Even if you are not required to have workers' compensation insurance, you may still wish to carry it because it can protect you from litigation.

This insurance can be obtained from most insurance companies and in many cases, it is not expensive. An employer may also:

✪   purchase a policy from the New York State Insurance Fund or

✪   self-insure upon proof of financial security and ability to pay claims.

If you have such coverage, you are protected against suits by employees or their heirs in case of accident and against other potentially ruinous claims.

Failure to provide workers' compensation insurance when required is a serious crime. It could result in a fine of up to $2,500, up to a year in prison, and an injunction against employing anyone. Failure to obtain the insurance within ten days of written notification can result in a fine of $250 per ten day period of noncompliance. If a person is injured on a job, even if another employee caused it or the injured person contributed to his or her own injury, you may be required to pay for all resulting losses.

Also, it is a misdemeanor to deduct the amount of the workers' compensation insurance premiums from an employee's wages.

Notice of coverage *must* be conspicuously posted on a form notice provided by the Workers' Compensation Board. This notice informs employees of what to do in the event of an injury. This law has been subject to frequent change lately so you should check with the New York State Workers' Compensation Board for the latest requirements. Call 518-486-9581 or go online to:

www.web.state.ny.us

Liability Insurance

In most cases, you are not required to carry liability insurance. Liability insurance can be divided into two main areas: coverage for injuries on your premises or by your employees and coverage for injuries caused by your products.

Coverage for the first type of injury is usually very reasonably priced. Injuries in your business or by your employees (such as in an auto accident) are covered by standard premises or auto policies. But coverage for injuries by products may be harder to find and more expensive.

If insurance is unavailable or unaffordable, you can go without and use a corporation and other asset protection devices to protect yourself from liability.

The best way to find out if insurance is available for your type of business is to check with other businesses. If there is a trade group for your industry, their newsletter or magazine may contain ads for insurers.

Umbrella Policy　As a business owner, you will be more visible as a target for lawsuits, even if there is little merit to them. Lawyers know that a *nuisance suit* is often settled for thousands of dollars. Because of your greater exposure, you should consider getting a personal umbrella policy. This is a policy that covers you for claims of up to a certain dollar amount (possibly even two or five million) and is very reasonably priced.

Hazard Insurance

One of the worst things that can happen to your business is a fire, flood, or other disaster. Due to lost customer lists, inventory, and equipment, many businesses have been forced to close after such a disaster.

The premium for hazard insurance is usually reasonable and could protect you from loss of your business. You can even get business interruption insurance, which will cover your losses while your business is getting back on its feet.

Home Business Insurance

There is a special insurance problem for home businesses. Most homeowner and tenant insurance policies do not cover business activities. In fact, under some policies, you may be denied coverage if you use your home for a business.

You probably will not have a problem and will not need extra coverage if you merely use your home to make business phone calls and send letters. If you own equipment or have dedicated a portion of your home exclusively to the business, you could have a problem. Check with your insurance agent for the options that are available to you.

If your business is a sole proprietorship and you have a computer that you use both personally and for your business, it would probably be covered under your homeowners policy. But if you incorporate your business and bought the computer in the name of the corporation, coverage might be denied. It is possible to get a special insurance policy in the company name covering just the computer if it is your main business asset. One company that offers such a policy is Safeware. They can be reached at 800-800-1492. Other specialty insurance may be located on the Internet.

Automobile Insurance

If you or any of your employees will be using an automobile for business purposes, be sure to have this use covered. Sometimes a policy may contain an exclusion for business use. Check to be sure your liability policy covers you if one of your employees causes an accident while running a business errand.

Health Insurance

While new businesses can rarely afford health insurance for their employees, the sooner they can obtain it, the better chance they will have to find and keep good employees. Those starting a business usually need insurance for themselves, and they can sometimes receive a better rate if they obtain a small business package.

Employee Theft

If you fear employees may be able to steal from your business, you may want to have them bonded. This means that you pay an insurance company a premium to guarantee employees' honesty and if they cheat you the insurance company pays you damages. This can cover all existing and new employees.

9 YOUR BUSINESS AND THE INTERNET

The Internet has opened up a world of opportunities for businesses. A few years ago, getting national visibility cost a fortune. Today a business can set up a Web page for a few hundred dollars, and with some clever publicity and a little luck, millions of people around the world will see it.

But this new world has new legal issues and new liabilities. Not all of them have been addressed by laws or by the courts. Before you begin doing business on the Internet, you should know the existing rules and the areas where legal issues exist.

Domain Names

A *domain name* is the address of your website. For example, **www.apple.com** is the domain name of Apple Computer Company. The last part of the domain name, the *.com* (or *dot com*) is the *top level domain*, or TLD. *Dot com* is the most popular, but others are currently available in the United States, including *.net* and *.org*. (Originally, *.net* was only available to network service providers and *.org* only to nonprofit organizations, but regulations have eliminated those requirements.) (See p.22 for a complete list of existing or soon-to-exist TLDs.)

It may seem like most words have been taken as a dot com name, but if you combine two or three short words or abbreviations, a nearly unlimited number of possibilities are available. For example, if you have a business dealing with automobiles, most likely someone has already registered automobile.com and auto.com. But you can come up with all kinds of variations, using adjectives or your name, depending on your type of business. Some examples include:

autos4u.com	joesauto.com	autobob.com
myauto.com	yourauto.com	onlyautos.com
greatauto.com	autosfirst.com	usautos.com
greatautos.com	firstautoworld.com	4autos.com

When the Internet first began, some individuals realized that major corporations would soon want to register their names. Since the registration was easy and cheap, people registered names they thought would ultimately be used by someone else.

At first, some companies paid high fees to buy their names from the registrants. But one company, Intermatic, filed a lawsuit instead of paying. The owner of the mark they wanted had registered numerous trademarks, such as britishairways.com and ussteel.com. The court ruled that since Intermatic owned a trademark on the name, the registration of their name by someone else violated that trademark and that Intermatic was entitled to it.

Since then, people have registered names that are not trademarks, such as CalRipkin.com, and have attempted to charge the individuals with those names to buy their domain. In 1998, Congress stepped in and passed the *Anti-Cybersquatting Consumer Protection Act*. This law makes it illegal to register a domain with no legitimate need to use it.

This law helped a lot of companies protect their names, but then some companies started abusing it and tried to stop legitimate users of similar names. This is especially likely against small companies. One organization that has been set up to help small companies protect their domains is the *Domain Name Rights Coalition*. Its website is:

www.domainnamerights.org

For extensive information on domains, refer to the *Domain Manual* at:

www.domainmanual.com

Registering a domain name for your own business is a simple process. There are many companies that offer registration services. For a list of those companies, visit the site of the *Internet Corporation for Assigned Names and Numbers* (ICANN) at **www.icann.org**. You can link directly to any member's site and compare the costs and registration procedures required for the different top-level domains.

Web Pages

There are many new companies eager to help you set up a website. Some offer turnkey sites for a low flat rate. Custom sites can cost tens of thousands of dollars. If you have plenty of capital, you may want to have your site handled by one of these professionals. However, setting up a website is a fairly simple process, and once you learn the basics, you can handle most of it in-house.

If you are new to the Web, you may want to look at the following sites that will familiarize you with the Internet jargon and give you a basic introduction to the Web:

www.learnthenet.com
www.webopedia.com

Site Set-Up　There are seven steps to setting up a website—purpose, design, content, structure, programming, testing, and publicity. Whether you do it yourself, hire a professional site designer, or use a college student, the steps toward creating an effective site are the same.

Before beginning your own site, look at other sites—including those of major corporations and small businesses. Look at the sites of all the companies that compete with you. Look at hundreds of sites and click through them to see how they work (or do not work).

Purpose. To know what to include on your site, decide what its purpose will be. Do you want to take orders for your products or services, attract new employees, give away samples, or show off your company headquarters? You might want to do several of these things.

Design. After looking at other sites, you can see that there are numerous ways to design a site. It can be crowded or open and airy, it can have several windows (frames) open at once or just one, and it can allow long scrolling or just click-throughs.

You will have to decide whether the site will have text only; text plus photographs and graphics; or, text plus photos, graphics, and other design elements, such as animation or Java script. Additionally, you will begin to make decisions about colors, fonts, and the basic graphic appearance of the site.

Content. You must create the content for your site. For this, you can use your existing promotional materials, you can write new material just for the website, or you can use a combination of the two. Whatever you choose, remember that the written material should be concise, free of errors, and easy for your target audience to read. Any graphics, including photographs, and written materials not created by you require permission. Obtain such permission from the lawful copyright holder in order to use any copyrighted material. Once you know your site's purpose, look, and content, you can begin to piece the site together.

Structure. You must decide how the content (text plus photographs, graphics, animation, etc.) will be structured, what content will be on which page, and how a user will link from one part of the site to another. For example, your first page may have the business name and then choices to click on, such as *about us*, *opportunities*, *product catalog*, etc. Have those choices connect to another page containing the detailed information so that a user will see the catalog when they click on *product catalog*. Or your site could have a choice to click on a link to another website related to yours.

Programming and setup. When you know nothing about setting up a website, it can seem like a daunting task that will require an expert. However, *programming* here means merely putting a site together. There are inexpensive computer programs available that make it very simple.

Commercial programs such as *Microsoft FrontPage, Dreamweaver, Pagemaker, Photoshop, MS Publisher,* and *PageMill* allow you to set up Web pages as easily as laying out a print publication. These programs will convert the text and graphics you create into HTML, the programming language of the Web. Before you choose Web design software and design your site, determine which Web hosting service you will use. Make sure that the design software you use is compatible with the host server's system. The Web host will be the provider who will give you space on their server and who may provide other services to you, such as secure order processing and analysis of your site to see who is visiting and linking to it.

If you have used a page layout program, you can usually get a simple Web page up and running within a day or two. If you do not have much experience with a computer, you might consider hiring a college student to set up a Web page for you.

Testing. Some of the website setup programs allow you to thoroughly check your new site to see if all the pictures are included and all the links are proper. There are also websites you can go to that will check out your site. Some even allow you to improve your site, such as by reducing the size of your graphics so they download faster. Use a major search engine (listed below) to look for companies that can test your site before you launch it on the Web.

Publicity. Once you set up your website, you will want to get people to look at it. *Publicity* means getting your site noticed as much as possible by drawing people to it.

The first thing to do to get noticed is to be sure your site is registered with as many *search engines* as possible. These are pages that people use to find things on the Internet, such as *Yahoo* and *Excite*. They do not automatically know about you just because you created a website. You must tell them about your site, and they must examine and catalog it.

For a fee, there are services that will register your site with numerous search engines. If you are starting out on a shoestring, you can easily do it yourself. While there are hundreds of search engines, most people use a dozen or so of the bigger ones. If your site is in a niche area, such as geneology services, then you would want to be listed on any specific geneology search engines. Most businesses should be mainly concerned with getting on the biggest ones. By far the biggest and most successful search engine today is *Google* (**www.google.com**). Some of the other big ones are:

www.altavista.com	www.infoseek.com
www.dejanews.com	www.lycos.com
www.excite.com	www.netcrawler.com
www.fastsearch.com	www.northernlight.com
www.goto.com	www.webcrawler.com
www.hotbot.com	www.yahoo.com

Most of these sites have a place to click to *add your site* to their system.

There are sites that rate the search engines, help you list on the search engines, or check to see if you are listed. One site is:

www.searchiq.com

A *meta tag* is an invisible subject word added to your site that can be found by a search engine. For example, if you are a pest control company, you may want to list all of the scientific names of the pests you control and all of the treatments you have available—but you may not need them to be part of the visual design of your site. List these words as meta tags when you set up your page so people searching for those words will find your site.

Some companies thought that a clever way to get viewers would be to use commonly searched names, or names of major competitors, as meta tags to attract people looking for those big companies. For example, a small delivery service that has nothing to do with UPS or FedEx might use those company names as meta tags so people looking for them would find the smaller company. While it may sound like a good idea, it has been declared illegal trademark infringement. Today, many companies have computer programs scanning the Internet for improper use of their trademarks.

Once you have made sure that your site is passively listed in all the search engines, you may want to actively promote your site. However, self-promotion is seen as a bad thing on the Internet, especially if its purpose is to make money.

Newsgroups are places on the Internet where people interested in a specific topic can exchange information. For example, expectant mothers have a group where they can trade advice and experiences. If you have a product that would be great for expectant mothers, that would be a good place for it to be discussed. However, if you log into the group and merely announce your product, suggesting people order it from your website, you will probably be *flamed* (sent a lot of hate mail).

If you join the group, however, and become a regular, and in answer to someone's problem, mention that you *saw this product that might help*, your information will be better received. It may seem unethical to plug your product without disclosing your interest, but this is a procedure used by many large companies. They hire people to plug their product (or *rock star*) all over the Internet. Perhaps it has become an acceptable marketing method and consumers know to take plugs with a grain of salt. Let your conscience be your guide.

Keep in mind that Internet publicity works both ways. If you have a great product and people love it, you will get a lot of business. If you sell a shoddy product, give poor service, and do not keep your customers happy, bad publicity on the Internet can kill your business. Besides being an equalizer between large and small companies, the Internet can be a filtering mechanism between good and bad products.

Advertising   There is no worse breach of Internet etiquette (*netiquette*) than to send advertising by email to strangers. It is called *spamming,* and doing it can have serious consequences.

The *Controlling the Assault of Non-Solicited Pornography And Marketing Act of 2003* (CANSPAM) has put numerous controls on how you can use email to solicit business for your company. Some of the prohibited activities under the Act are:

- ✪   false or misleading information in an email;

- ✪   deceptive subject heading;

- ✪   failure to include a functioning return address;

- ✪   mailing to someone who has asked not to receive solicitations;

- ✪   failure to include a valid postal address;

- ✪   omitting an opt-out procedure;

- ✪   failure to clearly mark the email as advertising; and,

- ✪   including sexual material without adequate warnings.

Some of the provisions contain criminal penalties as well as civil fines.

For more information on the CANSPAM Act see:
www.gigalaw.com/canspam

For text of the Act plus other Spam laws around the world, see:
www.spamlaws.com

Many states, including California, Colorado, Connecticut, Delaware, Idaho, Illinois, Iowa, Louisiana, Missouri, Nevada, North Carolina, Oklahoma, Pennsylvania, Rhode Island, Tennessee, Virginia, Washington, and West Virginia, have also enacted antispamming legislation. This legislation sets specific requirements for unsolicited bulk email and makes certain practices illegal. Check with an attorney to see if your business practices fall within the legal limits of these laws. Additionally, many Internet Service Providers (ISPs) have restrictions on unsolicited bulk email (spam). Check with your ISP to make sure you do not violate its policies.

Banner ads are the small rectangular ads on many Web pages that usually blink or move. Although most computer users seem to have become immune to them, there is still a big market in the sale and exchange of these ads.

If your site gets enough viewers, people may pay you to place their ads there. Another possibility is to trade ads with another site. In fact, there are companies that broker ad trades among websites. These trades used to be taxable transactions, but since January 5, 2000, such trades are no longer taxable under IRS Notice 2000-6.

Legal Issues

Before you set up a Web page, you should consider the legal issues described below.

Jurisdiction   *Jurisdiction* is the power of a court in a particular location to decide a particular case. Usually, you have to have been physically present in a jurisdiction or have done business there before you can be sued there. Since the Internet extends your business's ability to reach people in distant places, there may be instances when you could be subject to legal jurisdiction far from your own state (or country). There are a number of cases that have been decided in this country regarding the Internet and jurisdiction, but very few cases have been decided on this issue outside of the United States.

In most instances, U.S. courts use the pre-Internet test—whether you have been present in another jurisdiction or have had enough contact with someone in the other jurisdiction. The fact that the Internet itself is not a *place* will not shield you from being sued in another state when you have shipped your company's product there, have entered into a contract with a resident of that state, or have defamed a foreign resident with content on your website. The more interactive your site is with consumers, the more you target an audience for your goods in a particular location, and the farther you reach to send your goods out into the world, the more it becomes possible for someone to sue you outside of your own jurisdiction—possibly even in another country.

The law is not even remotely final on these issues. The American Bar Association, among other groups, is studying this topic in detail. At present, no final, global solution or agreement about jurisdictional issues exists.

One way to protect yourself from the possibility of being sued in a distant jurisdiction would be to have a statement on your website indicating that those using the site or doing business with you agree that *jurisdiction for any actions regarding this site* or your company will be in your home county.

For extra protection, you can have a preliminary page that must be clicked before entering your website. However, this may be overkill for a small business with little risk of lawsuits. If you are in any business for which you could have serious liability, review some competitors' sites and see how they handle the liability issue. They often have a place to click for *legal notice* or *disclaimer* on their first page.

You may want to consult with an attorney to discuss the specific disclaimer you will use on your website, where it should appear, and whether you will have users of your site actively *agree* to this disclaimer or just *passively* read it. However, these disclaimers are not enforceable everywhere in the world. Until there is global agreement on jurisdictional issues, this may remain an area of uncertainty for some time to come.

Libel

Libel is any publication that injures the reputation of another. This can occur in print, writing, pictures, or signs. All that is required for *publication* is that you transmit the material to at least one other person. When putting together your website you must keep in mind that it is visible to millions of people all over the planet and that if you libel a person or company you may have to pay damages. Many countries do not have the freedom of speech that we do and a statement that is not libel in the United States may be libelous elsewhere.

Copyright Infringement

It is so easy to copy and *borrow* information on the Internet that it is easy to infringe copyrights without even knowing it. A *copyright* exists for a work as soon as the creator creates it. There is no need to register the copyright or to put a copyright notice on it. So, practically everything on the Internet belongs to someone.

Some people freely give their works away. For example, many people have created web artwork (*gifs* and *animated gifs*) that they freely allow people to copy. There are numerous sites that provide hundreds or thousands of free gifs that you can add to your Web pages. Some require you to acknowledge the source, some do not. Always be sure that the works are free for the taking before using them.

Linking and Framing

One way to violate copyright laws is to improperly link other sites to yours, either directly or with framing. *Linking* is when you provide a place on your site to click that takes someone to another site. *Framing* occurs when you set up your site so that when you link to another site, your site is still viewable as a frame around the linked-to site.

While many sites are glad to be linked to others—some, especially providers of valuable information—object. Courts have ruled that linking and framing can be a copyright violation. One rule that has developed states that it is usually okay to link to the first page of a site, but not to link to a page with valuable information deeper within the site. The rationale for this is that the owner of the site wants visitors to go through the various levels of their site (viewing all the ads) before getting the information. By linking to the information, you are giving away their product without the ads.

The problem with linking to the first page of a site is that it may be a tedious or difficult task to find the needed page from there. Many sites are poorly designed and make it nearly impossible to find anything.

The best solution, if you wish to link to another page, is to ask permission. Email the Webmaster or other person in charge of the site, if one is given, and explain what you want to do. If they grant permission, be sure to print out a copy of their email for your records.

Privacy

Since the Internet is such an easy way to share information, there are many concerns that it will cause a loss of individual privacy. The two main concerns arise when you post information that others consider private and when you gather information from customers and use it in a way that violates their privacy.

While public actions of politicians and celebrities are fair game, details about their private lives are sometimes protected by law. Details about persons who are not public figures are often protected. The laws in each state are different and what might be allowable in one state could be illegal in another. If your site will provide any personal information about individuals, discuss the possibility of liability with an attorney.

Several well-known companies have been in the news lately for violations of their customers' privacy. They either shared what the customer was buying or downloading or looked for additional information on the customer's computer. To let customers know that you do not violate certain standards of privacy, you can subscribe to one of the privacy codes that have been promulgated for the Internet. These allow you to put a symbol on your site guarantying to your customers that you follow the code.

The following are websites of two of the organizations that offer this service and their fees at the time of this publication.

www.privacybot.com	$100
www.bbbonline.com	$200 to $7,000

Protecting Yourself

The easiest way to protect yourself personally from the various possible types of liability is to set up a corporation or limited liability company to own the website. This is not foolproof protection, since in some cases you could be sued personally as well, but it is one level of protection.

COPPA

If your website is aimed at children under the age of thirteen or if it attracts children of that age, then you must follow the federal *Children Online Privacy Protection Act of 1998* (COPPA). This law requires such websites to:

- ✪ give notice on the site of what information is being collected;

- ✪ obtain verifiable parental consent to collect the information;

- ✪ allow the parent to review the information collected;

- ✪ allow the parent to delete the child's information or to refuse to allow the use of the information;

- ✪ limit the information collected to only that necessary to participate on the site; and,

- ✪ protect the security and confidentiality of the information.

Financial Transactions

In the future, there will be easy ways to exchange money on the Internet. Some companies have already been started that promote their own kinds of electronic money. Whether any of these become universal is yet to be seen.

The existing services for sending money over the Internet, such as PayPal, usually offer more risk and higher fees than traditional credit card processing. Under their service agreements you usually must agree that they can freeze your account at any time and can take money out of your bank account at any time. Some offer no appeal process! Before signing up for any of these services you should read their service agreement carefully and check the Internet for other peoples' experiences with them. For example, for PayPal you can check **www.nopaypal.com**.

For now, the easiest way to exchange money on the Internet is through traditional credit cards. Because of concerns that email can be abducted in transit and read by others, most companies use a *secure* site in which customers are guarantied that their card data is encrypted before being sent.

When setting up your website, you should ask the provider if you can be set up with a secure site for transmitting credit card data. If they cannot provide it, you will need to contract with another software provider. Use a major search engine listed on page 59 to look for companies that provide credit card services to businesses on the web.

As a practical matter, there is very little to worry about when sending credit card data by email. If you do not have a secure site, another option is to allow purchasers to fax or phone in their credit card data. However, keep in mind that this extra step will lose some business unless your products are unique and your buyers are very motivated.

The least effective option is to provide an order form on the site, which can be printed out and mailed in with a check. Again, your customers must be really motivated or they will lose interest after finding out this extra work is involved.

FTC Rules

Because the Internet is an instrument of interstate commerce, it is a legitimate subject for federal regulation. The Federal Trade Commission (FTC) first said that all of its consumer protection rules applied to the Internet, but lately it has been adding specific rules and issuing publications. The following publications are available from the FTC website at **www.ftc.gov/bcp/menu-internet.htm** or by mail from Consumer Response Center, Federal Trade Commission, 600 Pennsylvania, NW, Room H-130, Washington, DC 20580-0001.

✪ *Advertising and Marketing on the Internet: The Rules of the Road*

✪ *Appliance Labeling Rule Homepage*

✪ *BBB-Online: Code of Online Business Practices*

✪ *Big Print. Little Print. What's the Deal? How to Disclose the Details*

✪ *Businessperson's Guide to the Mail and Telephone Order Mdse Rule*

✪ *Complying with the Telemarketing Sales Rule*

✪ *Disclosing Energy Efficiency Information: A Guide for Online Sellers of Appliances*

✪ *Dot Com Disclosures: Information About Online Advertising*

✪ *Electronic Commerce: Selling Internationally. A Guide for Business*

✪ *Frequently Asked Questions About the Children's Online Privacy Protection Rule*

✪ *How to Comply With The Children's Online Privacy Protection Rule*

✪ *Internet Auctions: A Guide for Buyer and Sellers*

✪ *Selling on the Internet: Prompt Delivery Rules*

✪ *TooLate.Com: The Lowdown on Late Internet Shipments*

✪ *Website Woes: Avoiding Web Service Scams*

✪ *What's Dot and What's Not: Domain Name Registration Scams*

✪ *You, Your Privacy Policy & COPPA*

Fraud

Because the Internet is somewhat anonymous, it is a tempting place for those with fraudulent schemes to look for victims. As a business consumer, exercise caution when dealing with unknown or anonymous parties on the Internet.

The U.S. Department of Justice, the FBI, and the National White Collar Crime Center launched the *Internet Fraud Complaint Center* (IFCC). If you suspect that you are the victim of fraud online, whether as a consumer or a business, you can report incidents to the IFCC on their website, **www.ifccfbi.gov**. The IFCC is currently staffed by FBI agents and representatives of the National White Collar Crime Center and will work with state and local law enforcement officials to prevent, investigate, and prosecute high-tech and economic crime online.

10 | HEALTH AND SAFETY LAWS

As a reaction to the terrible work conditions prevalent in the factories and mills of the nineteenth century industrial age, Congress and the states developed many laws intended to protect the health and safety of the nation's workers. These laws are difficult to understand and often seem to be very unfair to employers. Therefore, this is an area that you need to pay particular attention to as a new business. Failure to do so can result in terrible consequences for you.

Federal Laws

The federal government's laws regarding health and safety of workers are far-reaching and very important to consider in running your business, especially if you are a manufacturer or in the oil and gas, food production, or agriculture industries.

OSHA The point of the *Occupational Safety and Health Administration* (OSHA) is to place the duty on the employer to keep the workplace free from recognized hazards that are likely to cause death or serious bodily injury to workers. The regulations are not as cumbersome for small businesses as for larger enterprises. If you have ten or fewer employees or if you are in certain types of businesses you do not have to keep a record of illnesses, injuries, and exposure to hazardous substances of employees. If you have eleven or more employees, OSHA's rules will apply. One important rule to know is that within forty-eight hours of an on-the-job death of an employee or injury of five or more employees on the job, the area director of OSHA must be contacted.

For more information, write or call an OSHA office.

OSHA Regional Office
201 Varick St.
Room 670
New York, NY 10014
212-337-2378
(*fax*) 212-337-2371
www.osha.gov

You can obtain copies of OSHA publications, *OSHA Handbook for Small Business* (OSHA 2209) and *OSHA Publications and Audiovisual Programs Catalog* (OSHA 2019), from its website. They also have a poster that is required to be posted in the workplace by all employers. It is available on their website at **www.osha.gov/pls/publications/pubindex.list**.

Hazard Communication Standard

The *Hazard Communication Standard* requires that employees be made aware of the hazards in the workplace. (*Title 29, Code of Federal Regulations (C.F.R.), Section (Sec.) 1910.1200.*) It is especially applicable to those working with chemicals, but this can even include offices that use copy machines. Businesses using hazardous chemicals must have a comprehensive program for informing employees of the hazards and for protecting them from contamination.

For more information, you can contact OSHA at the previously-mentioned addresses, phone numbers, or websites. They can supply a copy of the regulation and a booklet called *OSHA 3084*, which explains the law.

EPA

The *Worker Protection Standard for Agricultural Pesticides* requires safety training, decontamination sites and, of course, posters. The Environmental Protection Agency will provide information on compliance with this law. It can be reached at 800-490-9198 or through its website at **www.epa.gov**.

FDA

The *Pure Food and Drug Act of 1906* prohibits the misbranding or adulteration of food and drugs. It also created the Food and Drug Administration (FDA), which has promulgated tons of regulations and which must give permission before a new drug can be introduced into the market. If you will be dealing with any food or drugs, keep abreast of FDA policies. Its website is **www.fda.gov**. Its small business site is **www.fda.gov/ora/fed_state/small_business/sb_guide/ default.htm** and its local small business representative can be reached at:

FDA, Northeast Region
158-15 Liberty Ave.
Jamaica, NY 11433
718-340-7000

Hazardous Materials Transportation

There are regulations that control the shipping and packing of hazardous materials. For more information, contact:

U.S. Department of Transportation
Research and Special Programs Administration
Office of Hazardous Materials Safety
400 Seventh Street, SW
Washington, DC 20590
202-366-8553
http://hazmat.dot.gov

CPSC

The *Consumer Product Safety Commission* has a set of rules that cover the safety of products. The commission feels that because its rules cover products, rather than people or companies, they apply to everyone producing such products. However, federal laws do not apply to small businesses that do not affect interstate commerce. Whether a small business would fall under a CPSC rule would depend on the size and nature of that business.

The CPSC rules are contained in the Code of Federal Regulations, Title 16 in the following parts. These can be found at most law libraries, some public libraries, and on the Internet at **www.access.gpo.gov/nara/cfr/cfr-table-search.html**. The CPSC's site is **www.cpsc.gov**.

PRODUCT	PART
Antennas, CB and TV	1402
Architectural Glazing Material	1201
Articles Hazardous to Children Under 3	1501
Baby Cribs—Full Size	1508
Baby Cribs—Non-Full Size	1509
Bicycle Helmets	1203
Bicycles	1512
Carpets and Rugs	1630, 1631
Cellulose Insulation	1209, 1404

Cigarette Lighters	1210
Citizens Band Base Station Antennas	1204
Coal and Wood Burning Appliances	1406
Consumer Products Containing Chlorofluorocarbons	1401
Electrically Operated Toys	1505
Emberizing Materials Containing Asbestos (banned)	1305
Extremely Flammable Contact Adhesives (banned)	1302
Fireworks	1507
Garage Door Openers	1211
Hazardous Lawn Darts (banned)	1306
Hazardous Substances	1500
Human Subjects	1028
Lawn Mowers—Walk-Behind	1205
Lead-Containing Paint (banned)	1303
Matchbooks	1202
Mattresses	1632
Pacifiers	1511
Patching Compounds Containing Asbestos (banned)	1304
Poisons	1700
Rattles	1510
Self-Pressurized Consumer Products	1401
Sleepwear-Childrens	1615, 1616
Swimming Pool Slides	1207
Toys, Electrical	1505
Unstable Refuse Bins (banned)	1301

Additional Regulations

Every day there are proposals for new laws and regulations. It would be impossible to include every conceivable one in this book. To be up to date on the laws that affect your type of business, join a trade association for your industry and subscribe to newsletters that cover your industry. Attending industry conventions is a good way to learn more and to discover new ways to increase your profits.

New York State Laws

The federal laws discussed previously are by far the most important with regard to the health and safety of your employees and customers. However, note that New York does have laws regarding smoking in certain places.

Employers Liability Law Under the 1921 *Employers Liability Law*, owners and employers can be found liable to employees due to any defect in the conditions of the workplace. The owners are liable for employee injuries or deaths unless they can rebut the presumption that they have not used reasonable care. When the employee is at fault, the damages are apportioned. Employers may not contract with employees to avoid the liability of this law.

Smoking Effective July 24, 2003, the amended New York State *Clean Indoor Air Act* (*Public Health Law, Article 13-E*) prohibits smoking in virtually all workplaces, including restaurants and bars. Localities may continue to adopt and enforce local laws regulating smoking. However, these regulations must be at least as strict as the *Clean Indoor Air Act*.

Where is smoking prohibited? The Act states that smoking shall not be permitted and that no person shall smoke in the following indoor areas:

✪ places of employment;

✪ bars;

✪ restaurants;

✪ enclosed indoor swimming areas;

✪ public transportation, including all ticketing, boarding and waiting areas; buses, vans, taxicabs and limousines;

✪ all places of employment where services are offered to children;

✪ all schools, including school grounds;

✪ all public and private colleges, universities and other educational and vocational institutions;

✪ general hospitals;

✪ residential health-care facilities, except separately designated smoking rooms for adult patients;

- commercial establishments used for the purpose of carrying on or exercising any trade, profession, vocation or charitable activity;

- all indoor arenas;

- zoos; and,

- bingo facilities.

Where is smoking permitted? Smoking is permitted in the following areas or businesses:

- private homes and private residences when not used for day care;

- private automobiles;

- hotel or motel rooms rented to one or more guests;

- retail tobacco businesses (primary activity is the retail sale of tobacco products and accessories, and the sale of other products is merely incidental);

- membership associations where all duties related to the operation of the association are performed by volunteers who are not compensated in any manner;

- cigar bars in existence prior to January 1, 2003 (where 10% or more of total annual gross income is from the sale of tobacco products); and,

- up to 25% of seating in outdoor areas of restaurants with no roof or ceiling enclosure may be designated smoking areas.

For more information go to the New York State Department of Health's website at:

www.health.state.ny.us/nysdoh/clean_indoor_air_act

II EMPLOYMENT AND LABOR LAWS

Like they have with health and safety laws, Congress and the states have heavily regulated the actions that employers can take with regard to hiring and firing, improper employment practices, and discrimination. Because the penalties can be severe, educate yourself on the proper actions to take and consult a labor and employment lawyer, if necessary, prior to making important employee decisions.

Hiring and Firing Laws

For small businesses, there are not many rules regarding who you may hire or fire. Fortunately, the ancient law that an employee can be fired at any time (or may quit at any time) still prevails for small businesses. But in certain situations, and as you grow, you will come under a number of laws that affect your hiring and firing practices.

One of the most important things to consider when hiring someone is that if you fire them, they may be entitled to unemployment compensation. If so, your unemployment compensation tax rate will go up, which can cost you a lot of money. Therefore, you should only hire people you are sure you will keep and you should avoid situations in which your former employees can make claims against your company.

One way this can be done is by hiring only part-time employees. The drawback to this is that you may not be able to attract the best employees. When hiring dishwashers or busboys, this may not be an issue; but when hiring someone to develop a software product, you do not want them to leave halfway through the development.

A better solution is to screen applicants first and only hire those who you feel certain will work out. Of course, this is easier said than done. Some people interview well but then turn out to be incompetent at the job.

The best record to look for is someone who has stayed a long time at each of their previous jobs. Next best is someone who has not stayed as long (for good reasons) but has always been employed. The worst type of hire would be someone who is or has been collecting unemployment compensation.

The reason those who have collected compensation are a bad risk is that if they collect in the future—even if it is not your fault—your employment of them could make you chargeable for their claim.

Example: You hire someone who has been on unemployment compensation and he or she works out well for a year, but then he or she quits to take another job and is fired after a few weeks. In this situation, you would be chargeable for most of the unemployment claim because his or her last five quarters of work are analyzed. Look for a steady job history.

The competence of an employee is often more important than his or her experience. An employee with years of typing experience may be fast, but may also be unable to figure out how to use your new computer, whereas a competent employee can learn the equipment quickly and eventually gain speed. Of course, common sense is important in all situations.

The bottom line is that you cannot know if an employee will be able to fill your needs from a résumé and interview. Once you have found someone who you think will work out, offer him or her a job with a ninety-day probationary period. If you are not completely satisfied with him or her after the ninety days, offer to extend the probationary period for an additional ninety days rather than end the relationship immediately. Of course, all of this should be in writing.

Background Checks Checking references is important, but beware that a former boss may be a good friend or even a relative. It has always been considered acceptable to exaggerate on résumés, but in recent years some applicants have been found to be completely fabricating sections of their education and experience.

Polygraph Tests Under the federal *Employee Polygraph Protection Act*, you cannot require an employee or prospective employee to take a polygraph test unless you are in the armored car, security alarm system, guard, or pharmaceutical business.

Drug Tests Under the *Americans with Disabilities Act* (ADA), drug testing can only be required of applicants who have been offered jobs conditioned upon passing the drug test. Unlike some states, Illinois does not have drug-testing laws that regulate the private sector. Therefore, you are free to implement a reasonable drug-testing program on applicants or employees.

Firing

In most cases, unless you have a contract with an employee for a set time period, you can fire him or her at any time. This is only fair, since the employee can quit at any time. The exceptions to this are if you fire someone based on: illegal discrimination; for filing some sort of health or safety complaint; or, for refusing your sexual advances or those of a coworker.

New Hire Reporting

In order to track down parents who do not pay child support, a federal law requires the reporting of new hires. The *Personal Responsibility and Work Opportunity Reconciliation Act of 1996* (PRWORA) provides that such information must be reported by employers to their state government.

Within twenty days of hiring a new employee, an employer must provide the state with information about the employee, including his or her name, Social Security number, and address. This information can be submitted in several ways, including mail, fax, magnetic tape, or over the Internet. There is a special form that can be used for this reporting. However, an employer can also use the **EMPLOYEE'S WITHHOLDING ALLOWANCE CERTIFICATE (IRS FORM W-4)** for this purpose. A copy of the **IRS FORM W-4** is included in Appendix C. (see form 7, p.221.) Since this form must be filled out for all employees anyway, it would be pointless to use a separate form for the new hire reporting.

Employment Agreements

To avoid misunderstanding with employees, you should use an employment agreement or an employee handbook. These can spell out in detail the policies of your company and the rights of your employees. They can protect your trade secrets and spell out clearly that employment can be terminated at any time by either party.

While it may be difficult or awkward to ask an existing employee to sign such an agreement, an applicant hoping you will hire him or her will usually sign whatever is necessary to obtain the job. However, because of the unequal bargaining position, do not use an agreement that would make you look bad if the matter ever went to court.

If having an employee sign an agreement is too awkward, you can usually obtain the same rights by putting the company policies in an employee manual. Each existing and new employee should be given a copy, along with a letter stating that the rules apply to all employees and that by accepting or continuing employment at your company, they agree to abide by the rules. Having an employee sign a receipt for the letter and manual is proof that they received it.

One danger of an employment agreement or handbook is that it may be interpreted to create a long-term employment contract. To avoid this, be sure that you clearly state in the agreement or handbook that the employment is *at will* and can be terminated at any time by either party.

Some other things to consider in an employment agreement or handbook include:

- ✪ what the salary and other compensation will be;

- ✪ what the hours of employment will be;

- ✪ what the probationary period will be;

✪   that the employee cannot sign any contracts binding the employer; and,

✪   that the employee agrees to arbitration rather than filing a lawsuit.

Independent Contractors

One way to avoid problems with employees and taxes at the same time is to have all of your work done through independent contractors. This can relieve you of most of the burdens of employment laws, as well as the obligation to pay Social Security and Medicare taxes for the workers.

An independent contractor is, in effect, a separate business that you pay to do a job. You pay them just as you pay any company from which you buy products or services. At the end of the year, if the amount paid exceeds $600, you will issue a 1099 form instead of the W-2 that you issue to employees.

This may seem too good to be true, and in some situations, it is. The IRS does not like independent contractor arrangements because it is too easy for the independent contractors to cheat on their taxes. To limit the use of independent contractors, the IRS has strict regulations on who may and may not be classified as an independent contractor. Also, companies who do not appear to pay enough in wages for their field of business are audited.

The highest at-risk jobs are those that are not traditionally done by independent contractors. For example, you could not get away with hiring a secretary as an independent contractor. One of the most important factors considered in determining if a worker can be an independent contractor is the amount of control the company has over his or her work.

Example 1:   If you need someone to paint your building and you agree to pay him or her a certain price to do it according to his or her own methods and schedule, you can pay him or her as an independent contractor. But if you tell him or her when to work, how to do the job, and provide the tools and materials, he or she will be classified as an employee.

Example 2: If you just need some typing done and you take it to a typing service and pick it up when it is ready, you will be safe in treating them as independent contractors. However, if you need someone to come into your office to type on your machine at your schedule, you will probably be required to treat that person as an employee for tax purposes.

The IRS has a form you can use in determining if a person is an employee or an independent contractor called **DETERMINATION OF WORKER STATUS FOR PURPOSE OF FEDERAL EMPLOYMENT TAXES AND INCOME TAX WITHHOLDING (IRS FORM SS-8)**. It is included in Appendix C of this book, along with instructions. (see form 9, p.235.)

Independent Contractors versus Employees

In deciding whether to make use of independent contractors or employees, you should weigh the following advantages and disadvantages.

Advantages.

✪ Lower taxes. You do not have to pay Social Security, Medicare, unemployment, or other employee taxes.

✪ Less paperwork. You do not have to handle federal withholding deposits or the monthly employer returns to the state or federal government.

✪ Less insurance. You do not have to pay workers' compensation insurance, and since the workers are not your employees, you do not have to insure against their possible liabilities.

✪ More flexibility. You can use independent contractors when you need them and not pay them when business is slow.

Disadvantages.

✪ The IRS and state tax offices are strict about when workers can qualify as independent contractors. They will audit companies whose use of independent contractors does not appear to be legitimate.

✪ If your use of independent contractors is found to be improper, you may have to pay back taxes and penalties and have problems with your pension plan.

✪ While employees usually cannot sue you for their injuries (if you have covered them with workers' compensation), independent contractors can sue you if their injuries were your fault.

✪ If you are paying someone to produce a creative work (writing, photography, artwork), you receive less rights to the work of an independent contractor.

✪ You have less control over the work of an independent contractor and less flexibility in terminating them if you are not satisfied that the job is being done the way you require.

✪ You have less loyalty from an independent contractor who works sporadically for you and possibly others than from your own full-time employees.

For some businesses, the advantages outweigh the disadvantages. For others, they do not. Consider your business plans and the consequences from each type of arrangement. Keep in mind that it will be easier to start with independent contractors and switch to employees than to hire employees and have to fire them to hire independent contractors.

Temporary Workers

Another way to avoid the hassles of hiring employees is to get workers from a temporary agency. In this arrangement, you may pay a higher amount per hour for the work, but the agency will take care of all of the tax and insurance requirements. Since these can be expensive and time-consuming, the extra cost may be well worth it.

Whether or not temporary workers will work for you depends upon the type of business you are in and the tasks you need performed. For jobs such as sales management, you would probably want someone who will stay with you long term and develop relationships with the buyers. For order fulfillment, temporary workers might work out well.

Another advantage of temporary workers is that you can easily stop using those who do not work out well for you, but if you find one who is ideal, you may be able to hire him or her on a full-time basis.

In recent years, a new wrinkle has developed in the temporary worker area. Many large companies are using temps because it is so much cheaper than paying the benefits demanded by full-time employees.

Example: *Microsoft Corp.* has had as many as 6,000 temporary workers, some of whom work for them for years. Some of the temporary workers recently won a lawsuit declaring that they are really employees and are entitled to the same benefits of other employees (such as pension plans).

The law is not yet settled in this area as to what arrangements will result in a temporary worker being declared an employee. That will take several more court cases, some of which have already been filed. The following are a few things you can do to protect yourself.

   ✪   Be sure that any of your benefit plans make it clear that they do not apply to workers obtained through temporary agencies.

   ✪   Do not keep the same temporary workers for longer than a year.

   ✪   Do not list temporary workers in any employee directories or hold them out to the public as your employees.

   ✪   Do not allow them to use your business cards or stationery.

Discrimination Laws

There are numerous federal laws forbidding discrimination based upon race, sex, pregnancy, color, religion, national origin, age, or disability. The laws apply to both hiring and firing, and to employment practices such as salaries, promotions, and benefits. Most of these laws only apply to an employer who has fifteen or more employees for twenty weeks of a calendar year or has federal contracts or subcontracts. Therefore, you most likely will not be required to comply with the law immediately upon opening your business. However, there are similar state laws that may apply to your business.

One exception is the *Equal Pay Act*. It applies to employers with two or more employees and requires that women be paid the same as men in the same type of job.

Employers with fifteen or more employees are required to display a poster regarding discrimination. This poster is available from the Equal Employment Opportunity Commission, 2401 E. Street, N.W., Washington, DC 20506. Employers with 100 or more employees are required to file an annual report with the EEOC.

When hiring employees, some questions are illegal or inadvisable to ask. The following subjects should not be included on your employment application or in your interviews, unless the information is somehow directly tied to the duties of the job.

- ✪ Do not ask about an applicant's citizenship or place of birth. After hiring an employee, you must ask about his or her right to work in this country.

- ✪ Do not ask a female applicant her maiden name. You can ask if she has been known by any other name in order to do a background check.

- ✪ Do not ask if applicants have children, plan to have them, or have child care. You can ask if an applicant will be able to work the required hours.

- ✪ Do not ask if the applicant has religious objections for working Saturday or Sunday. You can mention if the job requires such hours and ask whether the applicant can meet this job requirement.

- ✪ Do not ask an applicant's age. You can ask if an applicant is eighteen or over, or for a liquor-related job, if he or she is twenty-one or over.

- ✪ Do not ask an applicant's weight.

- ✪ Do not ask if an applicant has AIDS or is HIV positive.

- ✪ Do not ask if the applicant has filed a workers' compensation claim.

- ✪ Do not ask about the applicant's previous health problems.

✪ Do not ask if the applicant is married or whether his or her spouse would object to the job, hours, or duties.

✪ Do not ask if the applicant owns a home, furniture, or car, as it is considered racially-discriminatory.

✪ Do not ask if the applicant has ever been arrested. You can ask if the applicant has ever been *convicted* of a crime.

The most recent applicable law is the *Americans with Disabilities Act* (ADA). Under this law, employers who do not make *reasonable accommodations for disabled employees* will face fines of up to $100,000, as well as other civil penalties and civil damage awards.

The ADA currently applies to employers with fifteen or more employees. Employers who need more than fifteen employees might want to consider independent contractors to avoid problems with this law, particularly if the number of employees is only slightly larger than fifteen.

To find out how this law affects your business, review the publications available from the federal government to assist businesses with ADA compliance. The *Title III Technical Assistance Manual* and the *ADA Guide for Small Businesses* are available from the official ADA website at **www.usdoj.gov/crt/ada/publicat.htm** or by calling the ADA information line at 800-514-0301.

Tax benefits. There are three types of tax credits to help small businesses with the burden of these laws.

✪ Businesses can deduct up to $15,000 a year for making their premises accessible to the disabled and can depreciate the rest. (*Internal Revenue Code (IRC) Section 190.*)

✪ Small businesses (under $1,000,000 in revenue and under 30 employees) can get a tax credit each year for 50% of the cost of making their premises accessible to the disabled, but this only applies to the amount between $250 and $10,250. (*IRC Section 44.*)

✪ Small businesses can get a credit of up to 40% of the first $8,500 of wages paid to certain new employees who qualify. See IRS Publications

334 and 954, and **Pre-Screening Notice and Certification Request for the Work Opportunity and Welfare-to-Work Credits (IRS Form 8850)** and its instructions. (see form 11, p.245.)

New York Law

New York has its own laws regarding discrimination in employment practices. Section 296 of the Executive Law, known as the *Human Rights Law*, prohibits discrimination or classification based upon race, color, religion, sex, national origin, age, handicap, marital status, or sexual orientation. An employer who violates this law can be sued and be required to pay back pay, damages, and punitive damages. This statute also prohibits discrimination in compensation.

Sexual Harassment

In today's employment climate, any employer must pay attention to state and federal laws regarding sexual harassment in the workplace.

Federal Law

In the 1980s, the Equal Employment Opportunity Commission interpreted *Title VII* of the *Civil Rights Act of 1964* to forbid sexual harassment. After that, the courts took over and reviewed all types of conduct in the workplace. The numerous lawsuits that followed revealed a definite trend toward expanding the definition of sexual harassment and favoring employees.

The EEOC has held the following in sexual harassment cases.

- The victim and the harasser may be a woman or a man.

- The victim does not have to be of the opposite sex.

- The harasser can be the victim's supervisor, an agent of the employer, a supervisor in another area, a coworker, or a nonemployee.

- The victim does not have to be the person harassed but could be anyone affected by the offensive conduct.

- Unlawful sexual harassment may occur without economic injury to or discharge of the victim.

- The harasser's conduct must be unwelcome.

✪   An employer can be held liable for sexual harassment of an employee by a supervisor, even if the employer was unaware of the supervisor's conduct.

Some of the actions that have been considered harassment are:

✪   displaying sexually explicit posters in the workplace;

✪   requiring female employees to wear revealing uniforms;

✪   rating of sexual attractiveness of female employees as they passed male employees' desks;

✪   continued sexual jokes and innuendos;

✪   demands for sexual favors from subordinates;

✪   unwelcomed sexual propositions or flirtation;

✪   unwelcomed physical contact; and,

✪   whistling or leering at members of the opposite sex.

The law in the area of sexual harassment is still developing, so it is difficult to make clear rules of conduct.

Some things a business can do to protect against claims of sexual harassment include the following.

✪   Distribute a written policy against all kinds of sexual harassment to all employees.

✪   Encourage employees to report all incidents of sexual harassment.

✪   Insure there is no retaliation against those who complain.

✪   Make clear that your policy is *zero tolerance*.

✪   Explain that sexual harassment includes both requests for sexual favors and a work environment that some employees may consider hostile.

✪ Allow employees to report harassment to someone other than their immediate supervisor in case that person is involved in the harassment.

✪ Promise as much confidentiality as possible to complainants.

Wage and Hour Laws

The *Fair Labor Standards Act* (FLSA) applies to all employers who are engaged in *interstate commerce* or in the production of goods for interstate commerce (anything that will cross the state line) and all employees of hospitals, schools, residential facilities for the disabled or aged, or public agencies. It also applies to all employees of enterprises that gross $500,000 or more per year.

While many small businesses might not think they are engaged in interstate commerce, the laws have been interpreted so broadly that nearly any use of the mails, interstate telephone service, or other interstate services, however minor, is enough to bring a business under the law.

Minimum Wage   The federal wage and hour laws are contained in the federal *Fair Labor Standards Act.* The current minimum wage is $5.15. In certain circumstances a wage of $4.25 may be paid to employees under twenty years of age for a ninety-day training period.

For employees who regularly receive more than $30 a month in tips, the minimum wage is $2.13 per hour. But if the employee's tips do not bring him or her up to the full $5.15 minimum wage, then the employer must make up the difference.

Overtime   The general rule is that employees who work more than forty hours a week must be paid time-and-a-half for hours worked over forty. However, there are many exemptions to this general rule based on salary and position. These exceptions were completely revised in 2004 and an explanation of the changes, including a tutorial video, are available at **www.dol.gov/esa**. For answers to questions about the law, call the Department of Labor at 866-487-9243.

Exempt Employees

While nearly all businesses are covered, certain employees are exempt from the FLSA. Exempt employees include employees that are considered executives, administrative, and managerial, professionals, computer professionals, and outside salespeople.

Whether or not one of these exceptions applies to a particular employee is a complicated legal question. Thousands of court cases have been decided on this issue but they have given no clear answers. In one case a person could be determined to be exempt because of his or her duties, but in another, a person with the same duties could be found not exempt.

One thing that is clear is that the determination is made on the employee's function and not just the job title. You cannot make a secretary exempt by calling him or her a manager if most of his or her duties are clerical. For more information, contact:

U. S. Department of Labor
Wage and Hour Division
200 Constitution Avenue., N.W. Room S-3325
Washington, DC 20210
866-4USA-DOL
www.dol.gov/esa

On the Internet you can obtain information on the Department of Labor's *Small Business Handbook* at:

www.dol.gov/asp/programs/handbook/main.htm

New York Law

The New York *Labor Law*, Section 160 provides that eight hours constitutes a work day, under most circumstances.

Family and Medical Leave Law

Congress passed the *Family and Medical Leave Act of 1993* (FMLA), which requires an employee to be given up to twelve weeks of unpaid leave when:

✪ the employee or employee's spouse has a child;

✪ the employee adopts a child or takes in a foster child;

✪ the employee needs to care for an ill spouse, child, or parent; or,

✪ the employee becomes seriously ill.

The law only applies to employers with fifty or more employees. Also, the most highly paid ten percent of an employer's salaried employees can be denied this leave because of the disruption to business their loss could cause.

New York Law New York's *Executive Law, Section 296* (the *Human Rights Law*) declares it to be *an unlawful discriminatory practice* for an employer to force a pregnant employee to take a leave of absence during her pregnancy, unless the pregnancy prevents performance of the job *in a reasonable manner*. There is no exception made in the *Human Rights Law* for particular companies or companies with a certain number of employees.

New York's *Labor Law, Section 201-C* also requires that when an employer or governmental agency permits an employee to take a leave of absence upon the birth of such employee's child, the same leave must also be offered to adoptive parents.

Child Labor Laws

The federal *Fair Labor Standards Act* also contains rules regarding the hiring of children. The basic rules state that children under sixteen years old may not be hired, except in a few jobs (such as acting and newspaper delivery). Also, those under eighteen may not be hired for dangerous jobs. Children may not work more than three hours a day (eighteen hours a week) in a school week or more than eight hours a day (forty hours a week) in a nonschool week. If you plan to hire children, you should check the federal *Fair Labor Standards Act*, which is in Chapter 8, Title 29, United States Code (*29 USC Chapter 8*), as well as the related regulations that are in Title 29 of the Code of Federal Regulations (*29 C.F.R.*).

New York Law New York has rules that apply to child labor (called *minors* in New York) in addition to federal laws. (N.Y. *Labor Law*, beginning with Sec. 130.) The general rule is that no minor under 14 years of age may work in New York except as follows.

✪   Minors of any age may work as pages, in the entertainment industry, and in domestic or farm work for their parents. Children working for their parents may not do so during school hours.

✪   No child ten years of age or younger may engage in the sale and distribution of newspapers or the street trades.

✪   No child under fourteen years of age may be employed in any gainful occupation at any time except as described above.

✪   No minor of any age may work under any circumstances when attendance at school is required.

Other prohibited activities are:

✪   work in a factory;

✪   operation of oiling or cleaning machines;

✪   work in freezers or meat coolers;

✪   use of meat or vegetable slicers;

✪   operation of power-driven laundry or dry cleaning machinery;

✪   door-to-door sales of subscriptions or products except for merchandise of nonprofit organizations;

✪   spray painting;

✪   operating a motor vehicle;

✪   logging;

✪   operating an elevator;

✪   paint packing; and,

✪   construction work.

Employment Certificate. (*N.Y. Labor Law, Sec. 135.*) The employer of a minor must file the employment certificate (which the minor must get from the local board of education) in order to work.

Proof of child's age. (*N.Y. Labor Law, Sec. 135.*) A person who employs a child must keep proof of the child's age on file. Acceptable forms of proof of age are a photocopy of a birth certificate, a driver's license, a school age certificate, a passport, or a visa.

Children's hours. (*N.Y. Labor Law, Secs. 170, 172, 173.*) In addition to the previously mentioned requirements, no child fifteen years of age or younger may work more than twenty-eight hours a week, more than six days a week, or more than three school days per week. When school is not in session, permissible hours increase to forty-eight hours per week, six days a week, and eight hours a day.

No child fifteen years of age or younger may work before 7 A.M. or after 7 P.M. when school is scheduled the next day. No such child shall work more than eighteen hours a week or more than three hours in a day prior to a school day except in a vocational education program.

However, these rules do not apply during holiday and summer vacations, to sixteen or seventeen-year-old graduates, to students with school-authorized exemptions, to students with economic hardships, to children in domestic work in private homes, to children working for their parents, or to pages working for the legislature.

The employer is required to conspicuously post the hours of each child at the place of employment and keep the board of education informed of the child's employment status.

Another set of rules apply to minors that are 16 years old and another applies to minors age 17 and above. These rules increase the number of hours the minor may work. Again, it is advised that the law be consulted for your particular situation.

Immigration Laws

In 1986, a law was passed by Congress that imposed stiff penalties for any business that hires aliens who are not eligible to work. Under this law, you must verify both the identity and the employment eligibility of anyone you hire by using the **EMPLOYMENT ELIGIBILITY VERIFICATION (FORM I-9)**. (see form 5, p.209.) Both you and the employee must fill out the form and you must check an employee's identification cards or papers. Fines for hiring illegal aliens range from $250 to $2,000 for the first offense and up to $10,000 for the third offense. Failure to maintain the proper paperwork may result in a fine of up to $1,000. The law does not apply to independent contractors with whom you may contract and it does not penalize you if the employee used fake identification.

There are also penalties that apply to employers of four or more persons for discriminating against eligible applicants because they appear foreign or because of their national origin or citizenship status.

In Appendix B, there is a sample filled-in **FORM I-9**, and instructions. A blank form is in Appendix C. (see form 5, p.209.)

For more information call 800-870-3676 for the *Handbook for Employers (M-274)* or check the United States Citizenship and Immigration Services (USCIS) website:

> http://uscis.gov/graphics/lawsregs/handbook/hand_emp.pdf

For specific questions, call the USCIS (formerly the Immigration and Naturalization Service) Employer Business Investor hotline at 800-357-2099.

New York Law   It is unlawful for illegal aliens to claim unemployment insurance benefits in New York. (*N.Y. Labor Law, Sec. 590(9).*)

Hiring *Off the Books*

Because of the taxes, insurance, and red tape involved with hiring employees, some new businesses hire people *off the books*. The employers pay them in cash and never admit they are employees. While the cash paid in wages would not be deductible, they consider this a smaller cost than compliance. Some even use off the books receipts to cover it.

Except when your spouse or child is giving you some temporary help, this is a terrible idea. Hiring people off the books can result in civil fines, loss of insurance coverage, and even criminal penalties. When engaged in dangerous work, like roofing or using power tools, you are risking millions of dollars in potential damages if a worker is seriously injured or killed.

It may be more costly and time consuming to comply with the employment laws, but if you are focused on long-term growth with less risk, it is the wiser way to go.

Federal Contracts

Companies that do work for the federal government are subject to several laws.

The *Davis-Bacon Act* requires contractors engaged in U.S. government construction projects to pay wages and benefits that are equal to or better than the prevailing wages in the area.

The *McNamara-O'Hara Service Contract Act* sets wages and other labor standards for contractors furnishing services to agencies of the U.S. government.

The *Walsh-Healey Public Contracts Act* requires the Department of Labor to settle disputes regarding manufacturers supplying products to the U.S. government.

Miscellaneous Laws

Affirmative action. In most cases, the federal government does not yet tell employers who they must hire, especially small new businesses. The only situation in which a small business would need to comply with affirmative action requirements would be if it accepted federal contracts or subcontracts. These requirements could include the hiring of minorities or of Vietnam veterans.

Layoffs. Companies with one hundred or more full-time employees at one location are subject to the *Worker Adjustment and Retraining Notification Act* (*29 USC Chapter 23*). This law requires a sixty day notification prior to certain lay-offs, and has other strict provisions.

Unions. The *National Labor Relations Act of 1935 (29 USC Section 151 et seq.)* gives employees the right to organize or join a union. There are things employers can do to protect themselves, but you should consult a labor attorney or a book on the subject before taking action that might be illegal and could result in fines.

Poster laws. There are laws regarding what posters you may or may not display in the workplace. A federal judge in 1991 ruled that Playboy posters in a workplace were sexual harassment. This ruling is being appealed by the American Civil Liberties Union (ACLU). In addition, there are other poster laws that require certain posters to be displayed to inform employees of their rights. Not all businesses are required to display all posters. The following list provides guidance in determining the poster requirements for your business.

✪ All employers subject to minimum wage provisions must display the wage and hour poster available from:

U.S. Department of Labor
200 Constitution Avenue, NW
Washington, DC 20210
866-4-USWAGE
www.dol.gov/esa/regs/compliance/posters/flsa.htm

✪ Employers with fifteen or more employees for twenty weeks of the year and employers with federal contracts or subcontracts of $10,000 or more must display the sex, race, religion, ethnic, age, equal pay, and disability discrimination poster (see page 83), available from:

EEOC
1801 L Street, N.W.
Washington, DC 20507
202-693-0200

✪ The poster also specifically prohibits discrimination against Vietnam Era Veterans in the case of employers with federal contracts or subcontracts of $10,000 or more.

✪ Employers with government contracts subject to the *Service Contract Act* or the *Public Contracts Act* must display a notice to employees working on government contracts, which is available from:

Employment Standards Division
U.S. Department of Labor
200 Constitution Avenue, NW
Washington, DC 20210
202-693-0023

✪   Employers who employ fifty or more employees in twenty or more work weeks and who are engaged in commerce or in any industry or activity affecting commerce are required to post a notice explaining employees' rights under the federal *Family and Medical Leave Act*. The poster is available from the Employment Standards Division, or online at **www.dol.gov/esa/regs/compliance/posters/pdf/fmlaen.pdf.**

New York Law   *Threat of discharge for failing to trade with particular firm.* (*N.Y. Labor Law, Sec. 704.*) It is an unfair labor practice for an employer to require an employee to deal with or not to deal with any particular firm or person in his or her personal affairs or to discharge or threaten to discharge an employee for such a reason.

Wrongful combination against workers. (*N.Y. Labor Law, Sec. 704.*) It is an unfair labor practice for two or more persons to conspire to deny a person work or to cause the discharge of a person in a firm, or to threaten to injure the life, property, or business of any person for this purpose.

12 ADVERTISING AND PROMOTION LAWS

Because of the unscrupulous and deceptive advertising techniques and multitude of con artists trying to steal from innocent consumers, numerous federal and state statutes have been enacted that make it unlawful to use improper advertising and promotional techniques in soliciting business.

Advertising Laws and Rules

This section discusses various federal and New York laws and regulations relating to advertising.

Federal Law
The federal government regulates advertising through the Federal Trade Commission (FTC). The rules are contained in the Code of Federal Regulations (C.F.R.). You can find these rules in most law libraries and many public libraries. If you plan any advertising that you think may be questionable, you might want to check the rules. As you read the rules discussed, you will probably think of many violations you see every day.

Federal rules do not apply to every business. Small businesses that operate only within the state and do not use the postal service may be exempt.

Therefore, a violation could be prosecuted by the state rather than the federal government. Some of the important rules are summarized below. If you wish, you should obtain copies from your library.

Deceptive pricing. When prices are being compared, it is required that actual and not inflated prices are used.

Example: If an object would usually be sold for $7, you should not first offer it for $10 and then start offering it at 30% off.

It is considered misleading to suggest that a discount from list price is a bargain if the item is seldomly sold at list price. If most surrounding stores sell an item for $7 it is considered misleading to say it has a *retail value of $10*, even if there are some stores elsewhere selling it at that price. (*16 C.F.R. Ch. I, Part 233.*)

Bait advertising. Bait advertising is placing an ad when you do not really want the respondents to buy the product offered but to switch to another item. (*16 C.F.R. Ch. I, Part 238.*)

Use of free, half-off, and similar words. Use of words such as *free, 1¢ sale* and the like must not be misleading. This means that the *regular price* must not include a mark-up to cover the *free* item. The seller must expect to sell the product without the free item at some time in the future. (*16 C.F.R. Ch. I, Part 251.*)

Substantiation of claims. The FTC requires that advertisers be able to substantiate their claims. (*16 C.F.R. Sec 3.40; 48 F.R. Page 10471.*) Some information on this policy is contained on the Internet at:
www.ftc.gov/bcp/guides/ad3subst.htm

Endorsements. Rules forbid endorsements that are misleading. An example is a quote from a film review that is used in such a way as to change the substance of the review. It is not necessary to use the exact words of the person endorsing the product as long as the opinion is not distorted. If a product is changed, an endorsement that does not apply to the new version cannot be used. For some items, such as drugs, claims cannot be used without scientific proof. Endorsements by organizations cannot be used unless one is sure that the membership holds the same opinion. (*16 C.F.R. Ch. I, Part 255.*)

Unfairness. Any advertising practices that can be deemed to be *unfair* are forbidden by the FTC. (*15 USC Sec. 45.*) An explanation of this policy is located on the Internet at:

www.ftc.gov/bcp/policystmt/ad-unfair.htm

Negative option plans. When a seller uses a sales system in which the buyer must notify the seller if he or she does not want the goods, the seller must provide the buyer with a form to decline the sale and at least ten days in which to decline. Bonus merchandise must be shipped promptly and the seller must promptly terminate any who so request after completion of the contract. (*16 C.F.R. Ch. I, Part 425.*)

Food and dietary supplements. Under the *Nutrition Labeling Education Act of 1990* the FTC and the FDA regulate the packaging and advertising of food and dietary products. Anyone involved in this area should obtain a copy of these rules. (*21 USC Sec. 343.*) They are located on the Internet at:

www.ftc.gov/bcp/menu-health.htm#bized

Jewelry and precious metals. The FTC has numerous rules governing the sale and advertising of jewelry and precious metals. Anyone in this business should obtain a copy of these rules. (*61 F.R. Page 27212.*) They are located on the Internet at:

www.ftc.gov/bcp/guides/jewel-gd.htm

New York Law   *False advertising.* False advertising is a Class A misdemeanor under New York law. Misdemeanors are punishable by a fine of up to $1,000. False advertising is also a civil offense punishable by a fine of up to $500 in an action commenced by the New York Attorney General's Office.

False advertising is defined in *New York General Business Law*, Section 350-a as advertising in any form, including labeling, that is misleading in any form. In determining what is *misleading*, the following factors are taken into account:

✪   representations made by statement, word, design, device, sound, or any combination thereof and

✪   the extent to which the advertising fails to reveal important facts.

To display or announce the price of an item after rebate in print or over the TV or radio is also false advertising, unless the actual price is also shown.

Game promotion. (*N.Y. Gen. Bus. Law, Sec. 369-e.*) Gaming is generally illegal in New York. Any type of game, contest, sweepstakes, giveaway, or other game promotion must follow these rules.

✪ If the value of the prize is more than $5,000, the promoter must file a notice with the Secretary of State's office within thirty days of awarding of the prize that discloses the:

- minimum number of participants;

- minimum number of prizes;

- chances of winning; and,

- rules and regulations governing the promotion.

✪ The terms disclosed to the Secretary of State must be published and posted.

✪ The promoter must establish a special trust account sufficient to pay the prize.

✪ The promoter must file the names and addresses of winners of prizes of more than $25 within ninety days.

Failure to follow these rules is a criminal offense.

Insurance advertising. None of the above rules apply to insurance advertising, which is covered by insurance laws.

Names and photographs. (*N.Y. Gen. Bus. Law, Sec. 133.*) It is unlawful to use the name or likeness of any person that may deceive or mislead the public as to the identity of the person for trade or advertising purposes.

Internet Sales Laws

There are not yet specific laws governing Internet transactions that are different from laws governing other transactions. The FTC feels that its current rules regarding deceptive advertising, substantiation, disclaimers, refunds, and related matters must be followed by Internet businesses and that consumers are adequately protected by them. For some specific guidelines on Internet advertising, see the FTC's site at:

> http://ftc.gov/bcp/conline/pubs/buspubs/ruleroad.htm

Home Solicitation Laws

The Federal Trade Commission has rules governing door-to-door sales. In any such sale it is a deceptive trade practice to fail to furnish a receipt explaining the sale (in the language of the presentation) and giving notice that there is a right to back out of the contract within three days, known as a right of *rescission*. The notice must be supplied in duplicate, must be in at least 10-point type, and must be captioned either *Notice of Right to Cancel* or *Notice of Cancellation*. The notice must be worded as follows on the next page.

NOTICE OF CANCELLATION

_____
Date

YOU MAY CANCEL THIS TRANSACTION, WITHOUT ANY PENALTY OR OBLIGATION, WITHIN THREE BUSINESS DAYS FROM THE ABOVE DATE.

IF YOU CANCEL, ANY PROPERTY TRADED IN, ANY PAYMENTS MADE BY YOU UNDER THE CONTRACT OR SALE, AND ANY NEGOTIABLE INSTRUMENT EXECUTED BY YOU WILL BE RETURNED TO YOU WITHIN 10 BUSINESS DAYS FOLLOWING RECEIPT BY THE SELLER OF YOUR CANCELLATION NOTICE, AND ANY SECURITY INTEREST ARISING OUT OF THE TRANSACTION WILL BE CANCELLED.

IF YOU CANCEL, YOU MUST MAKE AVAILABLE TO THE SELLER AT YOUR RESIDENCE, IN SUBSTANTIALLY AS GOOD CONDITION AS WHEN RECEIVED, ANY GOODS DELIVERED TO YOU UNDER THIS CONTRACT OR SALE; OR YOU MAY IF YOU WISH, COMPLY WITH THE INSTRUCTIONS OF THE SELLER REGARDING THE RETURN SHIPMENT OF THE GOODS AT THE SELLER'S EXPENSE AND RISK.

IF YOU DO MAKE THE GOODS AVAILABLE TO THE SELLER AND THE SELLER DOES NOT PICK THEM UP WITHIN 20 DAYS OF THE DATE OF YOUR NOTICE OF CANCELLATION, YOU MAY RETAIN OR DISPOSE OF THE GOODS WITHOUT ANY FURTHER OBLIGATION. IF YOU FAIL TO MAKE THE GOODS AVAILABLE TO THE SELLER, OR IF YOU AGREE TO RETURN THE GOODS AND FAIL TO DO SO, THEN YOU REMAIN LIABLE FOR PERFORMANCE OF ALL OBLIGATIONS UNDER THE CONTRACT.

TO CANCEL THIS TRANSACTION, MAIL OR DELIVER A SIGNED AND DATED COPY OF THIS CANCELLATION NOTICE OR ANY OTHER WRITTEN NOTICE, OR SEND A TELEGRAM, TO _____, AT _____ _____ NOT LATER THAN MIDNIGHT OF _____ (date).

I HEREBY CANCEL THIS TRANSACTION.

_____   _____
(Buyer's signature)   (Date)

The seller must complete the notice and orally inform the buyer of the right to cancel. He or she cannot misrepresent the right to cancel, assign the contract until the fifth business day, nor include a confession of judgment in the contract. (For more specific details see the rules contained at 16 C.F.R. Ch. I, Part 429.)

New York Law   New York's *Personal Property Law*, Article 10-A is called the *Door-to-Door Sales Protection Act*. Sales activities covered by this law are much broader than the title indicates. The *Door-to-Door Sales Protection Act* actually covers *all* sales that are:

- ✪ consumer transactions (sale, rental, lease);

- ✪ over $25 (including all charges, interest, etc.);

- ✪ solicited other than at the seller's regular place of business; and,

- ✪ consummated other than at the seller's regular place of business.

Sales or rentals of real property, sales of insurance, and the sale of securities by a registered broker are not covered by the law. Sales resulting from a specific purchaser's request are included, unless the sale resulted from the purchaser's visit to a fixed location of the seller or the sale is a result of an emergency.

Sales of personal home security systems come under the *Door-to-Door Sales Protection Act*, even if the sale was done over the phone or by mail.

Right to cancel. Any such sale described in the *Door-to-Door Sales Protection Act* may be cancelled by the buyer by written notice postmarked any time before midnight of the *third business day* after the sales day. Business days do not include Sunday, New Year's Day, Washington's Birthday, Memorial Day, Independence Day, Labor Day, Columbus Day, Veterans Day, Thanksgiving Day, and Christmas Day. They *do* include Saturday. The notice of cancellation can be in any form.

Written agreement. Every sale contract covered by this law must be in writing and must contain the following notice.

BUYER'S RIGHT TO CANCEL

You, the buyer, may cancel this transaction at any time prior to midnight of the third business day after the date of this transaction. See the attached notice of cancellation form for an explanation of this right.

Refund. The refund must be made to the buyer within ten days. If it is not, the seller may be subject to criminal and civil penalties.

Buyer's Duty. Within a reasonable time after cancellation and demand by seller, a buyer must return any goods received under the contract unless the seller fails to refund the buyer's deposit as required. If the seller has not made a demand for the return of goods within twenty days, the buyer may keep the goods. If the seller does not refund the buyer's deposit, the buyer may retain possession of the goods. The buyer must take reasonable care of the goods in his or her possession, but does not have to deliver them to the seller at any place other than the buyer's residence.

Seller's Duty. All businesses conducting solicitation sales must orally inform the buyer of his or her right to cancel and provide a contract that conspicuously discloses the seller's refund policy.

Telephone Solicitation Laws

Federal Laws   *Phone calls.* Telephone solicitations are governed by the *Telephone Consumer Protection Act* (*47 USC Sec. 227*) and the Federal Communications Commission rules implementing the Act (*47 C.F.R. Sec. 64.1200*). Violators of the act can be sued for $500 in damages by consumers and can be fined $10,000 by the FCC. Some of the requirements under the law are:

✪   calls can only be made between 8 a.m. and 9 p.m.;

✪   solicitors must keep a *do not call* list and honor requests to not call;

✪ there must be a written policy stating that the parties called are told the name of the caller, the caller's business name, and the phone number or address. They must also be informed that the call is a sales call and the nature of the goods or services;

✪ personnel must be trained in the policies; and,

✪ recorded messages cannot be used to call residences.

In 2003, the FCC introduced the national *Do Not Call Registry*, where individuals could register their telephone numbers and prohibit certain telephone solicitors from calling the registered numbers. Once a person registers a telephone number, it remains on the registry for five years. Telemarketing firms can receive heavy fines for violating the registry statute, with fines ranging up to $11,000 per violation. Not all telephone solicitations are barred, however. The following solicitors may still contact a person whose telephone number has been entered in the registry:

✪ calls from companies with which the registered person has a prior business relationship;

✪ calls for which the recipient has given written consent;

✪ calls that do not include advertisements; and,

✪ calls from charitable organizations.

Faxes. It is illegal under the act to send advertising faxes to anyone who has not consented to receiving such faxes or is an existing customer.

New York Laws

The *Telephone Sales Protection Act* applies to any telephone transaction involving real or personal property normally used primarily for personal, family, or household purposes. (*N.Y. Pers. Prop. Law, Art. 10-B.*) It includes vacation clubs, time shares, the sale or rental of real property, and the sale of insurance or securities. By its own terms, the law is meant to provide a *cooling off period* from *high pressure* telephone sales. It does not apply to calls to businesses. The law contains the following main provisions.

Enforceability. A contract made pursuant to a telephone solicitation is not enforceable unless the seller does two things. First, the seller must inform the buyer of his or her right to cancel. Second, the seller must obtain a signed contract from the buyer that accurately describes the goods, that contains the name, address, and phone number of the seller, and that contains in bold, ten-point conspicuous type the following clause.

> **You, the buyer, may cancel this transaction without any penalty or obligation at any time prior to midnight of the third business day after receipt of this notice. If you cancel, any payments made by you under the sale will be credited to your charge account within ten business days following receipt by the seller of your written notice of cancellation and any security interest arising out of the transaction will be cancelled.**
>
> **If you cancel, you must make available to the seller at your residence, in substantially as good condition as when received, any goods delivered to you under this contract of sale; or you may, if you wish, comply with the instruction of the seller regarding the return shipment of the goods at the seller's expense and risk.**
>
> **If you do make the goods available to the seller and the seller does not pick them up within twenty days of the date of your notice of cancellation, you may retain or dispose of the goods without further obligation. If you fail to make the goods available to the seller, or if you agree to return the goods to the seller and fail to do so, then you remain liable for performance of all obligations under the contract.**
>
> **To cancel this transaction, mail or deliver a written notice of cancellation or send a telegram to (name of seller) at the following address (address of seller).**

Seller's Duties. The seller has thirty days from the date of cancellation to recredit the buyer's charge account. Failure to recredit the account may result in a $100 fine plus attorney's fees. The buyer may retain any goods delivered by the seller, and retain lien on the goods, until the seller complies with buyer's request for a recrediting of his or her charge account.

Buyer's Duties. Within reasonable time after a buyer cancels an order and upon demand by seller, a buyer must return any goods received under the contract unless the seller fails to refund or recredit buyer's credit card account. A *reasonable time* is presumed to be twenty days. If the seller has not made demand within twenty days, the buyer may keep the goods. If the seller does not refund any monies paid, the buyer may keep the goods. The buyer must take reasonable care of the goods in his or her possession, but does not have to deliver them to the seller anywhere other than the buyer's residence.

Exceptions. This law does not apply to catalog sales. Also exempt are real estate agents who make calls in response to yard signs or other ads by property owners.

Automatic Dialing. Except in limited circumstances, it is forbidden to use any machine for automatic dialing or playing a recorded message. (*N.Y. Gen. Bus. Law, Sec. 399-p.*) An automatic dialing system may be used with live messages if the calls are made only to persons who have requested information, if the dialing is screened to exclude persons who are on the *no solicitation calls* list or have unlisted numbers, or if the calls concern goods or services previously ordered or purchased. There are both civil and criminal penalties for violation of this law.

Fax Advertising. It is illegal to send unsolicited advertising materials by fax within the State of New York. (*N.Y. Gen. Bus. Law, Sec. 396-aa.*)

Weights and Labeling

Food Products

Beginning in 1994, all food products are required to have labels with information on the nutritional values, such as calories, fat, and protein. For most products, the label must be in the required format so that consumers can easily compare products. However, if such a format will not fit on the product label, the information may be presented in another form that is easily readable.

Metric Measures

In 1994, federal rules requiring metric measurement of products took effect. Metric measures do not have to be the first measurement on the container, but they must be included. Food items that are packaged as they are sold, such as delicatessen items, do not have to contain metric labels.

New York Law

Fraudulent practices. General Business Law, Section 392-b provides that it is a misdemeanor for a person, with intent to defraud, to:

✪   place upon an article for sale, any false descriptions of the kind, number, quantity, weight, or measure of the article;

- ✪ provide a false description of the point of origin or manufacturer of the article;

- ✪ provide a false description of the quality or grade of the article;

- ✪ provide a false description of the article; or,

- ✪ sell any goods in bulk without a name or trademark and states that the manufacturer is someone other than the real manufacturer.

Unit pricing. Agriculture and Markets Law, Section 214-i mandates the *conspicuous, clear, and plainly marked* disclosure of item or unit pricing on most food packages. Some exceptions include milk, fresh produce, eggs, and identical items sold within a multi-item package that is properly price marked.

Labeling and Pricing. New York's *Agriculture and Market Law* contains a comprehensive set of requirements for various kinds of foods regarding item labeling and packaging, including fair disclosure of quantities, weights, and points of origin.

Deceptive Practices

General Business Law, Section 349 provides that if a business engages in practices that may be regarded as *deceptive or unfair* in a consumer transaction, then it may be subject to the following penalties.

- ✪ The Attorney General may bring court action for injunctions, for damages to consumers, and for fines of up to $500 for each violation.

- ✪ A consumer may bring a suit to stop the deceptive practice and/or for damages up to $1,000 plus attorney's fees.

NOTE: *These penalties increase if the deceptive practice was committed against an elderly person.*

In any action brought against an alleged deceptive practice, it is a complete defense that the advertisement complies with the requirements of the Federal Trade Commission or any department or agency of the State of New York.

Refunds

If a retail establishment has a policy of no refunds or exchanges, a notice of such policy must be posted on one of the following four places:

- ✪ a sign attached to the item;

- ✪ a sign affixed to the cash register at the point of sale;

- ✪ a sign clearly visible to the buyer from the cash register; or,

- ✪ a sign posted at the store entrance.

  (*N.Y. Gen. Bus. Law, Sec. 218-a.*)

The sign required by this section must state whether or not it is the policy of the store to grant refunds, and, if so, under what conditions, including:

- ✪ items marked *sale* or *as is*;

- ✪ whether proof of purchase is required;

- ✪ any time limitations; and,

- ✪ whether cash refunds are available, or a store credit.

If no notice is posted, a seller must grant a refund to purchasers who request it within twenty days of purchase and who produce proof of purchase, provided that the merchandise is unused or undamaged. This rule does not apply to food that cannot be resold by a merchant because of a law or regulation, perishables, goods that are custom made or altered, or goods that cannot be resold.

Statement of Satisfaction
If a seller represents or guarantees that a full or partial credit or refund is available if the purchaser is not fully satisfied with the goods or services purchased, unless the seller specifically specifies otherwise, the purchaser alone decides whether such guarantee or representation is fulfilled by a refund or store credit. (*N.Y. Gen. Bus. Law, Sec. 396-0.*)

13 PAYMENT AND COLLECTION LAWS

Depending on the business you are in, you may be paid by cash, checks, credit cards, or some sort of financing arrangement, such as a promissory note or mortgage. Both state and federal laws affect the type of payments you collect. Failure to follow the laws can cost you considerably.

Cash

Cash is probably the easiest form of payment and it is subject to few restrictions. The most important one is that you keep an accurate accounting of your cash transactions and that you report all of your cash income on your tax return. Recent efforts to stop the drug trade have resulted in some serious penalties for failing to report cash transactions and for money laundering. The laws are so sweeping that even if you deal in cash in an ordinary business you may violate the law and face huge fines and imprisonment.

The most important law to be concerned with is the one requiring the filing of the **REPORT OF CASH PAYMENTS OVER $10,000 RECEIVED IN A TRADE OR BUSINESS (IRS FORM 8300)**. (see form 10, p.241.) A transaction does not have to happen in one day. If a person brings you smaller amounts of cash that add up to $10,000 and the government can construe them as one transaction, then the form must be filed. Under this law, *cash* also includes travelers' checks and money orders but not cashier's checks or bank checks.

Checks

It is important to accept checks in your business. While there is a small percentage which will be bad, most checks will be good and you will be able to accommodate more customers if you accept checks. To avoid having problems with checks, follow the following rules.

Accepting Checks   If a business requires a customer to provide a credit card number or expiration date in order to pay by or cash a check, it is illegal to record the account number of the credit card on the check. (*N.Y. Gen. Bus. Law, Sec. 520-a.*) The business can only request to see a card to establish that the customer is credit-worthy or for additional identification, and can record the type of credit card, issuing company, and/or expiration date. The penalty for a violation of this law is a fine of $250 for the first violation and $1000 for each subsequent violation.

Bad Checks   New York has a fairly effective bad check collection process. If you follow the rules you will probably be able to collect on a bad check. Some counties even have special divisions of the sheriff's department or district attorney's office that actively help you collect on bad checks.

The first requirement is that you are able to identify the person who gave you the check. To do this you should require identification and write down the sources of identification on the face of the check. Another common sense rule is that you should not accept post-dated checks. New York's *General Obligations Law, Section 71-104* provides that in many cases, provided sufficient notice is sent, you may collect from the person who gave you the check an amount equal to twice the amount or $750, whichever is less, if the person had no account with the bank, or twice its amount or $400, whichever is less, if the person had insufficient funds. First a notice must be sent by certified mail in both English and Spanish in at least ten-point type as follows.

DEMAND FOR PAYMENT OF DISHONORED CHECK

DATE:

TO: _____

NAME OF DRAWER

_____

_____

_____

LAST KNOWN RESIDENCE ADDRESS

OR PLACE OF BUSINESS

YOUR CHECK IN THE AMOUNT OF $_____ DATED _____PAYABLE TO THE ORDER OF _____ HAS BEEN DISHONORED BY THE BANK UPON WHICH IT WAS DRAWN, BECAUSE:

—YOU HAD NO ACCOUNT WITH THAT BANK.

—YOU HAD INSUFFICIENT FUNDS ON DEPOSIT WITH THAT BANK.

IF YOU DO NOT MAKE PAYMENT, YOU MAY BE SUED UNDER SECTION 11-104 OF THE GENERAL OBLIGATIONS LAW TO RECOVER PAYMENT. IF A JUDGMENT IS RENDERED AGAINST YOU IN COURT, IT MAY INCLUDE NOT ONLY THE ORIGINAL FACE AMOUNT OF THE CHECK, BUT ALSO ADDITIONAL LIQUIDATED DAMAGES, AS FOLLOWS:

—IF YOU HAD NO ACCOUNT WITH THE BANK UPON WHICH THE CHECK WAS DRAWN, AN ADDITIONAL SUM WHICH MAY BE EQUIVALENT TO TWICE THE FACE AMOUNT OF THE CHECK OR SEVEN HUNDRED FIFTY DOLLARS, WHICHEVER IS LESS; OR

—IF YOU HAD INSUFFICIENT FUNDS ON DEPOSIT WITH THE BANK UPON WHICH THE CHECK WAS DRAWN, AN ADDITIONAL SUM WHICH MAY BE EQUIVALENT TO TWICE THE FACE AMOUNT OF THE CHECK OR FOUR HUNDRED DOLLARS, WHICHEVER IS LESS.

PLEASE MAKE PAYMENT IN THE AMOUNT OF —   TO:

_____

NAME OF PAYEE

_____

_____

_____

ADDRESS TO WHICH PAYMENT

SHOULD BE DELIVERED

Refunds After Cashing a Check
A popular scam is for a person to purchase something using a check and then come back the next day demanding a cash refund. After making the refund the business discovers the initial payment check bounced. Do not make refunds until checks clear.

Credit Cards

In our buy-now, pay-later society, credit cards can add greatly to your sales potential, especially with large, discretionary purchases. For *MasterCard*, *Visa*, and *Discover*, the fees you pay are about two percent, and this amount is easily paid for by the extra purchases that the cards allow. (*American Express*, however, charges four to five percent.)

A business that has an account with a financial institution that allows the business to accept credit card transactions is said to have obtained *merchant status*. For businesses that have a *retail outlet* there is usually no problem getting merchant status. Most commercial banks can handle it. *Discover* can also set you up to accept their card as well as *MasterCard* and *Visa*, and they will wire the money into your bank account daily. However, for mail order businesses, especially those operating out of the home, it is much harder to get merchant status. (*American Express* will accept mail order companies operating out of the home. However, not as many people have their cards.)

Some companies open a small storefront (or share one) to get merchant status and then process mostly mail orders. The processors usually do not want to accept you if you will do more than fifty percent mail order. This is because credit card companies fear mail order fraud. However, if you have not had many complaints from your customers, you may be allowed to process mostly mail orders.

You might be tempted to try to run your charges through another business. This may be okay if you actually sell your products through them; however, if you run your business charges through their account, the other business may lose its merchant status. Someone who bought a book by mail from you and then has a charge on his or her statement from a florist shop will probably call the credit card company saying that they never bought anything from the florist shop. Too many of these complaints, and the account will be closed.

Financing Laws

Some businesses can make sales more easily if they finance the purchases themselves. If the business has enough capital to do this, it can earn extra profits on the financing terms. However, because of abuses, many consumer protection laws have been passed by both the federal and state governments.

Federal Law   Two important federal laws regarding financing are called the *Truth in Lending Act* and the *Fair Credit Billing Act*. These are implemented by what is called *Regulation Z* (commonly known as *Reg. Z*), issued by the Board of Governors of the Federal Reserve System. It is contained in Volume 12 of the *Code of Federal Regulations*, page 226.

The regulation covers all transactions in which the following four conditions are met:

1.   credit is offered;

2.   the offering of credit is regularly done;

3.   there is a finance charge for the credit or there is a written agreement with more than four payments; and,

4.   the credit is for personal, family, or household purposes.

It also covers credit card transactions in which only the first two conditions are met. It applies to leases if the consumer ends up paying the full value and keeping the item leased. It does not apply to the following transactions:

✪   transactions with businesses or agricultural purposes;

✪   transactions with organizations such as corporations or the government;

✪   transactions of over $25,000 which are not secured by the consumer's dwelling;

✪   credit involving public utilities;

✪   credit involving securities or commodities;

✪ home fuel budget plans; and,

✪ student loan programs.

The way for a small business to avoid Reg. Z violations is to avoid transactions that meet the conditions or to make sure all transactions fall under the exceptions. This is easy for many businesses. Instead of extending credit to customers, accept credit cards and let the credit card company extend the credit. However, if your customers usually do not have credit cards or if you are in a business that often extends credit (such as used car sales), consult a lawyer knowledgeable about Reg. Z.

New York Laws New York also has laws regarding financing arrangements. These laws specify what type size must be used in printed contracts, what notices must be included in them, and many other details. Anyone engaged in installment sales in New York should carefully review the latest versions of the following statutes:

✪ *Retail Installment Sales Act* (*Personal Property Law, Article 10*);

✪ *Motor Vehicle Detail Installment Sales Act* (*Personal Property Law, Article 9*);

✪ *Motor Vehicle Retail Leasing Act* (*Personal Property Law, Article 9-A*);

✪ Home Improvement Contracts (*General Business Law, Article 36-A*); and,

✪ Rental Purchase Agreements (*Personal Property Law, Article 11*).

These laws can be obtained at your local public law library, which is usually located at the Supreme Court building of your county. They are open to the public. Just tell the librarian that you are not a lawyer and he or she will point you in the right direction.

In addition to these acts, *Executive Law, Section 296-a* forbids discrimination based upon sex, marital status, or race in the areas of loaning money, granting credit, or providing equal pay for equal services performed. And *Executive Law, Section 296* forbids discrimination in the financing of residential real estate based upon race, color, national origin, sex, handicap, familial status, or religion. (This form of discrimination is known as *blockbusting*.)

Usury

Usury is the charging of an illegally high rate of interest. In New York, if you have a written agreement, the maximum rate of interest you may charge is 16%, except on loans of over $250,000 for which the maximum rate can be 25%. If there is no written agreement as to the rate of interest, the rate is set by law.

For banks, the penalty for charging interest in excess of the legal rate is that the borrower does not have to pay any interest and the lender has to repay double the amounts received. For other businesses, the contract is absolutely void.

Anyone charging or receiving interest at a rate of over 25% is guilty of a Class E felony. Anyone found guilty of a second offense is guilty of a Class C felony.

Securities Laws

Both the state and federal governments have long and complicated laws dealing with the sales of *securities*. There are also hundreds of court cases attempting to explain what these laws mean. A thorough explanation of this area of law is beyond the scope of this book.

Basically, securities have been held to exist in any case in which a person provides money with the expectation that he or she will profit through the efforts of another person. This can apply to any situation where someone buys stock in or makes a loan to your business. The laws require a disclosure of the risks involved and in some cases registration of the securities with the government. There are some exemptions, such as for small amounts of money and for limited numbers of investors.

Penalties for violation of securities laws are severe, including triple damages and prison terms. Consult a specialist in securities laws before letting anyone invest in your business. You can often get an introductory consultation at a reasonable rate to explain your options.

Collections

The *Fair Debt Collection Practices Act of 1977* bans the use of deception, harassment, and other unreasonable acts in the collection of debts. It has strict requirements whenever someone is collecting a debt for someone else. If you are in the collection business, you must obtain a copy of this law.

The Federal Trade Commission has issued some rules that prohibit deceptive representations, such as:

✪ pretending to be in the motion picture industry, the government, or a credit bureau;

✪ using questionnaires that do not say their purpose is collecting a debt; or,

✪ any combination of these.

New York Law The *Retail Installment Sales Act* (*Personal Property Law, Article 10, Sections 401-422*) applies to the sale of consumer goods or services where the price for such goods or services is payable in installments, including payments over time on credit. The statute is complicated and goes into much detail about the content of an installment contract and credit agreement. *Section 413* of the *Personal Property Law* deals in particular with the requirements of a retail installment credit agreement. This law is very complicated and could be the subject of its own book. Therefore, if you have any questions about complying with it, consult an attorney that specializes in business law. Failure to comply with Article 10 of the *Personal Property Law* is a misdemeanor punishable by a fine of up to $500, among other consequences.

General Business Law, Article 29-H, Sections 600-603 applies to the collection of debts owed by persons (not corporations) for transactions that were for personal, family, or household purposes. The law forbids:

✪ simulating a law enforcement officer or government agency;

✪ threatening to disclose the debt to others without explaining that there is a dispute over the debt that will also be disclosed;

- ✪ contacting or threatening to contact a debtor's employer prior to obtaining a final judgment, unless the debtor has given permission in writing or unless the debtor has agreed in writing as to the debt, after the debt goes to collection;

- ✪ disclosing information affecting the debtor's reputation to persons outside the debtor's family who do not have a legitimate business need for the information;

- ✪ disclosing information affecting the debtor's reputation, knowing the information to be false;

- ✪ disclosing information about a disputed debt without disclosing the dispute;

- ✪ willfully harassing the debtor or his or her family;

- ✪ attempting to collect a debt that is not legitimate;

- ✪ claiming a legal right knowing that the right does not exist;

- ✪ using communication that looks like it is from a court, government agency, or attorney if it is not; and,

- ✪ knowingly attempting to collect any collection fee, attorney's fee, court cost, or expense unless such charges are legitimately owed by the debtor.

Violation of this law is a misdemeanor, with each separate violation constituting a separate offense.

The New York State Attorney General or the District Attorney of any county may seek criminal penalties and injunctions for violations of this law.

14 | BUSINESS RELATIONS LAWS

At both the federal and state level there exist many laws regarding how businesses relate to one another. Some of the more important ones are discussed in this chapter.

The Uniform Commercial Code

The *Uniform Commercial Code (UCC)* is a set of laws regulating numerous aspects of doing business. In order to avoid having a patchwork of different laws around the fifty states, a national group drafted this set of uniform laws. Although some states have modified some sections of the laws, the code is basically the same in most states. In New York, the *UCC* is contained in three volumes of the *McKinney's Consolidated Laws of New York*. Each chapter of the UCC is concerned with a different aspect of commercial relations such as sales, warranties, bank deposits, commercial paper, and bulk transfers.

Businesses that wish to know their rights in all types of transactions should obtain a copy of the UCC and become familiar with it. It is especially useful in transactions between merchants. However, the meaning is not always clear from a reading of the statutes.

Commercial Discrimination

The *Robinson-Patman Act of 1936* prohibits businesses from injuring competition by offering the same goods at different prices to different buyers. This means that the large chain stores should not be getting a better price than a small shop. It also requires that promotional allowances must be made on proportionally the same terms to all buyers.

New York Law

New York *General Business Law*, Section 340 sets out New York law on commercial discrimination. It states that any business arrangement whereby *competition or the free exercise of any activity in the conduct of any business, trade or commerce or in the furnishing of any service in this state is or may be restrained is illegal and void*. It also subjects the offender to the penalties set forth in *Article 22* of the *General Business Law*.

Restraining Trade

One of the earliest federal laws affecting business is the *Sherman Antitrust Act of 1890*. The purpose of this law was to protect competition in the marketplace by prohibiting monopolies.

Examples of some prohibited actions are:

- ✪ agreements between competitors to sell at the same prices;

- ✪ agreements between competitors on how much will be sold or produced;

- ✪ agreements between competitors to divide up a market;

- ✪ refusing to sell one product without a second product; and,

- ✪ exchanging information among competitors that results in similarity of prices.

As a new business, you probably will not be in a position to violate the Act, but you should be aware of it in case a larger competitor tries to put you out of business.

New York Law   Under *General Business Law, Article 22*, it is unlawful to have any contract, combination, or conspiracy to restrain trade or to monopolize, attempt to monopolize, or combine or conspire with any other person to monopolize, any part of trade or commerce.

✪   Violation of this law is classified as a Class E felony.

✪   The penalty for any violation is up to $100,000 for a natural person or by imprisonment of up to four years, and up to $1,000,000 for a company.

✪   Anyone *knowingly* violating or knowingly aiding or advising a violation can be guilty of a felony and sentenced to up to three years in prison in addition to the fines.

✪   The Attorney General may bring an action against any person or company to restrain and prevent monopolies in New York State by the use of an injunction or other means, including penalties of up to $20,000, in addition to the monetary penalties specified above. (*N.Y. Gen. Bus. Law, Sec. 342.*)

Commercial Bribery

New York Law   The laws concerning commercial bribery are found in the *Penal Law*, Article 180. *Commercial bribe receiving* is defined as soliciting, accepting, or agreeing to accept a benefit with intent to influence the employer's conduct with intent to violate a law. It applies to:

✪   agents;

✪   employees;

✪   trustees;

- ✪   guardians;

- ✪   fiduciaries;

- ✪   lawyers;

- ✪   physicians;

- ✪   accountants;

- ✪   appraisers;

- ✪   other professional advisors;

- ✪   arbitrators;

- ✪   officers;

- ✪   directors;

- ✪   managers;

- ✪   partners; and,

- ✪   others in control of an organization.

Commercial bribery is committed by anyone on the other side of a transaction with one of the named individuals. Special laws apply to the bribery of labor officials and sports bribery. In most cases, commercial bribery and bribe receiving are misdemeanors

Intellectual Property Protection

As a business owner, you should know enough about intellectual property laws to protect your own creations and to keep from violating the rights of others. Intellectual property is the product of human creativity, such as writings, designs, inventions, melodies, and processes. Intellectual property is something that can be stolen without being physically taken. For example, if you write a book, someone can steal the words from your book without stealing a physical copy of it.

As the Internet grows, intellectual property is becoming more valuable. Smart business owners will take the actions necessary to protect their company's intellectual property. Additionally, business owners should know intellectual property laws to make certain they do not violate the rights of others. Even an unknowing violation of the law can result in stiff fines and penalties.

The following paragraphs explain the types of intellectual property and the ways to protect them.

Patent   A *patent* is protection given to new and useful inventions, discoveries and designs. To be entitled to a patent, a work must be completely *new* and *unobvious*. The first inventor who files for a patent gets it. Once an invention is patented, no one else can make use of that invention, even if they discover it independently. In general, a new patent lasts for twenty years from the date of filing the patent application with the United States Patent and Trademark Office (USPTO). Patents cannot be renewed. The patent application must clearly explain how to make the invention, so when the patent expires, others will be able to freely make and use the invention. Patents are registered with the United States Patent and Trademark Office. Patentable items include mechanical devices or new drug formulas.

Copyright   A *copyright* is protection given to *original works of authorship*, such as written works, musical works, visual works, performance works, or computer software programs. A copyright exists from the moment of creation, but one cannot register a copyright until it has been fixed in tangible form. Also, titles, names, or slogans cannot be copyrighted. A copyright currently gives the author and his or her heirs exclusive right to the work for the life of the author plus seventy years. Copyrights first registered before 1978 last for 95 years. This was previously 75 years, but was extended 20 years to match the European system. Copyrights are registered with the Register of Copyrights at the Library of Congress. The fee to register a copyright is $30. Examples of works that are copyrightable include books, paintings, songs, poems, plays, drawings, and films.

Contact the U.S. Copyright Office at:

Library of Congress
101 Independence Avenue, S.E.
Washington, DC 20559
202-707-3000
www.copyright.gov.

Trademark
A *trademark* is protection given to a name or symbol that is used to distinguish one person's goods or services from those of others. It can consist of letters, numbers, packaging, labeling, musical notes, colors, or a combination of these. If a trademark is used on services, as opposed to goods, it is called a *service mark*. A trademark lasts indefinitely if it is used continuously and renewed properly. Trademarks are registered with the United States Patent and Trademark Office and with individual states. (This is explained further in Chapter 3.) Examples of trademarks include the *Chrysler* name on automobiles, the red border on TIME magazine, and the shape of the *Coca-Cola* bottle.

Trade Secrets
A *trade secret* is information or a process that provides a commercial advantage that is protected by keeping it a secret. Examples of trade secrets may be a list of successful distributors, the formula for *Coca-Cola*, or some unique source code in a computer program. Trade secrets are not registered anywhere, but they are protected by the fact that they are not disclosed. They are protected only for as long as they are kept secret. If you independently discover the formula for *Coca-Cola* tomorrow, you can freely market it. (But you can't use the trademark *Coca-Cola* on your product to market it.)

Non-Protectable Creations
Some things are just not protectable, such as ideas, systems, and discoveries that are not allowed any protection under law. If you have a great idea, such as selling packets of hangover medicine in bars, you cannot stop others from doing the same thing. If you invent a new medicine you can patent it; if you pick a distinctive name for it you can register the name as a trademark; if you create a unique picture or instructions for the package, you can copyright it. However, you cannot stop others from using your basic business idea of marketing hangover medicine in bars.

Notice the subtle differences between the protective systems available. If you invent something two days after someone else does and that person has patented it, you cannot even use it for yourself. But if you write the same poem as someone else and neither of you copied the other, both of you can copyright the poem. If you patent something, you can have the exclusive rights to it for the term of the patent, but you must disclose how others can recreate it after the patent expires. However, if you keep it a trade secret, you have exclusive rights as long as no one learns the secret.

We are in a time of transition of the law of intellectual property. Every year new changes are made in the laws and new forms of creativity win protection. For more information, consult a new edition of a book on these types of property.

15 ENDLESS LAWS

The state of New York and the federal government have numerous laws and rules that apply to every aspect of every type of business. There are laws governing such things as fence posts, hosiery, rabbit raising, refund policies, frozen desserts, and advertising. Every business is affected by one or another of these laws.

Some activities are covered by both state and federal laws. In such cases, you must obey the stricter of the rules. In addition, more than one agency of the state or federal government may have rules governing your business. Each of these may have the power to investigate violations and impose fines or other penalties.

Penalties for violations of these laws can range from a warning to a criminal fine and even jail time. In some cases, employees can sue for damages. Since *ignorance of the law is no excuse*, it is your duty to learn what laws apply to your business.

Very few people in business know the laws that apply to their businesses. If you take the time to learn them, you can become an expert in your field and avoid problems with regulators. You can also fight back if one of your competitors uses an illegal method to compete with you.

The laws and rules that affect most businesses are explained in this section. Following the explanation is a list of more specialized laws. You should read through this list and see which ones may apply to your business. Then go to your public library or law library and read them. Some may not apply to your phase of the business. If any of them do apply, you should make copies to keep on hand.

Federal Laws

The federal laws that are most likely to affect small businesses are rules of the Federal Trade Commission (FTC). The FTC has some rules that affect many businesses; the rules about labeling, warranties, and mail order sales are just some examples. Other rules affect only certain industries.

If you sell goods by mail you should send for the FTC's booklet, *A Business Guide to the Federal Trade Commission's Mail or Telephone Order Merchandise Rule*. It is also available online at **www.ftc.gov/bcp/conline/pubs/buspubs/ mailorder.htm**. You should ask for their latest information on the subject if you are going to be involved in an industry such as those listed below, or using warranties or your own labeling. The address is:

Federal Trade Commission
Washington, DC 20580
202-326-2222

The rules of the FTC are contained in the Code of Federal Regulations (C.F.R.) in Title 16. Some of the industries covered are:

INDUSTRY	PART
Adhesive Compositions	235
Aerosol Products Used for Frosting Cocktail Glasses	417
Automobiles (New car fuel economy advertising)	259
Business Opportunities and Franchises	436
Cigarettes	408
Decorative Wall Paneling	243
Dog and Cat Food	241
Dry Cell Batteries	403
Extension Ladders	418
Fiber Glass Curtains	413

Food (Games of Chance)	419
Funerals	453
Gasoline (Octane posting)	306
Gasoline	419
Home Entertainment Amplifiers	432
Home Insulation	460
Household Furniture	250
Jewelry	23
Law Books	256
Luggage and Related Products	24
Mail Order Merchandise	435
Nursery	18
Ophthalmic Practices	456
Photographic Film and Film Processing	242
Private Vocational and Home Study Schools	254
Retail Food Stores (Advertising)	424
Sleeping Bags	400
Television Sets	410
Textile Wearing Apparel	423
Tires	228
Used Automobile Parts	20
Used Lubricating Oil	406
Used Motor Vehicles	455
Watches	245
Wigs and Hairpieces	252

Some other federal laws that affect businesses are as follows:

✪ *Alcohol Administration Act*

✪ *Child Protection and Toy Safety Act* (1969)

✪ *Clean Water Act*

✪ *Comprehensive Smokeless Tobacco Health Education Act* (1986)

✪ *Consumer Credit Protection Act* (1968)

✪ *Consumer Product Safety Act* (1972)

- ✪ *Energy Policy and Conservation Act*

- ✪ *Environmental Pesticide Control Act of 1972*

- ✪ *Fair Credit Reporting Act (1970)*

- ✪ *Fair Packaging and Labeling Act (1966)*

- ✪ *Flammable Fabrics Act (1953)*

- ✪ *Food, Drug, and Cosmetic Act*

- ✪ *Food Safety Enforcement Enhancement Act of 1997*

- ✪ *Fur Products Labeling Act (1951)*

- ✪ *Hazardous Substances Act (1960)*

- ✪ *Hobby Protection Act*

- ✪ *Insecticide, Fungicide, and Rodenticide Act*

- ✪ *Magnuson-Moss Warranty Act*

- ✪ *Nutrition Labeling and Education Act of 1990*

- ✪ *Poison Prevention Packaging Act of 1970*

- ✪ *Solid Waste Disposal Act*

- ✪ *Textile Fiber Products Identification Act*

- ✪ *Toxic Substance Control Act*

- ✪ *Wool Products Labeling Act (1939)*

Homeland Security Concerns The recent formation of the U.S. Department of Homeland Security (DHS) has caused a variety of new issues to arise that affect business. New laws designed to protect national interests have been and will continue to be enacted that will directly impact how businesses are operated. The DHS also has a need for products and services that will ensure national security. This, in turn, will provide for many opportunities for companies engaged in businesses that can deliver those goods and services. For more information about DHS opportunities, contact the Department at:

U.S. Department of Homeland Security
Washington, DC 20528
www.dhs.gov/dhspublic

Sarbanes-Oxley Act

In the wake of crises at Enron as well as other publicly-traded companies several years ago, Congress enacted the *Sarbanes-Oxley Act* in 2002. The purpose of this legislation is to, as Congress stated, *protect investors by improving the accuracy and reliability of corporate disclosures made pursuant to the securities law.* The Act applies to all publicly-traded companies, no matter how small. Among other things, the Act requires that:

✪ corporate officers certify that they have reviewed the company's financial reports and that no false or misleading information is contained therein;

✪ changes in the financial standing or operations of the company be disclosed;

✪ the company makes no loans to insiders; and,

✪ compliance with the Act is achieved by certain set deadlines.

The text of the *Sarbanes-Oxley Act* can be found online at **www.law.uc.edu/ CCL/SOact/soact.pdf**.

Punishment for violations of the Act includes multi-million dollar fines and prison time, so it is extremely important that the Sarbanes-Oxley requirements are followed. Firms offering assistance with compliance to companies is becoming big business in and of itself. It may pay off for you to consider hiring an expert to guide your business through the compliance process.

New York State Laws

New York has numerous laws regulating specific types of businesses or certain activities of businesses. They are contained in many different statutes that can be found in any law library. Regulations that govern the enforcement of these laws are found in the New York *Code of Rules and Regulations*, a loose-leaf bound set of volumes that are crossreferenced to each statute it supplements. They are also found in any law library. Unfortunately, it is not always easy to find a law library open to the general public for free. Most are contained in private law firms or law schools that severely restrict admittance by nonlawyers. However, every county has a county seat where the Supreme Court is located and most Supreme Courts operate a law library that is open to the public. A phone call or visit will provide information on hours of operation, etc.

The following is a list of those laws which are most likely to affect small businesses.

LAWS REGULATING BUSINESS IN NEW YORK

Adoption agencies	Provided for by various statutes in the Domestic Relations Law & Public Health Law
Adult congregate living facilities	Executive Law Sec. 543-a
Adult day care facilities	Social Services Law Article 7
Adult foster home care	Social Services Law Article 6
Air conditioning	Executive Law Article 18
Alcoholic beverages	Alcoholic Beverage Control Law
Ambulance service contracts	Public Health Law Sec. 2803-a, General Municipal Law Sec. 209-6
Anatomical matter	Public Health Law Article 43
Animals	See generally, Agriculture & Markets Law
Aquaculture	Town Law beginning with Sec. 191
Art & craft material	Arts & Cultural Affairs Law
Auctions	General Business Law, Art. 3
Automobile racing	Vehicle & Traffic Law Secs. 510, 1182, 1182-a
Bail bondsmen	Insurance Law Art. 68
Banking	Banking Law
Boiler safety	Labor Law Sec. 204
Bottles & boxes, markings	General Business Law Sec. 392-6

Boxing & fighting	Title 25, Ch. 1 Unconsolidated Laws
Brake fluid	Vehicle & Traffic Law Sec. 382
Budget planning	Banking Law Sec. 583-a
Buildings, radon resistance stds.	Energy Law, Part 7930
Burial contracts	Not-for-Profit Corp. Law Sec. 1509
Business opportunities	General Municipal Law Art. 19-A
Cemeteries	Various provisions in Town Law & Village Law
Charitable solicitation	Executive Law, Art. 7-A
Collection agencies	Judiciary Law Sec. 489, General Business Law Sec. 84
Commissions merchants	Agricultural & Markets Law, Art. 20
Condominiums	Real Property Law, Art. 9-B
Construction	Labor Law Sec. 241
Consumer Finance	Federal Truth in Lending Act
Cooperatives	Cooperative Corporation Law
Cosmetics	Education Law Sec. 6818-a
Credit cards	General Business Law Arts. 29-A, 29 AAA, 29-B
Credit service organizations	General Business Law, Art. 28-B
Dairies	Agricultural & Markets Law Sec. 75, Art. 4

Desserts, frozen	Agricultural & Markets Law, Art. 4-A
Dog racing & horse racing	Racing, Pari-mutuel, Wagering & Breeding Law
Drinking water	Public Health, Art. 11
Drugs	Public Health, Art. 33
Eggs & poultry	Agricultural & Markets Law, Art. 13 A & 5-D
Electrical code (towns)	Town Law Sec. 130(3)
Electronic repair	General Business Law Sec. 597
Elevators	Multiple Dwelling Law Sec. 51, Labor Law Sec. 255
Energy conservation standards	Energy Law Art. 11
Equity exchanges	Business Corp. Law Art. 16
Explosives	General Business Law Art. 28-D; Labor Law Art. 16
Factory built housing	Real Property Law Sec. 233, Vehicle & Traffic Law Art. 21
Fence Posts	Town Law Sec. 309
Fences & livestock at large	Agricultural & Markets Law Secs331, Art. 25-B
Fiduciary funds	Estate Planning & Trust Law Secs. 5-1.1; 5-1.1-A
Fireworks	Penal Law 270.00, 405.00
Food	Agricultural & Markets Law Art. 17

Franchises	General Business Law Art. 33
Fruits & vegetables	Agricultural & Markets Law Arts.13-C, 22, 23, 24, 25
Fuels, liquid	Environmental Conservation Law Sec. 23-230
Gambling & lotteries	Tax Law Art. 16
Gas, gasoline & oil	Environmental Conservation Law beginning with Sec. 23-0101
Glass	Environmental Conservation Law Art. 27
Hazardous substances	Various provisions in Environmental Conservation Law
Health care	Public Health Law
Health studios	General Business Law Art. 30
Home health agencies	Social Services Law Sec. 367-C; Public Health Law Art. 36
Home improvement sales & fin.	General Business Law Art 36-A
Honey	Agricultural & Markets Law Sec. 205, Art. 23
Horse sales, shows, exhibitions	Agricultural & Markets Law Secs. 358, 359-a, 364, 368
Hospices	Public Health Law, Art. 40
Hotels	General Business Law, Art. 12
Household products	Environmental Conservation Law, beginning with Sec. 35-0101

Housing codes, state minimum	N.Y.S. Uniform Fire Prevention & Building Code Act; Executive Law Art. 18
Insurance & service plans	Insurance Law
Land sales	Real Property Law, Arts. 8, 9, 12
Lasers & non-ionizing radiation	General Business Law, Art. 28-D
Lead acid batteries	Environmental Conservation Law Sec. 27-1701; Sec. 27-0719
Legal services	Judiciary Law Sec. 460, Sec. 474
Linen suppliers	General Business Law Sec. 396-e
Liquor	Alcoholic Beverage Control Law
Livestock	Agricultural & Markets Art. 35
Lodging	General Business Law, Art. 12
Marketing establishments	Agricultural & Markets Law Art. 25
Meats	Agr. & Mkt. Law, Art. 5-A, 5-B, 5-C
Mental health	Mental Hygiene Law
Metal recyclers	Environmental Conservation Law beginning with Sec. 71-2701
Milk & milk products	Agricultural & Markets Law, Art. 21 & 21-A
Mobile homes	Private Housing Finance Law Sec. 1122; Vehicle & Traffic Law Sec. 2124, 2125
Money orders	Banking Law Secs. 373, 453, 640

Motion pictures	Arts & Cultural Affairs Law Art. 19
Motor vehicle lemon law	General Business Law Secs. 198-a, 198-b
Motor vehicles	Vehicle & Traffic Law
Newsprint	General Business Law, Art. 21
Nursing homes	Public Health Law Sec. 2896, 2897
Obscene literature	General Business Law, Art. 21
Oil	Environmental Conservation Law beginning with 23-0101
Pari-mutuel wagering	Racing, Pari-mutuel Wagering & Breeding Law
Pest control	Agricultural & Markets Law, Art. 11 & 14
Photos of admission parks	Arts & Cultural Affairs Law Sec.31.01
Plants & nurseries	Agricultural & Markets Law, Art. 14
Plumbing	General City Law, Art. 4
Prostitution	Public Health Law beginning with Sec. 2320
Pyramid schemes	General Bus. Law Sec. 369-ee
Radiation	Agricultural & Markets Law Sec. 200, Public Health Sec. 225
Radio & television repairs	General Business Law Sec. 597

Real estate sales	Real Property Law, Arts. 8, 9, 12; Tax Law Sec. 1449
Rental housing	Landlord & Tenant Law; Real Property Actions & Proceedings law; Rent Control Law Unconsolidated Law beginning with Sec. 26-501; Rent Stabilization Law - Unconsolidated Law beginning with Sec. 26-501
Restaurants	Public Health Secs. 1350, 1351; Alcoholic Beverages Control Law Secs. 366, 101, 106, 98
Secondhand dealers	Town Law Sec. 136(1), 137
Securities transactions	General Business Law, Art. 23-A
Swimming & bathing places	General Municipal Law Sec. 242; Public Health Sec. 1340-1342
Syrup	Alcoholic Beverage Control Law 91, 91-a; Agr. & Mkts 203-204
Television picture tubes	General Business Law, Art. 29-C
Term papers, dissertations	Education Law Sec. 213-b
Thermal efficiency standards	Energy Law, Art. 12
Timber & lumber	Environmental Conservation Law beginning with Sec. 9-0101 .
Tires	Vehicle & Traffic Law 375(35); Gen. Bus. Law Sec. 391
Tobacco	Public Health Law beginning with Sec. 1399-aa. Tax Law Sec. 480-a

Tourist attraction	Economic Development Law, Arts. 5-A, 5-B
Tourist camps	Economic Development Law, Arts. 5-A, 5-B
Travel services	General Business Law, Art. 10-A
Sound & film, copying	Arts & Cultural Affairs Sec. 31.01
Viticulture	Tax Law Secs. 210, 606, 1115
Watches, used	General Business Law Sec. 392
Weapons & firearms	Penal Law, Art. 265, Art. 400; General Business Law, Art. 39-B

16 | BOOKKEEPING AND ACCOUNTING

It is beyond the scope of this book to explain all the intricacies of setting up a business's bookkeeping and accounting systems. However, if you do not set up an understandable bookkeeping system, your business will undoubtedly fail.

Without accurate records of where your income is coming from and where it is going, you will be unable to increase your profits, lower your expenses, obtain needed financing, or make the right decisions in all areas of your business. The time to decide how you will handle your bookkeeping is when you open your business, not a year later when it is tax time.

Initial Bookkeeping

If you do not understand business taxation, you should pick up a good book on the subject as well as the IRS tax guide for your type of business (proprietorship, partnership, or corporation). The IRS tax book for small businesses is Publication 334, *Tax Guide for Small Businesses*. There are also instruction booklets for each type of business's form, Schedule C for proprietorships, Form 1120 or 1120S for C corporations and S corporations, and 1165 for partnerships and businesses that are taxed like partnerships (LLCs and LLPs).

Keep in mind that the IRS does not give you the best advice for saving on taxes and does not give you the other side of contested issues. For that you need a private tax guide or advisor.

The most important thing to do is to set up your bookkeeping so that you can easily fill out your monthly, quarterly, and annual tax returns. The best way to do this is to get copies of the returns, note the totals that you will need to supply, and set up your bookkeeping system to group those totals.

For example, for a sole proprietorship you will use *Schedule C* to report business income and expenses to the IRS at the end of the year. Use the categories on that form to sort your expenses. To make your job especially easy, every time you pay a bill, put the category number on the check.

Accountants

Most likely your new business will not be able to afford hiring an accountant to handle your books, but that is good. Doing them yourself will force you to learn about business accounting and taxation. The worst way to run a business is to know nothing about the tax laws and turn everything over to an accountant at the end of the year to find out what is due.

You should know the basics of tax law before making basic decisions such as whether to buy or rent equipment or premises. You should understand accounting so you can time your financial affairs appropriately. If you were a boxer who only needed to win fights, you could turn everything over to an accountant. If your business needs to buy supplies, inventory, or equipment and provides goods or services throughout the year, you need to at least have a basic understanding of the system you are working within.

Once you can afford an accountant, weigh the cost against your time and the risk that you will make an error. Even if you think you know enough to do your own corporate tax return, you might take it to an accountant one year to see if you have been missing any deductions that you did not know about. You might decide that the money saved is worth the cost of the accountant's services.

Computer Programs

Today, every business should keep its books by computer. There are inexpensive programs, such as *Quicken*, that can instantly provide you with reports of your income and expenses and the right figures to plug into your tax returns. Most programs offer a tax program each year that will take all of your information and print it out on the current year's tax forms.

Tax Tips

Here are a few tax tips that may help businesses save money.

✪ Usually when you buy equipment for a business you must amortize the cost over several years. That is, you do not deduct the entire cost when you buy it, but take, say, 25% of the cost off your taxes each year for four years. (The time is determined by the theoretical usefulness of the item.) However, small businesses are allowed to write off the entire cost of a limited amount of items under *Internal Revenue Code, Section 179*. If you have income to shelter, use it.

✪ Owners of S corporations do not have to pay Social Security or Medicare taxes on the part of their profits that is not considered salary. As long as you pay yourself a reasonable salary, other money you take out is not subject to these taxes.

✪ Do not neglect to deposit withholding taxes for your own salary or profits. Besides being a large sum to come up with at once in April, there are penalties that must be paid for failure to do so.

✪ Be sure to keep track of, and remit, your employees' withholding. You will be personally liable for them even if your business is a corporation.

✪ If you keep track of your use of your car for business, you can deduct mileage (see IRS guidelines for the amount, as it can change each year). If you use your car for business a considerable amount of time, you may be able to depreciate it.

✪   If your business is a corporation and if you designate the stock as *section 1244 stock*, then if the business fails you are able to get a much better deduction for the loss.

✪   By setting up a retirement plan, you can exempt up to 20% of your salary from income tax. But do not use money you might need later. There are penalties for taking it out of the retirement plan.

✪   When you buy things that will be resold or made into products that will be resold (*i.e.*, you are buying from a wholesaler), you do not have to pay sales tax on those purchases.

17 | PAYING FEDERAL TAXES

As we all know, the federal government levies many different types of taxes on individuals and businesses. It is very important that you consult an accountant or attorney to properly comply with and take advantage of the incredibly complex federal tax code and regulations. The following discusses several of the most important federal taxes that will most likely affect your new business.

Income Tax

The following section describes the manner in which each type of business pays taxes.

Proprietorship A proprietor reports profits and expenses on Schedule C attached to the usual Form 1040 and pays tax on all of the net income of the business. Each quarter Form 1040ES (estimated tax) must be filed along with payment of one-quarter of the amount of income tax and Social Security tax estimated to be due for the year. Publication 334, *Tax Guide for Small Business*, is available online at **www.irs.gov**.

Partnership   The partnership files a return showing the income and expenses but pays no tax. Each partner is given a form showing his or her share of the profits or losses and reports these on Schedule E of Form 1040. Each quarter, Form 1040ES must be filed by each partner along with payment of one-quarter of the amount of income tax and Social Security tax estimated to be due for the year.

C Corporation   A regular corporation is a separate taxpayer and pays tax on its profits after deducting all expenses, including officers' salaries. If dividends are distributed, they are paid out of after-tax dollars and the shareholders pay tax a second time when they receive the dividends. If a corporation needs to accumulate money for investment, it may be able to do so at lower tax rates than the shareholders pay. But if all profits will be distributed to shareholders, the double-taxation may be excessive unless all income is paid as salaries. A C corporation files Form 1120.

S Corporation   A small corporation has the option of being taxed like a partnership. If Form 2553 *(Election by a Small Business Corporation)* is filed by the corporation and accepted by the Internal Revenue Service, the S corporation will only file an informational return listing profits and expenses. Each shareholder will be taxed on a proportional share of the profits (or be able to deduct a proportional share of the losses). Unless a corporation will make a large profit that will not be distributed, S-status is usually best in the beginning. An S corporation files Form 1120S and distributes Form K-1 *(Shareholder's Share of Income, Credits, Deductions,* etc.) to each shareholder. If any money is taken out by a shareholder that is not listed as wages subject to withholding, the shareholder will usually have to file Form 1040ES each quarter along with payment of the estimated withholding on the withdrawals.

Limited Liability Companies and Partnerships   Limited liability companies and limited liability partnerships are allowed to elect to be taxed either as a partnership or a corporation by the IRS. To make this election, you file Form 8832, *Entity Classification Election* with the IRS.

Tax Workshops and Booklets   The IRS conducts workshops to inform businesses about the tax laws. (Do not expect in-depth study of the loopholes.) For more information, call the IRS toll free at 800-829-1040 or write to the IRS at the following addresses:

IRS (Brooklyn)
10 Metrotech Center
625 Fulton St.
Brooklyn, NY 11201
718-488-3655

IRS (Buffalo)

P.O. Box 606

Buffalo, NY 14225

716-686-4777

IRS (Manhattan)

P.O. Box 3036

Church Street Station

New York, NY 10008

212-436-1021

They also offer online workshops for small businesses at **www.irs.gov/ businesses/small/index.html**.

Withholding, Social Security, and Medicare Taxes

If you need basic information on business tax returns, the IRS publishes a rather large booklet that answers most questions and is available free of charge. Call or write the IRS and ask for Publication No. 334. If you have any questions, look up their toll-free number in the phone book under United States Government/Internal Revenue Service. If you want more creative answers and tax saving information, find a good accountant. However, to get started, you will need the following.

Employer Identification Number

If you are a sole proprietor with no employees, you can use your Social Security number for your business. If you are a corporation, a partnership, or a proprietorship with employees, you must obtain an *Employer Identification Number*. This is done by filing the **APPLICATION FOR EMPLOYER IDENTIFICATION NUMBER (IRS FORM SS-4)**. (see form 6, p.215.) It usually takes a week or two to receive. You will need this number to open bank accounts for the business, so you should file this form as soon as you decide to go into business. A sample filled-in form and instructions are in Appendix B.

Employee's Withholding Allowance Certificate

You must have each employee fill out a W-4 form to calculate the amount of federal taxes to be deducted and to obtain his or her Social Security number. (see form 7, p.221.) The number of allowances on this form is used with IRS Publication 15, *Circular E, Employer's Tax Guide*, to figure out the exact deductions. A sample filled-in is included in Appendix B.

Federal Tax Deposit Coupons

After taking withholdings from employees' wages, you must deposit them at a bank that is authorized to accept such funds. Your required schedule for making deposits is explained in Publication 15 and depends upon the amount of taxes withheld from employees' wages. The deposit is made using the coupons in the Form 8109 booklet, which the IRS will provide.

Estimated Tax Payment Voucher

Sole proprietors and partners usually take draws from their businesses without the formality of withholding. However, they are still required to make deposits of income and FICA taxes each quarter. If more than $500 is due in April on a person's 1040 form, not enough money was withheld each quarter. In this situation, a penalty is assessed, unless the person falls under an exception. The quarterly withholding is submitted on Form 1040ES on April 15th, June 15th, September 15th, and January 15th each year. If these days fall on a weekend, the due date is the following Monday. The worksheet with Form 1040ES can be used to determine the amount to pay.

NOTE: *One exception to the rule is that if you withhold the same amount as last year's tax bill, you do not have to pay a penalty. This is usually much easier than filling out the 1040ES worksheet.*

Employer's Quarterly Tax Return

Each quarter you must file Form 941 to report your federal withholding and FICA taxes. If you owe more than $2500 at the end of a quarter, you are required to make a deposit to an authorized financial institution. Most banks are authorized to accept deposits. Consult the instructions for Form 941. In some cases, electronic deposit of taxes may be required.

Wage and Tax Statement

At the end of each year, you are required to issue a W-2 Form to each employee. This form shows the amount of wages paid to the employee during the year, as well as the amounts withheld for taxes, Social Security, Medicare, and other purposes.

Miscellaneous

If you pay at least $600 to a person (not a corporation) who is not an employee (such as independent contractors), you are required to file a Form 1099 for that person. Along with the 1099s, you must file a form 1096, which is a summary sheet.

Many people are not aware of this law and fail to file these forms, but the forms are required for such things as services, royalties, rents, awards, and prizes that you pay to individuals (but not corporations). The rules for this are quite complicated, so you should either obtain Instruction 1099 from the IRS or consult your accountant.

Earned Income Credit   People who are not liable to pay income tax may have the right to a check from the government because of the *Earned Income Credit*. You are required to notify your employees of this in one of the following ways:

- ✪ a W-2 Form with the notice on the back;

- ✪ a substitute for the W-2 Form with the notice on it;

- ✪ a copy of Notice 797; or,

- ✪ a written statement with the wording from Notice 797.

A Notice 797 can be obtained by calling 800-829-3676, or via the Internet at **www.irs.gov**.

Excise Tax

Excise taxes are taxes on certain activities or items. A few remain, but most federal excise taxes have been eliminated since World War II.

Some of the things that are subject to federal excise taxes are tobacco and alcohol, gasoline, tires and inner tubes, some trucks and trailers, firearms, ammunition, bows, arrows, fishing equipment, the use of highway vehicles of over 55,000 pounds, aircraft, wagering, telephone and teletype services, coal, hazardous wastes, and vaccines. If you are involved with any of these, obtain IRS publication No. 510, *Information on Excise Taxes*.

Unemployment Compensation Taxes

You must pay federal unemployment taxes (FUTA) if you paid wages of $1,500 in any quarter or if you had at least one employee for twenty calendar weeks. Temporary and part-time employees are included for purposes of FUTA. The federal tax amount is 0.8% of the first $7,000 of wages paid each employee.

If the FUTA tax is more than $100 at the end of a quarter, then the tax must be deposited quarterly; otherwise, it may be paid yearly with Form 940 or Form 940EZ. This is your annual report of federal unemployment taxes. You will receive an original form from the IRS.

Electronic Federal Tax Payment System

The Internal Revenue Service has initiated a program, called the Electronic Federal Tax Payment System (EFTPS), by which business owners can pay taxes online. For many businesses, this will be a more convenient and cost effective way of making deposits than using the Federal Tax Deposit coupons. Businesses that have deposited a total of more than $200,000 in taxes in a calendar year are *required* to use EFTPS starting the second year following the year the $200,000 threshold is reached. Enrollment in EFTPS is free of charge, and can be done by contacting EFTPS at 800-555-4477 or 800-945-8400, or online at **www.eftps.gov**.

18 PAYING NEW YORK STATE TAXES

In addition to the federal taxes a New York business must pay, the State of New York imposes several of its own.

Sales and Use Tax

If you will be selling or renting goods or services at retail, you must collect New York Sales and Use Tax. If you want to open a business in the Metropolitan Commuter Transportation District (New York City or Rockland, Nassau, Suffolk, Orange, Putnam, Dutchess or Westchester Counties), you must also collect the special 25% sales tax imposed in those counties. Some services, such as doctors and lawyer's fees and newspaper advertising are not taxed, but most others are. If you have any doubt, check with the New York Department of Taxation and Finance.

First, you must obtain a tax number by filling out form DTF-17. (see form 8, p.223.) (A sample, filled-in copy of the form is contained in Appendix B.) For more details about the tax you should obtain the booklet, *A Guide to Sales Tax in New York State and Vendor Registration Form*. You can obtain it from your local taxation and finance office or contact:

NYS Department of Taxation and Finance
W.A. Harriman Campus
Albany, NY 12227
800-972-1233

The state sales and use tax rate is 4%, plus local rates that can vary from 0% to 4.25%. Unless your sales exceed $300,000 in any quarter, in which event you must file monthly, the sales and use tax returns are due quarterly according to the following schedule.

Quarterly Period	Due Date
June 1 - Aug. 31	Sept. 20
Sept. 1 - Nov. 30	Dec. 20
Dec. 1 - Feb. 28 (29)	March 20
March 1 - May 31	June 20

You are allowed to deduct 1.5% of the 4% New York State portion of the sales tax as your reimbursement for collecting the tax. In some cases, if your sales are very limited (under $250 per year) you may be allowed to file returns annually.

Once you file your **APPLICATION FOR REGISTRATION AS A SALES TAX VENDOR** (form DF-17), you will have to start filing monthly returns whether you have any sales or not. (see form 8, p.223.) If you do not file the return, even if you had no sales, then you must pay a $50 penalty that rises if you have tax that is due. If you do not expect to have any sales during the first few months of your business, then you should probably wait before sending in the registration. Otherwise you may forget to file the returns marked with zeros and end up paying the penalties.

One reason to get a tax number early is to exempt your purchases from tax. When you buy a product to resell, or use as part of a product which you will sell, you are exempt from paying tax on it. To get this exemption you need to submit a Form ST-120 *Resales Certificate* to the seller. This form must contain your sales and use tax registration number.

If you will only be selling items wholesale or out-of-state, you will need to be registered to obtain the tax number to exempt your purchases.

If you have any sales before you get your monthly tax return forms, you should calculate the tax anyway and send it in. Otherwise, you will be charged a penalty, even if it was not your fault that you did not have the forms. After you obtain your tax number, you will be required to collect sales tax on all purchases.

If you sell to someone who claims to be exempt from sales and use taxes, (for example, if they plan to resell merchandise they have purchased from you) then you must have them complete the Resale Certificate previously mentioned. Following the application is an instruction sheet for filing a monthly return and collections charts for state and local sales and use tax.

Gas Stations   Gas station owners are required under certain circumstances to prepay sales tax on the sale of gasoline in New York. If your business is a gas station, you should carefully study the complicated provisions contained in Article 28, Section 1102 of the tax law.

Intangible Property Taxes

Intangible property tax is a tax on the value of things such as mortgages and transfers of stocks and bonds. Taxes on mortgages and deeds are due at the time the mortgage and deed are presented to the local county clerk's office for recording. In practice, these taxes are paid at the actual closing of title. The rate of the mortgage tax is 0.75% of the amount, minus a $25 credit for individuals. Customarily this is paid by the purchaser of the property. The deed tax is 0.4% of the purchase price, which is generally paid by the seller of the property.

The stock transfer tax is based on a sliding scale as follows:

✪   1.25¢ per share for a selling price less than $5 per share;

✪   2.5¢ per share for a selling price between $5 and $10 per share;

✪   3.75¢ per share for a selling price between $10 and $20 per share; and,

✪   5¢ per share for a selling price above $20 per share.

A corporation can pay the stock transfer tax on its own in lieu of the shareholders paying it. The advantage is that the corporation can deduct the tax as a business expense. Shareholders can deduct the tax only if they itemize their deductions, but they get a $20,000 exclusion, which may eliminate the tax completely.

Income Tax

New York has a personal income tax. It applies to individuals and corporations that are not S corporations and to limited liability companies. There is a withholding tax payable to New York in cases in which there are employees.

Forms and instructions can be obtained by contacting the New York State Department of Taxation and Finance at 800-462-8100.

Excise Tax

New York imposes excise taxes on the following businesses.

- ✪ Wholesale tobacco dealers and tobacco vending machine operators. (Contact the New York State Liquor Authority or the local county alcoholic beverage control board for more information.)

- ✪ Alcohol manufacturers and distributors. (Contact the New York State Liquor Authority or the local county alcoholic beverage control board for more information.)

- ✪ Motor Fuel dealers. (Contact the New York State Department of Taxation and Finance for more information.)

Selling to Tax Exempt Purchasers You are required to collect sales and use taxes for all sales you make unless you have documentation on file proving that a purchase was exempt from the tax. A tax exempt person can fill out a form for a particular sale or they can fill out one form to be used for all their dealings with you to meet this documentation requirement.

Unemployment Compensation Taxes

You are not liable to pay unemployment compensation taxes until you have paid an employee a minimum of $300 or more in any calender quarter. But once you reach that point, you are liable for all back taxes. The rate starts at 5.4%. The tax is paid on the first $7000 of wages of each employee.

You are required to notify the New York State Department of Labor upon becoming liable for unemployment insurance tax. You must also file an **EMPLOYER REGISTRATION FOR UNEMPLOYMENT INSURANCE, WITHHOLDING, AND WAGE REPORTING**. (see form 12, p.249.) Quarterly returns will be sent for you to fill out and are due April 30, July 31, October 31, and January 31.

19 OUT-OF-STATE TAXES

As a New York business, if you operate your business outside of the borders of the state of New York, you not only have to comply with New York and federal tax laws, but also with the laws of the states and other countries in which you do business. This can prove to be very complicated.

State Sales Taxes

In 1992, the United States Supreme Court struck a blow for the rights of small businesses by ruling that state tax authorities cannot force them to collect sales taxes on interstate mail orders (*Quill Corporation v. North Dakota*). Unfortunately, the court left open the possibility that Congress could allow interstate taxation of mail order sales, and since then several bills have been introduced that would do so.

At present, companies are only required to collect sales taxes for states in which they *do business*. Exactly what business is enough to trigger taxation is a legal question and some states try to define it as broadly as possible.

If you have an office in a state, clearly you are doing business there and any goods shipped to consumers in the state are subject to sales taxes. If you have a full-time employee working in the state much of the year, many states will consider you to be doing business there. In some states attending a two-day trade show is enough business to trigger taxation for the entire year for every order shipped to the state. One loophole that often works is to be represented at shows by persons who are not your employees.

Because the laws are different in each state you will have to do some research on a state-by-state basis to find out how much business you can do in a state without being subject to their taxation. You can request a state's rules from its department of revenue, but keep in mind that what a department of revenue wants the law to be is not always what the courts will rule that it is.

Business Taxes

Even worse than being subject to a state's sales taxes is to be subject to their income or other business taxes. For example, California charges every company doing business in the state a minimum $800 a year fee and charges income tax on a portion of the company's worldwide income. Doing a small amount of business in the state is clearly not worth getting mired in California taxation.

For this reason some trade shows have been moved from the state and this has resulted in a review of the tax policies and some *safe-harbor* guidelines to advise companies on what they can do without becoming subject to taxation.

Write to the department of revenue of any state with which you have business contacts to see what might trigger your taxation.

Internet Taxes

State revenue departments are drooling at the prospect of taxing commerce on the Internet. Theories have already been proposed that websites available to state residents mean a company is doing business in a state. Fortunately, Congress has passed a moratorium on taxation of the Internet.

Canadian Taxes

The Canadian government expects American companies that sell goods by mail order to Canadians to collect taxes for them and file returns with Revenue Canada, their tax department. Those who receive an occasional unsolicited order are not expected to register and Canadian customers who order things from the U.S. pay the tax plus a $5 fee upon receipt of the goods. But companies that solicit Canadian orders are expected to be registered if their worldwide income is $30,000 or more per year. In some cases a company may be required to post a bond and to pay for the cost of Canadian auditors visiting its premises and auditing its books. For these reasons you may notice that some companies decline to accept orders from Canada.

20 THE END...AND THE BEGINNING

If you have read through this whole book, you know more about the rules and laws for operating an New York business than most people in business today. However, after learning about all the governmental regulations, you may become discouraged. You are probably wondering how you can keep track of all the laws and how you will have any time left to make money after complying with the laws. It is not that bad. People are starting businesses every day and they are making money, lots of money.

Congratulations on deciding to start a business in New York! If you have any unusual experiences along the way, drop us a line at the following address. The information may be useful for a future book.

Sphinx Publishing/Sourcebooks, Inc.
P.O. Box 4410
Naperville, IL 60567-4410
www.info@SphinxLegal.com

GLOSSARY

A

acceptance. Agreeing to the terms of an offer and creating a contract.

affirmative action. Hiring an employee to achieve a balance in the workplace, and avoid existing or continuing discrimination based on minority status.

alien. A person who is not a citizen of the country.

articles of incorporation. The document that sets forth the organization of a corporation.

B

bait advertising. Offering a product for sale with the intention of selling another product.

bulk sales. Selling substantially all of a company's inventory.

C

C corporation. A corporation that pays taxes on its profits.

collections. The collection of money owed to a business.

common law. Laws that are determined in court cases rather than statutes.

consideration. The exchange of value or promises in a contract.

contract. An agreement between two or more parties.

copyright. Legal protection given to "original works of authorship."

corporation. An artificial person that is set up to conduct a business owned by shareholders and run by officers and directors.

D

deceptive pricing. Pricing goods or services in a manner intended to deceive the customers.

discrimination. The choosing among various options based on their characteristics.

domain name. The address of a website.

E

employee. Person who works for another under that person's control and direction.

endorsements. Positive statements about goods or services.

excise tax. A tax paid on the sale or consumption of goods or services.

express warranty. A specific guarantee of a product or service.

F

fictitious name. A name used by a business that is not its personal or legal name.

G

general partnership. A business that is owned by two or more persons.

goods. Items of personal property.

guarantee/guaranty. A promise of quality of a good or service.

I

implied warranty. A guarantee of a product or service that is not specifically made, but can be implied from the circumstances of the sale.

independent contractor. Person who works for another as a separate business, not as an employee.

intangible property. Personal property that does not have physical presence, such as the ownership interest in a corporation.

intellectual property. Legal rights to the products of the mind, such as writings, musical compositions, formulas and designs.

L

liability. The legal responsibility to pay for an injury.

limited liability company. An entity recognized as a legal "person" that is set up to conduct a business owned and run by members.

limited liability partnership. An entity recognized as a legal "person" that is set up to conduct a business owned and run by members that is set up for professionals such as attorneys or doctors.

limited partnership. A business that is owned by two or more persons of which one or more is liable for the debts of the business and one or more has no liability for the debts.

limited warranty. A guarantee covering certain aspects of a good or service.

M

merchant. A person who is in business.

merchant's firm offer. An offer by a business made under specific terms.

N

nonprofit corporation. An entity recognized as a legal "person" that is set up to run an operation in which none of the profits are distributed to controlling members.

O

occupational license. A government-issued permit to transact business.

offer. A proposal to enter into a contract.

overtime. Hours worked in excess of forty hours in one week, or eight hours in one day.

P

partnership. A business formed by two or more persons.

patent. Protection given to inventions, discoveries and designs.

personal property. Any type of property other than land and the structures attached to it.

pierce the corporate veil. When a court ignores the structure of a corporation and holds its owners responsible for its debts or liabilities.

professional association. An entity recognized as a legal "person" that is set up to conduct a business of professionals such as attorneys or doctors.

proprietorship. A business that is owned by one person.

R

real property. Land and the structures attached to it.

resident alien. A person who is not a citizen of the country but who may legally reside and work there.

S

S corporation. A corporation in which the profits are taxed to the shareholders.

sale on approval. Selling an item with the agreement that it may be brought back and the sale cancelled.

sale or return. An agreement whereby goods are to be purchased or returned to the vendor.

securities. Interests in a business such as stocks or bonds.

sexual harassment. Activity that causes an employee to feel or be sexually threatened.

shares. Units of stock in a corporation.

statute of frauds. Law that requires certain contracts to be in writing.

stock. Ownership interests in a corporation.

sublease. An agreement to rent premises from an existing tenant.

T

tangible property. Physical personal property such as desks and tables.

trade secret. Commercially valuable information or process that is protected by being kept a secret.

trademark. A name or symbol used to identify the source of goods or services.

U

unemployment compensation. Payments to a former employee who was terminated from a job for a reason not based on his or her fault.

usury. Charging an interest rate higher than that allowed by law.

W

withholding. Money taken out of an employee's salary and remitted to the government.

workers' compensation. Insurance program to cover injuries or deaths of employees.

APPENDIX A: TAX TIMETABLE

The following tax timetable may be photocopied or removed from this book and used immediately.

Tax Timetable

	New York				Federal			
	Sales	Unemployment	Income	Corp. Franchise	Est. Payment	Annual Return	Form 941[†]	Misc.
JAN.	20th*	31st	15th Estimated 31st Withholding		15th		31st	31st 940 W-2 508 1099
FEB.	20th*							
MAR.	20th			15th		15th Corp. & Partnership		
APR.	20th*	30th	15th Estimated 15th Annual 30th Withholding		15th	15th Personal	30th	30th 508
MAY	20th*							
JUN.	20th		15th Est.		15th			
JUL.	20th*	31st	31st Withholding				31st	31st 508
AUG.	20th*							
SEPT.	20th		15th Est.		15th			
OCT.	20th*	31st	31st Withholding				31st	31st 508
NOV.	20th*							
DEC.	20th							

*for $300,000 in taxable sales and purchases subject to use tax in any quarter.

[†]In addition to form 941, deposits must be made regularly if withholding exceeds $500 in any month.

Appendix B:
Sample Filled-in Forms

The following forms are selected filled-in forms for demonstration purposes. Most have a corresponding blank form in Appendix C. The form numbers in this appendix correspond to the form numbers in Appendix C. If there is no blank for a particular form, it is because you must obtain it from a government agency. If you need instructions for these forms as you follow how they are filled out, they can be found in Appendix C, or in those pages in the chapters that discuss those forms.

Certificate of Assumed Name
Pursuant to General Business Law, §130

NYS Department of State
Division of Corporations, State Records and UCC
41 State Street, Albany, NY 12231-0001
www.dos.state.ny.us

1. NAME OF ENTITY

1a. *FOREIGN ENTITIES ONLY.* If applicable, the fictitious name the entity agreed to use in New York State is:

2. NEW YORK LAW FORMED OR AUTHORIZED UNDER (CHECK ONE):

- ☒ Business Corporation Law
- ☐ Education Law
- ☐ Insurance Law
- ☐ Other (specify law):
- ☐ Limited Liability Company Law
- ☐ Not-for-Profit Corporation Law
- ☐ Revised Limited Partnership Act

3. ASSUMED NAME

Mason Inc., d/b/a Doe Company

4. PRINCIPAL PLACE OF BUSINESS IN NEW YORK STATE (MUST BE NUMBER AND STREET. IF NONE, INSERT OUT-OF-STATE ADDRESS)

123 North Street
Albany, NY 12208
Albany County

5. COUNTIES IN WHICH BUSINESS WILL BE CONDUCTED UNDER ASSUMED NAME

☒ ALL COUNTIES (if not, circle county[ies] below)

Albany	Clinton	Genesee	Monroe	Orleans	Saratoga	Tompkins
Allegany	Columbia	Greene	Montgomery	Oswego	Schenectady	Ulster
Bronx	Cortland	Hamilton	Nassau	Otsego	Schoharie	Warren
Broome	Delaware	Herkimer	New York	Putnam	Schuyler	Washington
Cattaraugus	Dutchess	Jefferson	Niagara	Queens	Seneca	Wayne
Cayuga	Erie	Kings	Oneida	Rensselaer	Steuben	Westchester
Chautauqua	Essex	Lewis	Onondaga	Richmond	Suffolk	Wyoming
Chemung	Franklin	Livingston	Ontario	Rockland	Sullivan	Yates
Chenango	Fulton	Madison	Orange	St. Lawrence	Tioga	

6. INSERT THE ADDRESS OF EACH LOCATION WHERE BUSINESS WILL BE CARRIED ON OR TRANSACTED UNDER THE ASSUMED NAME. Use a continuous sheet, if needed. (The address must be set forth in terms of a number and street, city, state and zip code. Please note that the address(es) reflected in paragraph 6 must be within the county(ies) circled in paragraph 5. If the entity does not have a specific location where it will conduct business under the assumed name please check the box.)

☐ No New York State Business Location

123 North Street
Albany, NY 12208
Albany County

456 South Street
New York, NY 10026
New York County

INSTRUCTIONS FOR SIGNATURE: If corporation, by an officer; if limited partnership, by a general partner; if limited liability company, by a member or manager or by an attorney-in-fact or authorized person for such corporation, limited partnership, or limited liability company.

John J. Doe
Name and Title

John J. Doe
Signature

CERTIFICATE OF ASSUMED NAME
OF

Doe Company

(Insert Entity Name)

Pursuant to §130, General Business Law

FILER'S NAME AND MAILING ADDRESS

123 North Street

Albany, NY 12208

Albany County

NOTE: This form was prepared by the New York State Department of State. You are not required to use this form. You may draft your own form or use forms available at legal stationery stores. The Department of State recommends that all documents be prepared under the guidance of an attorney. The certificate must be submitted with a $25 fee. The Department of State also collects the following, additional, county clerk fees for each county in which a **corporation** does or transacts business: $100 for each county within New York City (Bronx, Kings, New York, Queens and Richmond) and $25 for each county outside New York City. All checks over $500 must be certified.

(For Office Use Only)

Certificate of Assumed Name

I, <u>   John J. Doe   </u>, residing at <u>   </u>
Print or type full name

<u> 156 Second Street, NY 10956   </u>
HEREBY CERTIFY that I am conducting business under the name or designation of

<u>   Doe's Deli Shop   </u>

at
<u>   123 Any Street, Suffern NY, 10901   </u>

in the city or town of <u> Rampo   </u> County of <u> Rockland   </u>,
State of New York.

IN WITNESS WHEREOF, I have made and signed this certificate this <u> 5th </u> day of
<u>May   </u>, <u> 2004 </u>.

John J. Doe
—————————————————————

STATE OF NEW YORK   )
) ss.:

COUNTY OF <u>   Rockland   </u>)

     On this <u>5th</u> day of <u>May   </u>, <u> 2004 </u>, before me person-
ally appeared
<u>   John J. Doe   </u>
to me known to be the individual(s) described in and who executed the foregoing certificate, and he/she thereupon has duly acknowledged that he/she executed the same.

C. U. Sine
—————————————————————
Notary Public

NYS DEPARTMENT OF STATE
MISCELLANEOUS RECORDS
41 State Street
Albany, NY 12231-0001

REG NO

_____

Original Application to Register a Trademark

Please read the instructions prior to completing this form; attach additional sheets as needed.

1. APPLICANT NAME

    Doe Company, Inc.

2. ADDRESS | NUMBER AND STREET | CITY | STATE | ZIP
    123 Main Street | Albany | NY | 12208

3. IF A CORPORATION, ENTER STATE IN WHICH INCORPORATED AND
   IF A PARTNERSHIP, ENTER STATE IN WHICH ORGANIZED

4. IF A PARTNERSHIP, LIST THE NAMES OF ALL GENERAL PARTNERS

    N/A

5. DESCRIBE THE TRADEMARK, INCLUDING A **WRITTEN** DESCRIPTION OF DESIGN FEATURES, IF ANY (DO **NOT** GLUE A FACSIMILE TO THIS FORM)

    A blue bullseye on a light blue square

6. DESCRIBE THE SPECIFIC GOODS BEING PRODUCED ON WHICH THE TRADEMARK IS USED

    clothing

7. STATE THE MANNER IN WHICH THE TRADEMARK IS PLACED ON THE GOODS, CONTAINERS, ETC.

    embroidered

8. CLASS NUMBER(S) | | 9. DATE OF FIRST USE | (A) IN NEW YORK STATE | (B) ELSEWHERE
    39 | | | 1-1-04 | 1-1-04

FOR OFFICE USE ONLY

The applicant is the owner of the mark, the mark is in use, and, to the knowledge of the person verifying the application, no other person has registered, either federally or in this state, or has the to use such mark either in the identical form or in such near resemblance as to be likely, when app to the goods of such other person, to cause confusion, or to cause mistake, or to deceive.

The undersigned applies to register the aforesaid mark pursuant to Article 24 of the General Busir Law and affirms under the penalties of perjury that the statements herein made, including any attached papers, are true.

    Doe Company, Inc.
    (Corporation, Association, Firm, etc.)

By: **John J. Doe**   2-1-04
   (Signature and Title of Officer)   *(Date)*

DOS-241 (REV. 2/98)

U.S. Department of Justice
Immigration and Naturalization Service

OMB No. 1115-0136

Employment Eligibility Verification

Please read instructions carefully before completing this form. The instructions must be available during completion of this form. ANTI-DISCRIMINATION NOTICE: It is illegal to discriminate against work eligible individuals. Employers CANNOT specify which document(s) they will accept from an employee. The refusal to hire an individual because of a future expiration date may also constitute illegal discrimination.

Section 1. Employee Information and Verification. To be completed and signed by employee at the time employment begins.

Print Name: Last	First	Middle Initial	Maiden Name
Doe	John	J	

Address (Street Name and Number)	Apt. #	Date of Birth (month/day/year)
123 Liberty Lane		1-26-79

City	State	Zip Code	Social Security #
Albany	New York	12654	123-45-6789

I am aware that federal law provides for imprisonment and/or fines for false statements or use of false documents in connection with the completion of this form.

I attest, under penalty of perjury, that I am (check one of the following):
- [X] A citizen or national of the United States
- [ ] A Lawful Permanent Resident (Alien # A
- [ ] An alien authorized to work until ___/___/___
  (Alien # or Admission #)

Employee's Signature *John J. Doe*	Date (month/day/year) 1-29-05

Preparer and/or Translator Certification. *(To be completed and signed if Section 1 is prepared by a person other than the employee.) I attest, under penalty of perjury, that I have assisted in the completion of this form and that to the best of my knowledge the information is true and correct.*

Preparer's/Translator's Signature	Print Name

Address (Street Name and Number, City, State, Zip Code)	Date (month/day/year)

Section 2. Employer Review and Verification. To be completed and signed by employer. Examine one document from List A OR examine one document from List B and one from List C, as listed on the reverse of this form, and record the title, number and expiration date, if any, of the document(s)

	List A	OR	List B	AND	List C
Document title:	PASSPORT				
Issuing authority:	PASSPORT AGN				
Document #:	123456789				
Expiration Date (if any):	1 / 1 / 10		___/___/___		___/___/___
Document #:					
Expiration Date (if any):	___/___/___				

CERTIFICATION - I attest, under penalty of perjury, that I have examined the document(s) presented by the above-named employee, that the above-listed document(s) appear to be genuine and to relate to the employee named, that the employee began employment on (month/day/year) ___/___/___ **and that to the best of my knowledge the employee is eligible to work in the United States. (State employment agencies may omit the date the employee began employment.)**

Signature of Employer or Authorized Representative	Print Name	Title

Business or Organization Name	Address (Street Name and Number, City, State, Zip Code)	Date (month/day/year)

Section 3. Updating and Reverification. To be completed and signed by employer.

A. New Name (if applicable)	B. Date of rehire (month/day/year) (if applicable)

C. If employee's previous grant of work authorization has expired, provide the information below for the document that establishes current employment eligibility.

Document Title:_____ Document #:_____ Expiration Date (if any): ___/___/___

I attest, under penalty of perjury, that to the best of my knowledge, this employee is eligible to work in the United States, and if the employee presented document(s), the document(s) I have examined appear to be genuine and to relate to the individual.

Signature of Employer or Authorized Representative	Date (month/day/year)

Form **SS-4**

(Rev. December 2001)

Department of the Treasury
Internal Revenue Service

Application for Employer Identification Number

(For use by employers, corporations, partnerships, trusts, estates, churches, government agencies, Indian tribal entities, certain individuals, and others.)

▶ See separate instructions for each line. ▶ Keep a copy for your records.

EIN

OMB No. 1545-0003

Type or print clearly.

1 Legal name of entity (or individual) for whom the EIN is being requested	
Doe Company	

2 Trade name of business (if different from name on line 1)	**3** Executor, trustee, "care of" name

4a Mailing address (room, apt., suite no. and street, or P.O. box)	**5a** Street address (if different) (Do not enter a P.O. box.)
123 Main Street	
4b City, state, and ZIP code	**5b** City, state, and ZIP code
Albany, NY 12231	

6 County and state where principal business is located
Albany, New York

7a Name of principal officer, general partner, grantor, owner, or trustor	**7b** SSN, ITIN, or EIN
John Doe	

8a **Type of entity** (check only one box)

- ☐ Sole proprietor (SSN) _____
- ☒ Partnership
- ☐ Corporation (enter form number to be filed) ▶ _____
- ☐ Personal service corp.
- ☐ Church or church-controlled organization
- ☐ Other nonprofit organization (specify) ▶ _____
- ☐ Other (specify) ▶

- ☐ Estate (SSN of decedent)   123 45 6789
- ☐ Plan administrator (SSN) _____
- ☐ Trust (SSN of grantor) _____
- ☐ National Guard   ☐ State/local government
- ☐ Farmers' cooperative   ☐ Federal government/military
- ☐ REMIC   ☐ Indian tribal governments/enterprises
- Group Exemption Number (GEN) ▶ _____

8b If a corporation, name the state or foreign country (if applicable) where incorporated

State	Foreign country

9 **Reason for applying** (check only one box)

- ☒ Started new business (specify type) ▶_____
  - **bistro**
- ☐ Hired employees (Check the box and see line 12.)
- ☐ Compliance with IRS withholding regulations
- ☐ Other (specify) ▶

- ☐ Banking purpose (specify purpose) ▶ _____
- ☐ Changed type of organization (specify new type) ▶ _____
- ☐ Purchased going business
- ☐ Created a trust (specify type) ▶ _____
- ☐ Created a pension plan (specify type) ▶ _____

10 Date business started or acquired (month, day, year)	**11** Closing month of accounting year
10-15-04	December

12 First date wages or annuities were paid or will be paid (month, day, year). **Note:** *If applicant is a withholding agent, enter date income will first be paid to nonresident alien. (month, day, year)* . . . . ▶ 10-22-04

13 Highest number of employees expected in the next 12 months. **Note:** *If the applicant does not expect to have any employees during the period, enter "-0-."* . . . . ▶

Agricultural	Household	Other
		3

14 Check **one** box that best describes the principal activity of your business.

- ☐ Construction
- ☐ Real estate
- ☐ Rental & leasing
- ☐ Manufacturing
- ☐ Transportation & warehousing
- ☐ Finance & insurance
- ☐ Health care & social assistance
- ☒ Accommodation & food service
- ☐ Other (specify)
- ☐ Wholesale–agent/broker
- ☐ Wholesale–other
- ☐ Retail

15 Indicate principal line of merchandise sold; specific construction work done; products produced; or services provided.
restaurant

16a Has the applicant ever applied for an employer identification number for this or any other business? . . . . . ☐ **Yes** ☒ **No**
Note: *If "Yes," please complete lines 16b and 16c.*

16b If you checked "Yes" on line 16a, give applicant's legal name and trade name shown on prior application if different from line 1 or 2 above.
Legal name ▶ _____ Trade name ▶ _____

16c Approximate date when, and city and state where, the application was filed. Enter previous employer identification number if known.

Approximate date when filed (mo., day, year)	City and state where filed	Previous EIN

Third Party Designee	Complete this section **only** if you want to authorize the named individual to receive the entity's EIN and answer questions about the completion of this form.	
	Designee's name	Designee's telephone number (include area code) ( )
	Address and ZIP code	Designee's fax number (include area code) ( )

Under penalties of perjury, I declare that I have examined this application, and to the best of my knowledge and belief, it is true, correct, and complete.

Name and title (type or print clearly) ▶ John J. Doe, Partner	Applicant's telephone number (include area code) (518) 555-0000
Signature ▶ *John J. Doe* Date ▶ 10/15/04	Applicant's fax number (include area code) ( )

For Privacy Act and Paperwork Reduction Act Notice, see separate instructions.   Cat. No. 16055N   Form **SS-4** (Rev. 12-2001)

Form W-4 (2004)

Purpose. Complete Form W-4 so that your employer can withhold the correct Federal income tax from your pay. Because your tax situation may change, you may want to refigure your withholding each year.

Exemption from withholding. If you are exempt, complete only lines 1, 2, 3, 4, and 7 and sign the form to validate it. Your exemption for 2004 expires February 16, 2005. See **Pub. 505,** Tax Withholding and Estimated Tax.

Note: *You cannot claim exemption from withholding if: (a) your income exceeds $800 and includes more than $250 of unearned income (e.g., interest and dividends) and (b) another person can claim you as a dependent on their tax return.*

Basic instructions. If you are not exempt, complete the **Personal Allowances Worksheet** below. The worksheets on page 2 adjust your withholding allowances based on itemized

deductions, certain credits, adjustments to income, or two-earner/two-job situations. Complete all worksheets that apply. **However, you may claim fewer (or zero) allowances.**

Head of household. Generally, you may claim head of household filing status on your tax return only if you are unmarried and pay more than 50% of the costs of keeping up a home for yourself and your dependent(s) or other qualifying individuals. See line **E** below.

Tax credits. You can take projected tax credits into account in figuring your allowable number of withholding allowances. Credits for child or dependent care expenses and the child tax credit may be claimed using the **Personal Allowances Worksheet** below. See **Pub. 919,** How Do I Adjust My Tax Withholding? for information on converting your other credits into withholding allowances.

Nonwage income. If you have a large amount of nonwage income, such as interest or dividends, consider making estimated tax payments using

Form 1040-ES, Estimated Tax for Individuals. Otherwise, you may owe additional tax.

Two earners/two jobs. If you have a working spouse or more than one job, figure the total number of allowances you are entitled to claim on all jobs using worksheets from only one Form W-4. Your withholding usually will be most accurate when all allowances are claimed on the Form W-4 for the highest paying job and zero allowances are claimed on the others.

Nonresident alien. If you are a nonresident alien, see the **Instructions for Form 8233** before completing this Form W-4.

Check your withholding. After your Form W-4 takes effect, use Pub. 919 to see how the dollar amount you are having withheld compares to your projected total tax for 2004. See Pub. 919, especially if your earnings exceed $125,000 (Single) or $175,000 (Married).

Recent name change? If your name on line 1 differs from that shown on your social security card, call 1-800-772-1213 to initiate a name change and obtain a social security card showing your correct name.

Personal Allowances Worksheet (Keep for your records.)

A Enter "1" for **yourself** if no one else can claim you as a dependent . . . . **A** __1__

B Enter "1" if: {
 ● You are single and have only one job; or
 ● You are married, have only one job, and your spouse does not work; or
 ● Your wages from a second job or your spouse's wages (or the total of both) are $1,000 or less. } . . **B** _____

C Enter "1" for your **spouse.** But, you may choose to enter "-0-" if you are married and have either a working spouse or more than one job. (Entering "-0-" may help you avoid having too little tax withheld.) . . . . . . **C** _____

D Enter number of **dependents** (other than your spouse or yourself) you will claim on your tax return . . . . **D** _____

E Enter "1" if you will file as **head of household** on your tax return (see conditions under **Head of household** above) . . **E** _____

F Enter "1" if you have at least $1,500 of **child or dependent care expenses** for which you plan to claim a credit . . **F** _____
 (**Note:** *Do not include child support payments. See Pub. 503, Child and Dependent Care Expenses, for details.*)

G **Child Tax Credit** (including additional child tax credit):
 ● If your total income will be less than $52,000 ($77,000 if married), enter "2" for each eligible child.
 ● If your total income will be between $52,000 and $84,000 ($77,000 and $119,000 if married), enter "1" for each eligible child plus "1" **additional** if you have four or more eligible children. **G** _____

H Add lines A through G and enter total here. **Note:** *This may be different from the number of exemptions you claim on your tax return.* ▶ **H** __1__

For accuracy, complete all worksheets that apply. {
 ● If you plan to **itemize or claim adjustments to income** and want to reduce your withholding, see the **Deductions and Adjustments Worksheet** on page 2.
 ● If you have **more than one job** or are **married and you and your spouse both work** and the combined earnings from all jobs exceed $35,000 ($25,000 if married) see the **Two-Earner/Two-Job Worksheet** on page 2 to avoid having too little tax withheld.
 ● If **neither** of the above situations applies, **stop here** and enter the number from line H on line 5 of Form W-4 below.
}

Cut here and give Form W-4 to your employer. Keep the top part for your records.

Form **W-4**
Department of the Treasury
Internal Revenue Service

Employee's Withholding Allowance Certificate

▶ Your employer must send a copy of this form to the IRS if: (a) you claim more than 10 allowances or (b) you claim "Exempt" and your wages are normally more than $200 per week.

OMB No. 1545-0010

2004

1 Type or print your first name and middle initial	Last name	2 Your social security number
John J.	Doe	123 : 45 : 6789

Home address (number and street or rural route)	3 [X] Single [ ] Married [ ] Married, but withhold at higher Single rate.
456 South Street	Note: *If married, but legally separated, or spouse is a nonresident alien, check the "Single" box.*

City or town, state, and ZIP code	4 If your last name differs from that shown on your social security
Northtown, NY 00000	card, check here. You must call 1-800-772-1213 for a new card. ▶ [ ]

		5	1
5	Total number of allowances you are claiming (from line **H** above **or** from the applicable worksheet on page 2)		
6	Additional amount, if any, you want withheld from each paycheck	6	$ 0

7 I claim exemption from withholding for 2004, and I certify that I meet **both** of the following conditions for exemption:
 ● Last year I had a right to a refund of **all** Federal income tax withheld because I had **no** tax liability **and**
 ● This year I expect a refund of **all** Federal income tax withheld because I expect to have **no** tax liability.
 If you meet both conditions, write "Exempt" here . . . . ▶ | 7 |

Under penalties of perjury, I certify that I am entitled to the number of withholding allowances claimed on this certificate, or I am entitled to claim exempt status.

Employee's signature
(Form is not valid
unless you sign it.) ▶ *John J. Doe*

Date ▶ 08-25-2004

8 Employer's name and address (Employer: Complete lines 8 and 10 only if sending to the IRS.)	9 Office code (optional)	10 Employer identification number (EIN)

For Privacy Act and Paperwork Reduction Act Notice, see page 2. Cat. No. 10220Q Form **W-4** (2004)

Deductions and Adjustments Worksheet

Note: *Use this worksheet **only** if you plan to itemize deductions, claim certain credits, or claim adjustments to income on your 2004 tax return.*

1 Enter an estimate of your 2004 itemized deductions. These include qualifying home mortgage interest, charitable contributions, state and local taxes, medical expenses in excess of 7.5% of your income, and miscellaneous deductions. (For 2004, you may have to reduce your itemized deductions if your income is over $142,700 ($71,350 if married filing separately). See **Worksheet 3** in Pub. 919 for details.) . . . **1** $ _____

2 Enter:
{ $9,700 if married filing jointly or qualifying widow(er)
$7,150 if head of household
$4,850 if single
$4,850 if married filing separately } . . . . . **2** $ _____

3 **Subtract** line 2 from line 1. If line 2 is greater than line 1, enter "-0-". . . . . . **3** $ _____

4 Enter an estimate of your 2004 adjustments to income, including alimony, deductible IRA contributions, and student loan interest **4** $ _____

5 **Add** lines 3 and 4 and enter the total. (Include any amount for credits from **Worksheet 7** in Pub. 919) . **5** $ _____

6 Enter an estimate of your 2004 nonwage income (such as dividends or interest) . . . . **6** $ _____

7 **Subtract** line 6 from line 5. Enter the result, but not less than "-0-" . . . . **7** $ _____

8 **Divide** the amount on line 7 by $3,000 and enter the result here. Drop any fraction . . . . . . **8** _____

9 Enter the number from the **Personal Allowances Worksheet,** line H, page 1 . . . . **9** _____

10 **Add** lines 8 and 9 and enter the total here. If you plan to use the **Two-Earner/Two-Job Worksheet,** also enter this total on line 1 below. Otherwise, **stop here** and enter this total on Form W-4, line 5, page 1 . **10** _____

Two-Earner/Two-Job Worksheet (See **Two earners/two jobs** on page 1.)

Note: *Use this worksheet **only** if the instructions under line H on page 1 direct you here.*

1 Enter the number from line H, page 1 (or from line 10 above if you used the **Deductions and Adjustments Worksheet**) **1** _____

2 Find the number in **Table 1** below that applies to the **LOWEST** paying job and enter it here . . . . **2** _____

3 If line 1 is **more than or equal to** line 2, subtract line 2 from line 1. Enter the result here (if zero, enter "-0-") and on Form W-4, line 5, page 1. **Do not** use the rest of this worksheet . . . . **3** _____

Note: *If line 1 is **less than** line 2, enter "-0-" on Form W-4, line 5, page 1. Complete lines 4-9 below to calculate the additional withholding amount necessary to avoid a year-end tax bill.*

4 Enter the number from line 2 of this worksheet . . . . **4** _____

5 Enter the number from line 1 of this worksheet . . . . **5** _____

6 **Subtract** line 5 from line 4 . . . . **6** _____

7 Find the amount in **Table 2** below that applies to the **HIGHEST** paying job and enter it here . . . . **7** $ _____

8 **Multiply** line 7 by line 6 and enter the result here. This is the additional annual withholding needed . . **8** $ _____

9 Divide line 8 by the number of pay periods remaining in 2004. For example, divide by 26 if you are paid every two weeks and you complete this form in December 2003. Enter the result here and on Form W-4, line 6, page 1. This is the additional amount to be withheld from each paycheck . . . . **9** $ _____

Table 1: Two-Earner/Two-Job Worksheet

Married Filing Jointly			Married Filing Jointly			All Others	
If wages from **HIGHEST** paying job are-	AND, wages from **LOWEST** paying job are-	Enter on line 2 above	If wages from **HIGHEST** paying job are-	AND, wages from **LOWEST** paying job are-	Enter on line 2 above	If wages from **LOWEST** paying job are-	Enter on line 2 above
$0 - $40,000	$0 - $4,000	0	$40,001 and over	31,001 - 38,000	6	$0 - $6,000	0
	4,001 - 8,000	1		38,001 - 44,000	7	6,001 - 11,000	1
	8,001 - 17,000	2		44,001 - 50,000	8	11,001 - 18,000	2
	17,001 and over	3		50,001 - 55,000	9	18,001 - 25,000	3
$40,001 and over	$0 - $4,000	0		55,001 - 65,000	10	25,001 - 31,000	4
	4,001 - 8,000	1		65,001 - 75,000	11	31,001 - 44,000	5
	8,001 - 15,000	2		75,001 - 85,000	12	44,001 - 55,000	6
	15,001 - 22,000	3		85,001 - 100,000	13	55,001 - 70,000	7
	22,001 - 25,000	4		100,001 - 115,000	14	70,001 - 80,000	8
	25,001 - 31,000	5		115,001 and over	15	80,001 - 100,000	9
						100,001 and over	10

Table 2: Two-Earner/Two-Job Worksheet

Married Filing Jointly		All Others	
If wages from **HIGHEST** paying job are-	Enter on line 7 above	If wages from **HIGHEST** paying job are-	Enter on line 7 above
$0 - $60,000	$470	$0 - $30,000	$470
60,001 - 110,000	780	30,001 - 70,000	780
110,001 - 150,000	870	70,001 - 140,000	870
150,001 - 270,000	1,020	140,001 - 320,000	1,020
270,001 and over	1,090	320,001 and over	1,090

DTF-17 (8/00)

form 8 ◆ 183

New York State Department of Taxation and Finance

Application for Registration as a Sales Tax Vendor

Department use only

Please print or type

1 Type of certificate you are applying for
(You must check one box; see instructions): [X] Regular [ ] Temporary [ ] Show [ ] Entertainment

2 Legal name of vendor
John J. Doe

3 Trade name or DBA (if different from item 2)
Doe Masonry, Inc. d/b/a Doe Company

4 Federal employer identification number

5 Address of business location (show/entertainment or temporary vendors use home address)

Number and street	City	County	State	ZIP code	Country, if not U.S.
123 Anywhere Street	Albany	Albany	NY	12208	

6 Business telephone number (include area code)
(518) 555-5555

7 Date you will begin business in New York State *(see instructions)*
1 / 1 / 04

8 Temporary vendors: Enter the date you will end business in New York
/ /

9 Mailing address, if different from business address on line 5
c/o name   Number and street   City   State   ZIP code

10 Type of organization: [ ] Individual (sole proprietor) [ ] Partnership [ ] Trust [ ] Governmental [ ] Exempt organization
[X] Corporation [ ] Limited Liability Partnership [ ] Limited Liability Company [ ] Other *(specify)* _____

11 Reason for applying: [ ] Started new business [ ] Purchased existing business [ ] Adding a new location [ ] Change in organization [ ] Other *(specify)* _____

12 Regular vendors — Will you operate more than one place of business?
[ ] Yes *(check appropriate box below)*   [ ] No
A [ ] Separate sales tax return will be filed for each business location.
B [ ] One sales tax return will be filed for all business locations *(complete Form DTF-17-ATT and attach it to this application)*.

13 List all owners/officers. Attach a separate sheet if necessary. All applicants must complete this section.

Name	Title	Social security number
John J. Doe	President	123-45-6789

Home address	City	State	ZIP code	Telephone number
123 Anywhere Street	Albany	NY	12208	(518) 555-5552

Name	Title	Social security number
Jane E. Doe	Treasurer	123-45-6788

Home address	City	State	ZIP code	Telephone number
124 Anywhere Street	Albany	NY	12208	(518) 555-5553

Name	Title	Social security number
William Q. Doe	Secretary	123-45-6787

Home address	City	State	ZIP code	Telephone number
125 Anywhere Street	Albany	NY	12208	(518) 555-5554

14 If your business currently files New York State returns for the following taxes, check the box for the appropriate tax type and enter the identification number used on the return:
[X] Corporation tax   ID # 12-3456789
[X] Withholding tax   ID # 12-3456789
[ ] Other *(explain)* _____   ID # _____

15 If you have ever registered as a sales tax vendor with New York State, enter the information shown on the last sales tax return you filed:
Name _____   Identification number _____

16 Do you expect to **collect** any sales or use tax or **pay** any sales or use tax directly to the Department of Taxation and Finance? .... [X] Yes [ ] No

17 Describe your major business activity and enter your six-digit NAICS code:

Describe your business activity in detail *(attach a separate sheet if necessary)*	North American Industry Classification System (NAICS)
Stone cutting and sculpture	c 1 7 4 1

18 Are you a sidewalk vendor? .... [ ] Yes [X] No
   If *Yes*, do you sell food? .... [ ] Yes [X] No
19 Do you participate solely in flea markets, antique shows, or other "shows"? .... [ ] Yes [X] No
20 Do you intend to make retail sales of cigarettes or other tobacco products? .... [ ] Yes [X] No
21 If you withhold or will withhold New York State tax from employees, do you need withholding tax forms or information? .... [X] Yes [ ] No

22 If you acquired this business from a registered vendor, did you file Form AU-196.10, *Notification of Sale, Transfer or Assignment in Bulk,* with the Tax Department? ..... ☐ Yes ☒ No

Former owner's name _____ Address _____ ID # _____

23 Have you been notified that you owe any New York State tax? .... ☐ Yes ☒ No

Type of tax	Amount due	Assessment number (if any)	Assessment date	Assessment currently being protested? ..... ☐ Yes ☐ No

24 Do any responsible officers, directors, partners, or employees owe New York State or local sales and use taxes on your behalf, on behalf of another person, or as a vendor of property or services? .... ☐ Yes ☒ No

Individual's name		Street address	City	State	ZIP code
Social security number	Amount due	Assessment number (if any)	Assessment date	Assessment currently being protested? ..... ☐ Yes ☐ No	

25 Have you been convicted of a crime under the Tax Law during the past year? .... ☐ Yes ☒ No

Date of conviction	Court of conviction	Disposition (fine, imprisonment, probation, etc.)

26 During the past year, has any responsible officer, director, partner, or employee of the applicant been convicted of a crime under the Tax Law? .... ☐ Yes ☒ No

Individual's name		Street address	City	State	ZIP code
Social security number	Date of conviction	Court of conviction	Disposition (fine, imprisonment, probation, etc.)		

27 If previously registered as a New York State sales tax vendor, was your *Certificate of Authority* revoked or suspended during that past year? ☐ Yes ☒ No   If *Yes*, please indicate why_____ .

_____

Questions 28, 29, and 30 apply to corporations only.

28 If any shareholder owns more than half of the shares of voting stock of the applicant, has this shareholder ever owned more than half of the shares of voting stock of another corporation? ☐ Yes   ☐ No   **If *Yes*, complete questions 29 and 30.**

29 Did this shareholder own these shares of another corporation when the corporation had a tax liability that remains unpaid? .... ☐ Yes ☒ No

Shareholder's name		Corporation name		Federal identification number	
Street address		City		State	ZIP code
Type of tax	Amount due	Assessment number *(if any)*	Assessment date	Assessment currently being protested? ..... ☐ Yes ☐ No	

30 Did this shareholder own these shares of another corporation at a time during the past year when the corporation was convicted of a crime under the Tax Law? .... ☐ Yes ☒ No

Corporation name		Federal identification number	
Street address		City	State	ZIP code
Date of conviction	Court of conviction	Disposition (fine, imprisonment, probation, etc.)	

I certify that the information in this application is true and correct. Willfully filing a false application is a misdemeanor punishable under the Tax Law.

Signature	Title	Telephone number	Date
John Doe	President	518-555-1950	12-1-04

☐ Check this box if you want your sales tax returns mailed to a tax preparer rather than the address on the front of this application. Enter preparer information in the box below:

Name of preparer	Street Address	City	State	ZIP code

This application will be returned if it is not signed or if any other information is missing.

Mail your application to: NYS Tax Department, Sales Tax Registration Unit, W A Harriman Campus, Albany NY 12227, at least 20 days (but not more than 90 days) before you begin doing business in New York State.

Form SS-8
(Rev. June 2003)
Department of the Treasury
Internal Revenue Service

Determination of Worker Status
for Purposes of Federal Employment Taxes
and Income Tax Withholding

OMB No. 1545-0004

Name of firm (or person) for whom the worker performed services	Worker's name
W & J Printing	Samuel S. Samuelson

Firm's address (include street address, apt. or suite no., city, state, and ZIP code)	Worker's address (include street address, apt. or suite no., city, state, and ZIP code)
123 Main St., Northtown NY 12345	456 South St, Grane, NY 12345

Trade name	Telephone number (include area code)	Worker's social security number
	(412) 555-2222	444 : 55 : 6666

Telephone number (include area code)	Firm's employer identification number	Worker's employer identification number (if any)
(412) 555-1111	11 : 222 3333	N/A :

If the worker is paid by a firm other than the one listed on this form for these services, enter the name, address, and employer identification number of the payer.

Important Information Needed To Process Your Request

We must have your permission to disclose your name and the information on this form and any attachments to other parties involved with this request. **Do we have your permission to disclose this information?** . . . . [X] **Yes** [ ] **No**
If you answered "No" or did not mark a box, we will not process your request and will not issue a determination.

You must answer ALL items OR mark them "Unknown" or "Does not apply." If you need more space, attach another sheet.

A This form is being completed by: [X] Firm [ ] Worker; for services performed __1/5/05__ to __7/15/05__ .
(beginning date)   (ending date)

B Explain your reason(s) for filing this form (e.g., you received a bill from the IRS, you believe you received a Form 1099 or Form W-2 erroneously, you are unable to get worker's compensation benefits, you were audited or are being audited by the IRS). ____
Unable to collect worker's compensation benefits. ____

C Total number of workers who performed or are performing the same or similar services __three__ .

D How did the worker obtain the job? [X] Application [ ] Bid [ ] Employment Agency [ ] Other (specify) ____ .

E Attach copies of all supporting documentation (contracts, invoices, memos, Forms W-2, Forms 1099, IRS closing agreements, IRS rulings, etc.). In addition, please inform us of any current or past litigation concerning the worker's status. If no income reporting forms (Form 1099-MISC or W-2) were furnished to the worker, enter the amount of income earned for the year(s) at issue $ __see attachments__ .

F Describe the firm's business. Printing of books, catalogs, manuals, and flyers. ____

G Describe the work done by the worker and provide the worker's job title. operated presses and heavy machinery ____
Printer/Machinist ____

H Explain why you believe the worker is an employee or an independent contractor. I have worked at W & J eight hours a day, five days a week, for the past six months. ____

I Did the worker perform services for the firm before getting this position? . . . . [ ] Yes [X] No [ ] N/A
If "Yes," what were the dates of the prior service? N/A ____
If "Yes," explain the differences, if any, between the current and prior service. N/A ____

J If the work is done under a written agreement between the firm and the worker, attach a copy (preferably signed by both parties). Describe the terms and conditions of the work arrangement. see attachments ____

For Privacy Act and Paperwork Reduction Act Notice, see page 5. Cat. No. 16106T Form **SS-8** (Rev. 6-2003)

Form SS-8 (Rev. 6-2003)   Page **2**

Part I   Behavioral Control

1 What specific training and/or instruction is the worker given by the firm? <u>instructions of new operating system,</u>
<u>forklift operation</u>

2 How does the worker receive work assignments? <u>from manager – verbally</u>

3 Who determines the methods by which the assignments are performed? <u>manager</u>

4 Who is the worker required to contact if problems or complaints arise and who is responsible for their resolution?
<u>contact manager who will instruct me in resolution</u>

5 What types of reports are required from the worker? Attach examples. <u>N/A</u>

6 Describe the worker's daily routine (i.e., schedule, hours, etc.). <u>7 AM – 3 PM, half-hour lunch break. Manual</u>
<u>operation of presses, organizing warehouse with lift twice daily.</u>

7 At what location(s) does the worker perform services (e.g., firm's premises, own shop or office, home, customer's location, etc.)?
<u>firm's premises</u>

8 Describe any meetings the worker is required to attend and any penalties for not attending (e.g., sales meetings, monthly meetings, staff
meetings, etc.). <u>Two safety meetings in first week</u>

9 Is the worker required to provide the services personally? . . . .   ☒ **Yes**   ☐ **No**

10 If substitutes or helpers are needed, who hires them? <u>N/A</u>

11 If the worker hires the substitutes or helpers, is approval required? . . . .   ☐ **Yes**   ☐ **No**
If "Yes," by whom?

12 Who pays the substitutes or helpers? <u>N/A</u>

13 Is the worker reimbursed if the worker pays the substitutes or helpers? . . . . . .   ☐ **Yes**   ☐ **No**
If "Yes," by whom? <u>N/A</u>

Part II   Financial Control

1 List the supplies, equipment, materials, and property provided by each party:
The firm <u>all equipment and supplies</u>
The worker <u>uniform and hard hat</u>
Other party <u>clients provide original material to be printed</u>

2 Does the worker lease equipment? . . . .   ☐ **Yes**   ☐ **No**
If "Yes," what are the terms of the lease? (Attach a copy or explanatory statement.)
<u>N/A</u>

3 What expenses are incurred by the worker in the performance of services for the firm? <u>transportation</u>

4 Specify which, if any, expenses are reimbursed by:
The firm <u>N/A</u>
Other party

5 Type of pay the worker receives: ☐ Salary   ☐ Commission   ☐ Hourly Wage   ☒ Piece Work
☐ Lump Sum   ☐ Other (specify)
If type of pay is commission, and the firm guarantees a minimum amount of pay, specify amount $ _____ .

6 Is the worker allowed a drawing account for advances? . . . .   ☐ **Yes**   ☒ **No**
If "Yes," how often? <u>N/A</u>
Specify any restrictions. <u>N/A</u>

7 Whom does the customer pay? . . . .   ☒ **Firm**   ☐ **Worker**
If worker, does the worker pay the total amount to the firm? ☐ **Yes**   ☐ **No** If "No," explain. <u>N/A</u>

8 Does the firm carry worker's compensation insurance on the worker? <u>(UNKNOWN)</u> . . . .   ☐ **Yes**   ☐ **No**

9 What economic loss or financial risk, if any, can the worker incur beyond the normal loss of salary (e.g., loss or damage of equipment,
material, etc.)? <u>N/A</u>

Form **SS-8** (Rev. 6-2003)

Part III   Relationship of the Worker and Firm

1 List the benefits available to the worker (e.g., paid vacations, sick pay, pensions, bonuses). N/A

2 Can the relationship be terminated by either party without incurring liability or penalty? (UNKNOWN)   ☐ Yes ☐ No
If "No," explain your answer.

3 Does the worker perform similar services for others?   ☐ Yes ☒ No
If "Yes," is the worker required to get approval from the firm?   ☐ Yes ☐ No

4 Describe any agreements prohibiting competition between the worker and the firm while the worker is performing services or during any later period. Attach any available documentation. (UNKNOWN)

5 Is the worker a member of a union?   ☐ Yes ☒ No

6 What type of advertising, if any, does the worker do (e.g., a business listing in a directory, business cards, etc.)? Provide copies, if applicable.
N/A

7 If the worker assembles or processes a product at home, who provides the materials and instructions or pattern?
N/A

8 What does the worker do with the finished product (e.g., return it to the firm, provide it to another party, or sell it)?
deliver to manager

9 How does the firm represent the worker to its customers (e.g., employee, partner, representative, or contractor)?
(UNKNOWN)

10 If the worker no longer performs services for the firm, how did the relationship end? with injury from forklift accident,
I could no longer perform my duties, and was asked to leave.

Part IV   For Service Providers or Salespersons- Complete this part if the worker provided a service directly to customers or is a salesperson.

1 What are the worker's responsibilities in soliciting new customers? N/A

2 Who provides the worker with leads to prospective customers? N/A

3 Describe any reporting requirements pertaining to the leads. N/A

4 What terms and conditions of sale, if any, are required by the firm? N/A

5 Are orders submitted to and subject to approval by the firm?   ☐ Yes ☒ No

6 Who determines the worker's territory? N/A

7 Did the worker pay for the privilege of serving customers on the route or in the territory?   ☐ Yes ☒ No
If "Yes," whom did the worker pay? N/A
If "Yes," how much did the worker pay? $ N/A

8 Where does the worker sell the product (e.g., in a home, retail establishment, etc.)? N/A

9 List the product and/or services distributed by the worker (e.g., meat, vegetables, fruit, bakery products, beverages, or laundry or dry cleaning services). If more than one type of product and/or service is distributed, specify the principal one. N/A

10 Does the worker sell life insurance full time?   ☐ Yes ☐ No

11 Does the worker sell other types of insurance for the firm?   ☐ Yes ☐ No
If "Yes," enter the percentage of the worker's total working time spent in selling other types of insurance.   N/A %

12 If the worker solicits orders from wholesalers, retailers, contractors, or operators of hotels, restaurants, or other similar establishments, enter the percentage of the worker's time spent in the solicitation.   N/A %

13 Is the merchandise purchased by the customers for resale or use in their business operations?   ☐ Yes ☐ No
Describe the merchandise and state whether it is equipment installed on the customers' premises. N/A

Part V   Signature (see page 4)

Under penalties of perjury, I declare that I have examined this request, including accompanying documents, and to the best of my knowledge and belief, the facts presented are true, correct, and complete.

Signature ▶ *Samuel S. Samson*   Title ▶ printer/machinist   Date ▶ *8/25/05*
(Type or print name below)
Samuel S. Samson

Department of Taxation and Finance and
Department of Labor-Unemployment Insurance Div Reg Sec
W A Harriman State Campus Bldg 12
Albany NY 12240-0339

NYS-100
(12/99)

**New York State Employer Registration
for Unemployment Insurance,
Withholding, and Wage Reporting**

For office use only: U.I.
Employer Registration No.

Return completed form (*type or print in ink*) to the
address above, **or fax to (518) 485-8010**

Need Help? Call (518) 485-8057

PART A - Employer Information

1. Type (*check one*):
   - [X] Business (*complete parts A, B, D, and E*)
   - [ ] Household Employer of Domestic
     Services (*complete parts A, C, D, and E-1*)

   * If nonprofit IRC 501 (C) (3), agricultural, or
   governmental employer, **do not** complete
   this form. Phone (518) 485-8589 or write to the
   above address to request the applicable form.

2. Legal entity (*check one - do not complete if household employer*):
   - [X] Corporation (*includes Sub-Chapter S*)
   - [ ] Sole proprietorship
   - [ ] Partnership
   - [ ] Other (please describe) _____
   - [ ] Limited liability company
   - [ ] Limited liability partnership

3. FEIN (*Fed. Id. no.*) |5|9|–|1|2|3|4|5|6|7|

4. Telephone no. (518) 555-5555

5. Fax no. (518) 444-4444

6. Legal name   Doe Masonry, Inc.

7. Trade name (*doing business as*), if any   Doe Masonry, Inc. d/b/a Doe Company

PART B - Business Employer

1. Enter date of first operations in New York State.................... |0|1|0|1|0|4| *(mmddyy)*

2. Enter the date of the first payroll from which you withheld or
   will withhold NYS Income Tax from your employees' pay................... |0|1|0|1|0|4| *(mmddyy)*

3. Indicate the first calendar quarter and enter the year you paid (*or expect to pay*) total remuneration of **$300** or more. (*Remuneration is every form of compensation, including payments to employees or to corporate and Sub-Chapter S officers for services*) ....

[X] Jan 1 - Mar 31	[ ] Apr 1 - Jun 30	[ ] Jul 1 - Sep 30	[ ] Oct 1 - Dec 31	Tax Year
1	2	3	4	Y Y

4. Total number of employees _____

5. Do persons work for you whom you do not consider employees? [ ] Yes [X] No If *Yes*, explain the services performed and the reason you do not consider these persons employees. _____

6. Have you acquired the business of another employer liable for NYS Unemployment Insurance? [ ] Yes [X] No If *Yes*, did you acquire [ ] All or [ ] Part? Date of acquisition | | | | | | | *(mmddyy)* Enter previous owner information below:

   Business name and address _____

   Employer Registration No. _____   FEIN _____

7. Have you changed legal entity? [X] Yes [ ] No. If *Yes*, enter the date of legal entity change.................. |0|1|0|1|0|4| *(mmddyy)*

   Previous Employer Registration Number _____   Previous FEIN _____

PART C - Household Employer of Domestic Services

1. Indicate the first calendar quarter and enter the year you paid (*or expect to pay*) total cash wages of **$500** or more.

[ ] Jan 1 - Mar 31	[ ] Apr 1 - Jun 30	[ ] Jul 1 - Sep 30	[X] Oct 1 - Dec 31	Tax Year
1	2	3	4	0 4 / Y Y

2. Enter the total number of persons employed in your home _____

3. Will you withhold New York State income tax from these employees? [ ] Yes [ ] No

PART D - Address/Telephone Information

Please enter your mailing and/or physical location address, as well as the physical location of your books/records. If you wish to provide us with **ADDITIONAL** addresses to direct specific forms, please indicate below.

1. **MAILING ADDRESS:** This is **YOUR** business mailing address (*NOT your agent or paid preparer*) where all your Unemployment Insurance/ Withholding Tax mail will be directed unless otherwise indicated.
   *If all your Unemployment Insurance/Withholding Tax mail (*including Forms NYS-45 and NYS-1*) is to be received at this mailing address, **do not** complete sections 4 through 6.

Street or PO Box	123 Anywhere St.		
City	State		ZIP Code
Albany	NY		12208-0110

2. **PHYSICAL ADDRESS:** This is the **ACTUAL** location of your business if different from the mailing address, or if your mailing address is a P.O. Box. If you have more than one location, list your primary location.

Street	same		
City		State	ZIP Code

3. **BOOKS/RECORDS ADDRESS:** This is the physical location where your **BOOKS/RECORDS** can be found.

   [X] Same as no. 1   [ ] Same as no. 2

   [ ] Other - please complete

c/o			
Street			
City		State	ZIP Code

ADDITIONAL ADDRESSES

4. **AGENT ADDRESS (*C/O*):** This is the address of your **AGENT**, where all your Unemployment Insurance mail will be directed unless other addresses have been provided for the mailing of specific forms in sections 5 and/or 6.
   Note: All withholding tax mail (*except quarterly return NYS-45 and Return of Tax Withheld coupon NYS-1*) must be sent to your mailing address (*no. 1*). However, the quarterly return NYS-45 and coupon NYS-1 may be directed to a separate address if no. 5 below is completed.

c/o	none		
Street or PO Box			
City		State	ZIP Code
Telephone ( )			

5. **QUARTERLY COMBINED WITHHOLDING, WAGE REPORTING AND UNEMPLOYMENT INSURANCE RETURN (*Form NYS-45*) AND RETURN OF TAX WITHHELD (*Form NYS-1*) ADDRESS:** If completed, this is the address to which your NYS-45 and NYS-1 will be directed.

   [ ] Same as no. 4   [ ] Other - please complete

c/o			
Street or PO Box			
City		State	ZIP Code

6. **NOTICE OF ENTITLEMENT AND POTENTIAL CHARGES ADDRESS:** If completed, this is the address to which the Notice of Entitlement and Potential Charges will be mailed. This form is mailed each time a former employee files a claim for Unemployment Insurance benefits. Please attach a separate sheet if you need to indicate different Notice of Entitlement and Potential Charges addresses for more than one physical location.

c/o			
Street or PO Box			
City		State	ZIP Code

PART E - Business Information

1. Complete the following for **sole proprietor, household employer of domestic services**, all **partners** (*including partners of LLP or RLLP*), all **members** (*of LLC or PLLC*), and all **corporate officers**, whether or not remuneration is received or services are performed in New York State.

Name	Social Security no.	Title	Residence Address
Jane Doe		President	123 Anywhere Street
John Doe		Vice President	123 Anywhere Street
William Doe		Treasurer	123 Anywhere Street

Enter legal name

For office use only

PART E- Business Information (*Continued*)

2. For **each** of your establishments in New York State, answer A-E below. Use a separate sheet for each establishment.

A. Location ___123 Anywhere Street___ ___Albany___ ___Albany___ ___12208___
No. and Street   City or Town   County   ZIP Code

B. Approximately how many persons do you employ there? ___10___

C. Check the principal activity at the above location

☐ Manufacturing	☐ Transportation	☐ Scientific/professional & technical services
☐ Wholesale trade	☐ Computer services	☐ Finance and insurance
☐ Retail trade	☐ Educational services	☐ Arts, entertainment, & recreation
☒ Construction	☐ Health & social assistance	☐ Food service, drinking, & accommodations
☐ Warehousing	☐ Real estate	☐ Corporate, subsidiary managing office
☐ Other (*Please specify*) _____		

D. If you are primarily engaged in manufacturing, complete the following:

Principal Products Produced	Percent of Total Sales Value	Principal Raw Materials Used

E. If your principal activity is not manufacturing, indicate products sold or services rendered:

Type of Establishment	Principal Product Sold or Service Rendered	Percent of Total Revenue
Masonry	Stone blocks and sculpture	100%

I affirm that I have read the above questions and that the answers provided are true to the best of my knowledge and belief.

Jane Doe   *President*   *1/1/04*

Signature of Officer, Partner, Proprietor, Member or Individual   Official Position   Date

Instructions

General Information:

- If you are a business employer or a household employer of domestic services, complete and return Form NYS-100.
- If you are a nonprofit, agricultural, or governmental employer, **do not** complete Form NYS-100. Phone (518) 485-8589 or write to the address on page one of this form to request information and necessary forms.
- Voluntary Coverage for U.I. purposes - if you are not liable for UI tax but want to provide voluntary coverage for employees, phone (518) 457-2635.

Part - A

Item 3   Enter your nine digit Federal Identification Number. This number is used to certify your payments to the IRS under the Federal Unemployment Tax Act.

Item 6-7   Enter the legal name of the employer and the trade name, firm name, registered name, etc., if any, used for business purposes. If the employer is a partnership, enter the full name of each partner. If the employer is a corporation, enter the corporate name shown in its Certificate of Incorporation or other official document. In the case of an estate of a decedent, insolvent, incompetent, etc., enter the name of the estate, and the name of the administrator or other fiduciary.

Part - B

Item 2   Any person or organization qualifying as an employer on the basis of instructions contained in federal Circular E that maintains an office or transacts business in New York State is an employer for New York State withholding tax purposes and must withhold from compensation paid to its employees.

Item 3   Enter the first calendar quarter in which you paid (*or expect to pay*) total remuneration of $300 or more. Do not go back beyond 3 years from January of the current year. Remuneration includes compensation such as: salary, cash wages, commissions, bonuses, payments to corporate officers for services rendered regardless of their stock ownership and without regard to how such payments are treated under Sub-Chapter S of the IRS Code or any other tax law, reasonable money value of board, rent, housing, lodging, or any similar advantage received, and the value of tips or other gratuities received from persons other than the employer. Note: **do not** include compensation paid to: daytime elementary or secondary students working after school or during vacation periods; the spouse or child (*under 21*) of an individual owner; children under age 14; employees who perform no services in New York State; or employees whose services are considered agricultural employment. If you have employees who work both within and outside NY State, please request a ruling from the Liability and Determination Section of the Department of Labor. Phone (518) 457-2635 for information.

Item 5   Answer *Yes*, if there are persons working for you whom you do not consider to be your employees. Do not include those described in Part B instructions for Item 3 which follow the Note. Attach a separate sheet if additional lines are required to accommodate your explanation.

Item 6   Answer *Yes,* if one or more of the following are true: you employed substantially the same employees as the previous owner; you continued or resumed the business of the previous owner at the same or another location; you assumed the previous owner's obligations; and/or you acquired the previous owner's good will.

Instructions (*Continued*)

Item 7   Answer *Yes*, if legal entity has changed. Types of legal entity appear in Part A, Item 2 of this form. A New York State Employer Registration Number is assigned to an employer who is liable to pay Unemployment Insurance tax. It is used to identify an individual account for recording tax payments due and Unemployment Insurance benefits paid.

Part C

Item 1   Enter the first calendar quarter and year in which you paid (*or expect to pay*) total cash wages of $500 or more to your household employees. Do not go back beyond 3 years from January of the current year. **Do not** include as cash wages payments to: household employees for carfare or other travel expenses; your spouse or your child under 21 years of age; elementary or secondary school students who attend school in the daytime; children under 14 years of age; babysitters under age 18, or casual laborers under age 21.

Item 3   Withholding of New York State, New York City or Yonkers income tax from household employees performing domestic services is voluntary. Answer *Yes* to this question only if there is a voluntary agreement in effect between you and the domestic employee to withhold New York State, New York City, or Yonkers income tax.

Part E

Item 2   Describe (1) principal activity or (2) product which produces greatest gross sales value. Examples:
(C - E)

Manufacturing	State type of establishment (*e.g., sawmill, vegetable cannery, printing and publishing*). Show principal products, percent of total sales value, and principal raw materials used. Specify principal products (*e.g., upholstered household furniture, ladies' sweaters hand knit from yarn*).
Trade	State principal product distributed. If sold to businesses (*wholesale*) or general public (*retail*), indicate which is primary.
Construction	Specify general or special trade contractor and show usual type of work (*e.g., general contractor-apartment houses or trade contractor-plumbing*).
Warehousing	State type of storage (*e.g., refrigerated, general, self-storage units for the public*).
Transportation	Includes establishments in railroading; local and suburban transit; interurban highway passenger transportation; motor freight transportation; water transportation (*deep sea foreign transportation, lighterage, etc.*); transportation by air, etc. Be specific.
Computer services	State primary activity (*e.g., computer analysis and design, custom programming, Internet access or data processing, etc.*).
Educational services	Includes all schools (*e.g., elementary, colleges, universities, vocational schools*). Be specific in Section E.
Health & social services	Includes health referral agencies, operation of clinics, hospital or homes. Be specific.
Real estate	Include owners/operators of real estate and agents. If owner/operator, specify type of property (*e.g., commercial or residential building*).
Scientific/professional & technical services	Includes lawyers, accountants, business consultants (*contractors*), architects, engineers, doctors, surveyors, etc. Be specific in Section E.
Finance & insurance	Includes bank and trust companies, credit agencies other than banks, insurance carriers. State if national or commercial banks, charter, and if accepting deposits from the general public. Insurance underwriters are classified by type of insurance (*e.g., life, accident and health, etc*).
Arts, entertainment & recreation	Includes theater operation, entertainers, commercial parks, casinos, professional athletes, sports recreational facilities, etc. Be specific.
Food service, drinking & accommodations	State type of service rendered (*e.g., operation of hotel, sports camp, restaurant [full or limited service], taverns or catering service*). Be specific.
Corporate, subsidiary managing office	Includes administrative, management consultant, and human resource consultants. Be specific.
Other activities	Indicate type of activity not covered by above paragraphs (*e.g., agriculture, forestry, fisheries, mining, motion picture or television production, etc*).

APPENDIX C: BLANK FORMS

The following forms may be photocopied or removed from this book and used immediately. Some of the tax forms explained in this book are not included here because you should use original returns provided by the IRS (940, 941) or the New York State Department of Taxation and Finance (quarterly unemployment compensation form). Many of these forms have a sample, filled-in copy in Appendix B.

These forms are included on the following pages:

Certificate of Assumed Name
Pursuant to General Business Law, §130

NYS Department of State
Division of Corporations, State Records and UCC
41 State Street, Albany, NY 12231-0001
www.dos.state.ny.us

1. NAME OF ENTITY

1a. *FOREIGN ENTITIES ONLY.* If applicable, the fictitious name the entity agreed to use in New York State is:

2. NEW YORK LAW FORMED OR AUTHORIZED UNDER (CHECK ONE):

☐ Business Corporation Law   ☐ Limited Liability Company Law

☐ Education Law   ☐ Not-for-Profit Corporation Law

☐ Insurance Law   ☐ Revised Limited Partnership Act

☐ Other (specify law):

3. ASSUMED NAME

4. PRINCIPAL PLACE OF BUSINESS IN NEW YORK STATE (MUST BE NUMBER AND STREET. IF NONE, INSERT OUT-OF-STATE ADDRESS)

5. COUNTIES IN WHICH BUSINESS WILL BE CONDUCTED UNDER ASSUMED NAME

☐ ALL COUNTIES (if not, circle county[ies] below)

Albany	Clinton	Genesee	Monroe	Orleans	Saratoga	Tompkins
Allegany	Columbia	Greene	Montgomery	Oswego	Schenectady	Ulster
Bronx	Cortland	Hamilton	Nassau	Otsego	Schoharie	Warren
Broome	Delaware	Herkimer	New York	Putnam	Schuyler	Washington
Cattaraugus	Dutchess	Jefferson	Niagara	Queens	Seneca	Wayne
Cayuga	Erie	Kings	Oneida	Rensselaer	Steuben	Westchester
Chautauqua	Essex	Lewis	Onondaga	Richmond	Suffolk	Wyoming
Chemung	Franklin	Livingston	Ontario	Rockland	Sullivan	Yates
Chenango	Fulton	Madison	Orange	St. Lawrence	Tioga	

6. INSERT THE ADDRESS OF EACH LOCATION WHERE BUSINESS WILL BE CARRIED ON OR TRANSACTED UNDER THE ASSUMED NAME. Use a continuous sheet, if needed. (The address must be set forth in terms of a number and street, city, state and zip code. Please note that the address(es) reflected in paragraph 6 must be within the county(ies) circled in paragraph 5. If the entity does not have a specific location where it will conduct business under the assumed name please check the box.)

☐ No New York State Business Location

INSTRUCTIONS FOR SIGNATURE: If corporation, by an officer; if limited partnership, by a general partner; if limited liability company, by a member or manager or by an attorney-in-fact or authorized person for such corporation, limited partnership, or limited liability company.

_____

Name and Title   Signature

CERTIFICATE OF ASSUMED NAME
OF

_____

(Insert Entity Name)

Pursuant to §130, General Business Law

FILER'S NAME AND MAILING ADDRESS

_____

_____

_____

NOTE: This form was prepared by the New York State Department of State. You are not required to use this form. You may draft your own form or use forms available at legal stationery stores. The Department of State recommends that all documents be prepared under the guidance of an attorney. The certificate must be submitted with a $25 fee. The Department of State also collects the following, additional, county clerk fees for each county in which a **corporation** does or transacts business: $100 for each county within New York City (Bronx, Kings, New York, Queens and Richmond) and $25 for each county outside New York City. All checks over $500 must be certified.

(For Office Use Only)

Certificate of Assumed Name

I, _____, residing at _____
Print or type full name

_____

HEREBY CERTIFY that I am conducting business under the name or designation of

_____

at

_____

in the city or town of _____ County of _____,
State of New York.

IN WITNESS WHEREOF, I have made and signed this certificate this _____ day of

_____, _____.

_____

STATE OF NEW YORK   )
) ss.:
COUNTY OF _____   )

     On this _____ day of _____, _____, before me person-
ally appeared

_____
to me known to be the individual(s) described in and who executed the foregoing certificate, and he/she thereupon has duly acknowledged that he/she executed the same.

_____
Notary Public

This page intentionally left blank.

NYS DEPARTMENT OF STATE
MISCELLANEOUS RECORDS
41 State Street
Albany, NY 12231-0001

REG NO

Original Application to Register a Trademark

Please read the instructions prior to completing this form; attach additional sheets as needed.

1. APPLICANT NAME

2. ADDRESS   NUMBER AND STREET   CITY   STATE   ZIP

3. IF A CORPORATION, ENTER STATE IN WHICH INCORPORATED AND
   IF A PARTNERSHIP, ENTER STATE IN WHICH ORGANIZED

4. IF A PARTNERSHIP, LIST THE NAMES OF ALL GENERAL PARTNERS

5. DESCRIBE THE TRADEMARK, INCLUDING A **WRITTEN** DESCRIPTION OF DESIGN FEATURES, IF ANY (DO **NOT** GLUE A FACSIMILE TO THIS FORM)

6. DESCRIBE THE SPECIFIC GOODS BEING PRODUCED ON WHICH THE TRADEMARK IS USED

7. STATE THE MANNER IN WHICH THE TRADEMARK IS PLACED ON THE GOODS, CONTAINERS, ETC.

8. CLASS NUMBER(S)   9. DATE OF   (A) IN NEW YORK STATE   (B) ELSEWHERE
                                                         FIRST USE

FOR OFFICE USE ONLY

The applicant is the owner of the mark, the mark is in use, and, to the knowledge of the person verifying the application, no other person has registered, either federally or in this state, or has the right to use such mark either in the identical form or in such near resemblance as to be likely, when applied to the goods of such other person, to cause confusion, or to cause mistake, or to deceive.

The undersigned applies to register the aforesaid mark pursuant to Article 24 of the General Business Law and affirms under the penalties of perjury that the statements herein made, including any attached papers, are true.

_____
(Corporation, Association, Firm, etc.)

By: _____   _____
       (Signature and Title of Officer)   *(Date)*

Instructions: Please refer to the instruction sheet for completion of items 1 through 9 of the registration form.

Definition: The term *"trademark"* means any word, name, symbol or device or any combination thereof used by a person to identify and distinguish the goods of such person, including a unique product, from those manufactured and sold by others, and to indicate the source of the goods, even if the source is unknown.

General Classes of Goods: New York State's classification of goods conforms to the classification adopted by the United States Patent and Trademark Office. Please refer to the classification of goods and services enclosure.

Please note there is a $50 filing fee for EACH CLASSIFICATION claimed for registration.

Application Form: The application must be on a current form supplied by the Department of State and be completed in the English language and plainly written or typed. If the mark or any part thereof is not in the English language, it must be accompanied by a sworn translation.

Specimens of the Mark: The application must be accompanied by three specimens showing the mark as actually used.

Mail to: Please mail the completed application form together with the filing fee and three specimens of the mark to: New York State Department of State, Miscellaneous Records Unit, 41 State Street, Albany, NY 12231-0001.

Questions: If you have any questions or require assistance completing this form, please write to the Department of State, Miscellaneous Records Unit at the above address or call (518) 474-4770.

Payment: Checks or money orders should be made payable to the "Department of State." Please do not send cash through the mail.

NYS Department of State
Miscellaneous Records Unit
41 State Street
Albany, NY 12231-0001

INSTRUCTIONS FOR THE COMPLETION OF AN ORIGINAL APPLICATION TO REGISTER A TRADEMARK OR SERVICEMARK

Item 1 - Name of Applicant: If the applicant is a corporation, set forth the true name of the corporation. If the applicant is a partnership, set forth the name of the partnership. If the applicant is one or more persons, set forth the name of each person in terms of first name, middle initial and last name. If the applicant is one or more persons using a dba, set forth the names of all such persons using first name, middle initial, last name and then the dba business name; e.g., John T. Doe and Jane E. Roe d/b/a Doe-Roe Company.

Item 2 - Address: Set forth the business address of the applicant in terms of street and number, city, state and zip code.

Item 3: If the applicant is a corporation, set forth the state of incorporation and if the applicant is a partnership, set forth the state in which the partnership is organized.

Item 4: If the applicant is a partnership, set forth the names of all the general partners.

Item 5: Set forth a written description of the design features being claimed of the mark; e.g., the mark is a one inch circle containing the head of a unicorn facing to the left with a cratered moon and three five-pointed stars in the background. The unicorn head, moon and stars are white on a black background.

If the mark is a name, signature or portrait of any living individual, that person's verified consent must accompany the application. If the mark consists of the name of an individual but is merely a fanciful name, a statement should follow the description declaring that such name is fanciful and not intended to identify or be identified with that of any living individual.

Item 6: Set forth specific goods or services on or in connection with which the mark is used.

Item 7: Set forth the manner in which the mark is affixed to the goods or used in connection with the services; e.g., the mark appears on a label sewn into the inside collar of the shirt, or the mark appears on letterhead, business cards and all advertising material.

Item 8: Set forth the classification number of each category of goods or services for which the mark will be used. Please note that there is a $50 fee for each classification claimed.

Item 9: Set forth the date of first use of the mark by akin or predecessor in interest: (a) in New York State, (b) or used anywhere else. The term "use" means the bonified use of a mark in the ordinary course of trade and not merely to reserve a right in a mark. For the purposes of filing under Article 24 of the General Business Law, a mark shall be deemed to be in use: (1) on the goods when it is placed in any manner on the goods or other containers or the displays associated therewith, or on the tags or labels affixed thereto, or if the nature of the goods makes such placement impractical, then on documents associated with the goods or their sale and the goods are sold or transported in commerce in this state; and (2) on services when it is used or displayed in the sale or advertising of service and the services are rendered in this state.

Signing: The application must be signed by: (1) in the case of a corporation or association, by an officer of the corporation or association; (2) in the case of a partnership, by a member or partner of the firm; and (3) in the case of an individual, by the individual or individuals.

NYS Department of State
Miscellaneous Records Unit
41 State Street
Albany, N.Y. 12231-0001

CLASSIFICATION OF GOODS AND SERVICES
FOR REGISTRATION OF A TRADEMARK OR SERVICEMARK

GOODS:

1. Chemical products used in industry, science, photography, agriculture, horticulture, forestry; artificial and synthetic resins; plastics in the form of powders, liquids or pastes, for industrial use; manures (natural and artificial); fire extinguishing compositions; tempering substances and chemical preparations for soldering; chemical substances for preserving foodstuffs; tanning substances; adhesive substances used in industry.

2. Paint, varnishes, lacquers; preservatives against rust and against deterioration of wood; coloring matters, dyestuff; mordants; natural resins; metals in foil and powder form for painters and decorators.

3. Bleaching preparations and other substances for laundry use; cleaning, polishing, scouring, and abrasive preparations; soaps; perfumery, essential oils, cosmetics, hair lotions; dentifrices.

4. Industrial oils and greases (other than edible oils and fats and essential oils); lubricants; dust laying and absorbing compositions; fuels (including motor spirit) and illuminants; candles, tapers, night lights and wicks.

5. Pharmaceutical, veterinary, and sanitary substances; infants' and invalids' foods; plasters, material for bandaging; material for stopping teeth, a dental sax; disinfectants; preparations for killing weeds and destroying vermin.

6. Unwrought and partly wrought common metals and their alloys; anchors, anvils, bells, rolled and cast building materials; rails and other metallic materials for railway tracks; chains (except driving chains for vehicles); cables and wires (nonelectric); locksmiths' work; metallic pipes and tubes; safes and cash boxes; steel balls; horseshoes; nails and screws; other goods in nonprecious metal not included in other classes; ores.

7. Machines and machine tools; motors (except for land vehicles); machine couplings and belting (except for land vehicles); large size agricultural implements; incubators.

8. Hand tools and instruments; cutlery, forks, and spoons; side arms.

9. Scientific, nautical, surveying and electrical apparatus and instruments (including wireless), photographic, cinematographic, optical, weighing, measuring, signaling, checking (supervision), life saving and teaching apparatus and instruments; coin or counter-freed apparatus; talking machines; cash registers; calculating machines; fire extinguishing apparatus.

10. Surgical, medical, dental, and veterinary instruments and apparatus (including artificial limbs, eyes, and teeth).

11. Installations for lighting, heating, steam generating, cooking, refrigerating, drying, ventilating, water supply and sanitary purposes.

12. Vehicles; apparatus for locomotion by land, air, or water.

13. Firearms; ammunition and projectiles; explosive substances; fireworks.

14. Precious metals and their alloys and goods in precious metals or coated therewith (except cutlery, forks, and spoons); jewelry, precious stones, horological, and other chronometric instruments.

15. Musical instruments (other than talking machines and wireless apparatus).

16. Paper and paper articles, cardboard and cardboard articles; printed matter, newspaper and periodicals, books; bookbinding material; photographs; stationery, adhesive materials (stationery); artists' materials; paint rushes; typewriters and office requisites (other than furniture); instruction and teaching material (other than apparatus); playing cards; printers' type and cliches (stereotype).

17. Gutta percha, indiarubber, balata, and substitutes, articles made from these substances and not included in other classes; plastics in the form of sheets, blocks, and rods, being for use in manufacture; materials for packing, stopping, or insulating; asbestos, mica and their products; hose pipes (nonmetallic),

18. Leather and imitations of leather, and articles made from these materials and not included in other classes; skins, hides; trunks and traveling bags; umbrellas, parasols, and walking sticks; whips, harness, and saddlery.

19. Building materials, natural and artificial stone, cement, lime, mortar, plaster, and gravel; pipes of earthenware or cement; road-making materials; asphalt, pitch, and bitumen; portable buildings; stone monuments; chimney pots.

20. Furniture, mirrors, picture frames; articles (not included in other classes) of wood, cork, reeds, cane, wicker, horn bone, ivory, whalebone, shell, amber, mother-of-pearl, meerschaum, celluloid, substitutes for all these materials, or of plastics.

21. Small domestic utensils and containers (not of precious metals, or coated therewith); combs and sponges; brushes (other than paint brushes); brush making materials; instruments and material for cleaning purposes, steel wool; unworked or semiworked glass (excluding glass used in building); glassware, porcelain, and earthenware, not included in other classes.

22. Ropes, string, nets, tents, awnings, tarpaulins, sails, sacks; padding and stuffing materials (hair, kapok, feathers, seaweed, etc.); raw fibrous textile materials.

23. Yarns, threads.

24. Tissues (piece goods); bed and table covers; textile articles not included in other classes.

25. Clothing, including boots, shoes, and slippers.

26. Lace and embroidery, ribands and braid; buttons, press buttons, hooks and eyes, pins and needles; artificial flowers.

27. Carpets, rugs, mats, and matting; linoleums and other materials for covering existing floors; wall hangings (nontextile).

28. Games and playthings; gymnastic and sporting articles (except clothing); ornaments and decorations for Christmas trees.

29. Meat, fish, poultry, and game; meat extracts; preserved, dried and cooked fruits and vegetables; jellies, jams; eggs, milk, and other dairy products; edible oils and fats; preserves, pickles.

30. Coffee, tea, cocoa, sugar, rice, tapioca, sago, coffee substitutes; flour, and preparations made from cereals; bread, biscuits, cakes, pastry and confectionery, ices; honey treacle; yeast, baking powder; salt, mustard, pepper, vinegar, sauces, spices; ice.

31. Agricultural, horticultural, and forestry products and grains not included in other classes; living animals; fresh fruits and vegetables; seeds; live plants and flowers; foodstuffs for animals, malt.

32. Beer, ale, and porter; mineral and aerated waters and other nonalcoholic drinks; syrups and other preparations for making beverages.

33. Wines, spirits, and liqueurs.

34. Tobacco, raw or manufactured; smokers' articles; matches.

SERVICES:

35. Advertising and business.

36. Insurance and financial.

37. Construction and repair.

38. Communication.

39. Transportation and storage.

40. Material treatment.

41. Education and entertainment.

42. Miscellaneous.

This page intentionally left blank.

NYS DEPARTMENT OF STATE
MISCELLANEOUS RECORDS
41 State Street
Albany, NY 12231-0001

REG NO

Original Application to Register a Servicemark

Please read the instructions prior to completing this form; attach additional sheets as needed.

1. APPLICANT NAME

2. ADDRESS   NUMBER AND STREET   CITY   STATE   ZIP

3. IF A CORPORATION, ENTER STATE IN WHICH INCORPORATED AND
   IF A PARTNERSHIP, ENTER STATE IN WHICH ORGANIZED

4. IF A PARTNERSHIP, LIST THE NAMES OF ALL GENERAL PARTNERS

5. DESCRIBE THE SERVICEMARK, INCLUDING A **WRITTEN** DESCRIPTION OF DESIGN FEATURES, IF ANY (DO **NOT** GLUE A FACSIMILE TO THIS FORM)

6. STATE THE SPECIFIC SERVICES FOR WHICH THE MARK IS USED

7. DESCRIBE THE MODE OR MANNER IN WHICH THE MARK IS USED

8. CLASS NUMBER(S)   9. DATE OF   (A) IN NEW YORK STATE   (B) ELSEWHERE
                                             FIRST USE

FOR OFFICE USE ONLY

The applicant is the owner of the mark, the mark is in use, and, to the knowledge of the person verifying the application, no other person has registered, either federally or in this state, or has the right to use such mark either in the identical form or in such near resemblance as to be likely, when applied to the services of such other person, to cause confusion, or to cause mistake, or to deceive.

The undersigned applies to register the aforesaid mark pursuant to Article 24 of the General Business Law and affirms under the penalties of perjury that the statements herein made, including any attached papers, are true.

_____
(Corporation, Association, Firm, etc.)

By: _____
    (Signature and Title of Officer)   *(Date)*

DOS-246 (REV. 2/98)

Instructions: Please refer to the instruction sheet for completion of items 1 through 9 of the registration form.

Definition: The term "*servicemark*" means any word, name, symbol or device or any combination thereof used by a person to identify and distinguish the services of one person, including a unique service, from the services of others, and to indicate the source of the services, even if the source is unknown. Titles, character names used by a person, and other distinctive features of radio or television programs may be registered as servicemarks not withstanding that they, or the programs, may advertise the goods of the sponsor.

General Classes of Services: New York State's classification of services conforms to the classification adopted by the United States Patent and Trademark Office:

Class	Title		Class	Title
35	Advertising and Business		39	Transportation and Storage
36	Insurance and Financial		40	Material treatment
37	Construction and Repair		41	Education and Entertainment
38	Communication		42	Miscellaneous

Please note there is a $50 filing fee for EACH CLASSIFICATION claimed for registration.

Application Form: The application must be on a current form supplied by the Department of State and be completed in the English language and plainly written or typed. If the mark or any part thereof is not in the English language, it must be accompanied by a sworn translation.

Specimens of the Mark: The application must be accompanied by three specimens showing the mark as actually used.

Mail to: Please mail the completed application form together with the filing fee and three specimens of the mark to: New York State Department of State, Miscellaneous Records Unit, 41 State Street, Albany, NY 12231-0001.

Questions: If you have any questions or require assistance completing this form, please write to the Department of State, Miscellaneous Records Unit at the above address or call (518) 474-4770.

Payment: Checks or money orders should be made payable to the "Department of State." Please do not send cash through the mail.

INSTRUCTIONS FOR THE COMPLETION OF AN ORIGINAL APPLICATION TO REGISTER A TRADEMARK OR SERVICEMARK

Item 1 - Name of Applicant: If the applicant is a corporation, set forth the true name of the corporation. If the applicant is a partnership, set forth the name of the partnership. If the applicant is one or more persons, set forth the name of each person in terms of first name, middle initial and last name. If the applicant is one or more persons using a dba, set forth the names of all such persons using first name, middle initial, last name and then the dba business name; e.g., John T. Doe and Jane E. Roe d/b/a Doe-Roe Company.

Item 2 - Address: Set forth the business address of the applicant in terms of street and number, city, state and zip code.

Item 3: If the applicant is a corporation, set forth the state of incorporation and if the applicant is a partnership, set forth the state in which the partnership is organized.

Item 4: If the applicant is a partnership, set forth the names of all the general partners.

Item 5: Set forth a written description of the design features being claimed of the mark; e.g., the mark is a one inch circle containing the head of a unicorn facing to the left with a cratered moon and three five-pointed stars in the background. The unicorn head, moon and stars are white on a black background.

If the mark is a name, signature or portrait of any living individual, that person's verified consent must accompany the application. If the mark consists of the name of an individual but is merely a fanciful name, a statement should follow the description declaring that such name is fanciful and not intended to identify or be identified with that of any living individual.

Item 6: Set forth specific goods or services on or in connection with which the mark is used.

Item 7: Set forth the manner in which the mark is affixed to the goods or used in connection with the services; e.g., the mark appears on a label sewn into the inside collar of the shirt, or the mark appears on letterhead, business cards and all advertising material.

Item 8: Set forth the classification number of each category of goods or services for which the mark will be used. Please note that there is a $50 fee for each classification claimed.

Item 9: Set forth the date of first use of the mark by akin or predecessor in interest: (a) in New York State, (b) or used anywhere else. The term "use" means the bonified use of a mark in the ordinary course of trade and not merely to reserve a right in a mark. For the purposes of filing under Article 24 of the General Business Law, a mark shall be deemed to be in use: (1) on the goods when it is placed in any manner on the goods or other containers or the displays associated therewith, or on the tags or labels affixed thereto, or if the nature of the goods makes such placement impractical, then on documents associated with the goods or their sale and the goods are sold or transported in commerce in this state; and (2) on services when it is used or displayed in the sale or advertising of service and the services are rendered in this state.

Signing: The application must be signed by: (1) in the case of a corporation or association, by an officer of the corporation or association; (2) in the case of a partnership, by a member or partner of the firm; and (3) in the case of an individual, by the individual or individuals.

This page intentionally left blank.

U.S. Department of Justice
Immigration and Naturalization Service

OMB No. 1115-0136

Employment Eligibility Verification

Please read instructions carefully before completing this form. The instructions must be available during completion of this form. ANTI-DISCRIMINATION NOTICE: It is illegal to discriminate against work eligible individuals. Employers CANNOT specify which document(s) they will accept from an employee. The refusal to hire an individual because of a future expiration date may also constitute illegal discrimination.

Section 1. Employee Information and Verification. To be completed and signed by employee at the time employment begins.

Print Name: Last	First	Middle Initial	Maiden Name

Address (Street Name and Number)		Apt. #	Date of Birth (month/day/year)

City	State	Zip Code	Social Security #

I am aware that federal law provides for imprisonment and/or fines for false statements or use of false documents in connection with the completion of this form.	I attest, under penalty of perjury, that I am (check one of the following): ☐ A citizen or national of the United States ☐ A Lawful Permanent Resident (Alien # A ☐ An alien authorized to work until ___/___/___ (Alien # or Admission #)

Employee's Signature	Date (month/day/year)

Preparer and/or Translator Certification. *(To be completed and signed if Section 1 is prepared by a person other than the employee.) I attest, under penalty of perjury, that I have assisted in the completion of this form and that to the best of my knowledge the information is true and correct.*

Preparer's/Translator's Signature	Print Name

Address (Street Name and Number, City, State, Zip Code)	Date (month/day/year)

Section 2. Employer Review and Verification. To be completed and signed by employer. Examine one document from List A OR examine one document from List B and one from List C, as listed on the reverse of this form, and record the title, number and expiration date, if any, of the document(s)

List A	OR	List B	AND	List C
Document title:_____		_____		_____
Issuing authority:_____		_____		_____
Document #:_____		_____		_____
Expiration Date (if any): ___/___/___		___/___/___		___/___/___
Document #:_____				
Expiration Date (if any): ___/___/___				

CERTIFICATION - I attest, under penalty of perjury, that I have examined the document(s) presented by the above-named employee, that the above-listed document(s) appear to be genuine and to relate to the employee named, that the employee began employment on *(month/day/year)* **___/___/___ and that to the best of my knowledge the employee is eligible to work in the United States. (State employment agencies may omit the date the employee began employment.)**

Signature of Employer or Authorized Representative	Print Name	Title

Business or Organization Name	Address (Street Name and Number, City, State, Zip Code)	Date (month/day/year)

Section 3. Updating and Reverification. To be completed and signed by employer.

A. New Name (if applicable)	B. Date of rehire (month/day/year) (if applicable)

C. If employee's previous grant of work authorization has expired, provide the information below for the document that establishes current employment eligibility.

Document Title:_____	Document #:_____	Expiration Date (if any): ___/___/___

I attest, under penalty of perjury, that to the best of my knowledge, this employee is eligible to work in the United States, and if the employee presented document(s), the document(s) I have examined appear to be genuine and to relate to the individual.

Signature of Employer or Authorized Representative	Date (month/day/year)

INSTRUCTIONS
PLEASE READ ALL INSTRUCTIONS CAREFULLY BEFORE COMPLETING THIS FORM.

Anti-Discrimination Notice. It is illegal to discriminate against any individual (other than an alien not authorized to work in the U.S.) in hiring, discharging, or recruiting or referring for a fee because of that individual's national origin or citizenship status. It is illegal to discriminate against work eligible individuals. Employers **CANNOT** specify which document(s) they will accept from an employee. The refusal to hire an individual because of a future expiration date may also constitute illegal discrimination.

Section 1 - Employee.
All employees, citizens and noncitizens, hired after November 6, 1986, must complete Section 1 of this form at the time of hire, which is the actual beginning of employment. **The employer is responsible for ensuring that Section 1 is timely and properly completed.**

Preparer/Translator Certification. The Preparer/Translator Certification must be completed if Section 1 is prepared by a person other than the employee. A preparer/translator may be used only when the employee is unable to complete Section 1 on his/her own. However, the employee must still sign Section 1.

Section 2 - Employer.
For the purpose of completing this form, the term "employer" includes those recruiters and referrers for a fee who are agricultural associations, agricultural employers or farm labor contractors.

Employers must complete Section 2 by examining evidence of identity and employment eligibility within three (3) business days of the date employment begins. If employees are authorized to work, but are unable to present the required document(s) within three business days, they must present a receipt for the application of the document(s) within three business days and the actual document(s) within ninety (90) days. However, if employers hire individuals for a duration of less than three business days, Section 2 must be completed at the time employment begins. **Employers must record: 1)** document title; **2)** issuing authority; **3)** document number, **4)** expiration date, if any; and **5)** the date employment begins. Employers must sign and date the certification. Employees must present original documents. Employers may, but are not required to, photocopy the document(s) presented. These photocopies may only be used for the verification process and must be retained with the I-9. **However, employers are still responsible for completing the I-9.**

Section 3 - Updating and Reverification.
Employers must complete Section 3 when updating and/or reverifying the I-9. Employers must reverify employment eligibility of their employees on or before the expiration date recorded in Section 1. Employers **CANNOT** specify which document(s) they will accept from an employee.

- If an employee's name has changed at the time this form is being updated/ reverified, complete Block A.

- If an employee is rehired within three (3) years of the date this form was originally completed and the employee is still eligible to be employed on the same basis as previously indicated on this form (updating), complete Block B and the signature block.

- If an employee is rehired within three (3) years of the date this form was originally completed and the employee's work authorization has expired **or** if a current employee's work authorization is about to expire (reverification), complete Block B and:
  - examine any document that reflects that the employee is authorized to work in the U.S. (see List A **or** C),
  - record the document title, document number and expiration date (if any) in Block C, and complete the signature block.

Photocopying and Retaining Form I-9. A blank I-9 may be reproduced, provided both sides are copied. The Instructions must be available to all employees completing this form. Employers must retain completed I-9s for three (3) years after the date of hire or one (1) year after the date employment ends, whichever is later.

For more detailed information, you may refer to the INS Handbook for Employers, (Form M-274). You may obtain the handbook at your local INS office.

Privacy Act Notice. The authority for collecting this information is the Immigration Reform and Control Act of 1986, Pub. L. 99-603 (8 USC 1324a).

This information is for employers to verify the eligibility of individuals for employment to preclude the unlawful hiring, or recruiting or referring for a fee, of aliens who are not authorized to work in the United States.

This information will be used by employers as a record of their basis for determining eligibility of an employee to work in the United States. The form will be kept by the employer and made available for inspection by officials of the U.S. Immigration and Naturalization Service, the Department of Labor and the Office of Special Counsel for Immigration Related Unfair Employment Practices.

Submission of the information required in this form is voluntary. However, an individual may not begin employment unless this form is completed, since employers are subject to civil or criminal penalties if they do not comply with the Immigration Reform and Control Act of 1986.

Reporting Burden. We try to create forms and instructions that are accurate, can be easily understood and which impose the least possible burden on you to provide us with information. Often this is difficult because some immigration laws are very complex. Accordingly, the reporting burden for this collection of information is computed as follows: **1)** learning about this form, 5 minutes; **2)** completing the form, 5 minutes; and **3)** assembling and filing (recordkeeping) the form, 5 minutes, for an average of 15 minutes per response. If you have comments regarding the accuracy of this burden estimate, or suggestions for making this form simpler, you can write to the Immigration and Naturalization Service, HQPDI, 425 I Street, N.W., Room 4034, Washington, DC 20536. OMB No. 1115-0136.

LISTS OF ACCEPTABLE DOCUMENTS

LIST A		LIST B		LIST C

Documents that Establish Both Identity and Employment Eligibility

OR

Documents that Establish Identity

AND

Documents that Establish Employment Eligibility

LIST A
Documents that Establish Both Identity and Employment Eligibility

1. U.S. Passport (unexpired or expired)

2. Certificate of U.S. Citizenship (INS Form N-560 or N-561)

3. Certificate of Naturalization (INS Form N-550 or N-570)

4. Unexpired foreign passport, with I-551 stamp or attached INS Form I-94 indicating unexpired employment authorization

5. Permanent Resident Card or Alien Registration Receipt Card with photograph (INS Form I-151 or I-551)

6. Unexpired Temporary Resident Card (INS Form I-688)

7. Unexpired Employment Authorization Card (INS Form I-688A)

8. Unexpired Reentry Permit (INS Form I-327)

9. Unexpired Refugee Travel Document (INS Form I-571)

10. Unexpired Employment Authorization Document issued by the INS which contains a photograph (INS Form I-688B)

LIST B
Documents that Establish Identity

1. Driver's license or ID card issued by a state or outlying possession of the United States provided it contains a photograph or information such as name, date of birth, gender, height, eye color and address

2. ID card issued by federal, state or local government agencies or entities, provided it contains a photograph or information such as name, date of birth, gender, height, eye color and address

3. School ID card with a photograph

4. Voter's registration card

5. U.S. Military card or draft record

6. Military dependent's ID card

7. U.S. Coast Guard Merchant Mariner Card

8. Native American tribal document

9. Driver's license issued by a Canadian government authority

For persons under age 18 who are unable to present a document listed above:

10. School record or report card

11. Clinic, doctor or hospital record

12. Day-care or nursery school record

LIST C
Documents that Establish Employment Eligibility

1. U.S. social security card issued by the Social Security Administration (other than a card stating it is not valid for employment)

2. Certification of Birth Abroad issued by the Department of State (Form FS-545 or Form DS-1350)

3. Original or certified copy of a birth certificate issued by a state, county, municipal authority or outlying possession of the United States bearing an official seal

4. Native American tribal document

5. U.S. Citizen ID Card (INS Form I-197)

6. ID Card for use of Resident Citizen in the United States (INS Form I-179)

7. Unexpired employment authorization document issued by the INS (other than those listed under List A)

Illustrations of many of these documents appear in Part 8 of the Handbook for Employers (M-274)

This page intentionally left blank.

Form **SS-4**
(Rev. December 2001)
Department of the Treasury
Internal Revenue Service

Application for Employer Identification Number

(For use by employers, corporations, partnerships, trusts, estates, churches, government agencies, Indian tribal entities, certain individuals, and others.)

▶ See separate instructions for each line. ▶ Keep a copy for your records.

EIN

OMB No. 1545-0003

Type or print clearly.

1 Legal name of entity (or individual) for whom the EIN is being requested	

2 Trade name of business (if different from name on line 1)	**3** Executor, trustee, "care of" name

4a Mailing address (room, apt., suite no. and street, or P.O. box)	**5a** Street address (if different) (Do not enter a P.O. box.)
4b City, state, and ZIP code	**5b** City, state, and ZIP code

6 County and state where principal business is located

7a Name of principal officer, general partner, grantor, owner, or trustor	**7b** SSN, ITIN, or EIN

8a Type of entity (check only one box)

- ☐ Sole proprietor (SSN) _____
- ☐ Partnership
- ☐ Corporation (enter form number to be filed) ▶ _____
- ☐ Personal service corp.
- ☐ Church or church-controlled organization
- ☐ Other nonprofit organization (specify) ▶ _____
- ☐ Other (specify) ▶

- ☐ Estate (SSN of decedent) _____
- ☐ Plan administrator (SSN) _____
- ☐ Trust (SSN of grantor) _____
- ☐ National Guard   ☐ State/local government
- ☐ Farmers' cooperative   ☐ Federal government/military
- ☐ REMIC   ☐ Indian tribal governments/enterprises

Group Exemption Number (GEN) ▶ _____

8b If a corporation, name the state or foreign country (if applicable) where incorporated

State	Foreign country

9 **Reason for applying** (check only one box)

- ☐ Started new business (specify type) ▶ _____
- ☐ Hired employees (Check the box and see line 12.)
- ☐ Compliance with IRS withholding regulations
- ☐ Other (specify) ▶

- ☐ Banking purpose (specify purpose) ▶ _____
- ☐ Changed type of organization (specify new type) ▶ _____
- ☐ Purchased going business
- ☐ Created a trust (specify type) ▶ _____
- ☐ Created a pension plan (specify type) ▶ _____

10 Date business started or acquired (month, day, year)	**11** Closing month of accounting year

12 First date wages or annuities were paid or will be paid (month, day, year). **Note:** *If applicant is a withholding agent, enter date income will first be paid to nonresident alien. (month, day, year)* . . . . ▶

13 Highest number of employees expected in the next 12 months. **Note:** *If the applicant does not expect to have any employees during the period, enter "-0-."* . . . . ▶	Agricultural	Household	Other

14 Check **one** box that best describes the principal activity of your business.

- ☐ Construction   ☐ Rental & leasing   ☐ Transportation & warehousing
- ☐ Real estate   ☐ Manufacturing   ☐ Finance & insurance
- ☐ Health care & social assistance   ☐ Wholesale–agent/broker
- ☐ Accommodation & food service   ☐ Wholesale–other   ☐ Retail
- ☐ Other (specify)

15 Indicate principal line of merchandise sold; specific construction work done; products produced; or services provided.

16a Has the applicant ever applied for an employer identification number for this or any other business? . . . . . ☐ **Yes**   ☐ **No**
Note: *If "Yes," please complete lines 16b and 16c.*

16b If you checked "Yes" on line 16a, give applicant's legal name and trade name shown on prior application if different from line 1 or 2 above.
Legal name ▶   Trade name ▶

16c Approximate date when, and city and state where, the application was filed. Enter previous employer identification number if known.

Approximate date when filed (mo., day, year)	City and state where filed	Previous EIN

Third Party Designee	Complete this section **only** if you want to authorize the named individual to receive the entity's EIN and answer questions about the completion of this form.	
	Designee's name	Designee's telephone number (include area code) ( )
	Address and ZIP code	Designee's fax number (include area code) ( )

Under penalties of perjury, I declare that I have examined this application, and to the best of my knowledge and belief, it is true, correct, and complete.

Name and title (type or print clearly) ▶

Applicant's telephone number (include area code) ( )

Signature ▶   Date ▶

Applicant's fax number (include area code) ( )

For Privacy Act and Paperwork Reduction Act Notice, see separate instructions.   Cat. No. 16055N   Form **SS-4** (Rev. 12-2001)

Do I Need an EIN?

File Form SS-4 if the applicant entity does not already have an EIN but is required to show an EIN on any return, statement, or other document.[1] **See also the separate instructions for each line on Form SS-4.**

IF the applicant...	AND...	THEN...
Started a new business	Does not currently have (nor expect to have) employees	Complete lines 1, 2, 4a-6, 8a, and 9-16c.
Hired (or will hire) employees, including household employees	Does not already have an EIN	Complete lines 1, 2, 4a-6, 7a-b (if applicable), 8a, 8b (if applicable), and 9-16c.
Opened a bank account	Needs an EIN for banking purposes only	Complete lines 1-5b, 7a-b (if applicable), 8a, 9, and 16a-c.
Changed type of organization	Either the legal character of the organization or its ownership changed (e.g., you incorporate a sole proprietorship or form a partnership)[2]	Complete lines 1-16c (as applicable).
Purchased a going business[3]	Does not already have an EIN	Complete lines 1-16c (as applicable).
Created a trust	The trust is other than a grantor trust or an IRA trust[4]	Complete lines 1-16c (as applicable).
Created a pension plan as a plan administrator[5]	Needs an EIN for reporting purposes	Complete lines 1, 2, 4a-6, 8a, 9, and 16a-c.
Is a foreign person needing an EIN to comply with IRS withholding regulations	Needs an EIN to complete a Form W-8 (other than Form W-8ECI), avoid withholding on portfolio assets, or claim tax treaty benefits[6]	Complete lines 1-5b, 7a-b (SSN or ITIN optional), 8a-9, and 16a-c.
Is administering an estate	Needs an EIN to report estate income on Form 1041	Complete lines 1, 3, 4a-b, 8a, 9, and 16a-c.
Is a withholding agent for taxes on non-wage income paid to an alien (i.e., individual, corporation, or partnership, etc.)	Is an agent, broker, fiduciary, manager, tenant, or spouse who is required to file **Form 1042,** Annual Withholding Tax Return for U.S. Source Income of Foreign Persons	Complete lines 1, 2, 3 (if applicable), 4a-5b, 7a-b (if applicable), 8a, 9, and 16a-c.
Is a state or local agency	Serves as a tax reporting agent for public assistance recipients under Rev. Proc. 80-4, 1980-1 C.B. 581[7]	Complete lines 1, 2, 4a-5b, 8a, 9, and 16a-c.
Is a single-member LLC	Needs an EIN to file **Form 8832,** Classification Election, for filing employment tax returns, **or** for state reporting purposes[8]	Complete lines 1-16c (as applicable).
Is an S corporation	Needs an EIN to file **Form 2553,** Election by a Small Business Corporation[9]	Complete lines 1-16c (as applicable).

[1] For example, a sole proprietorship or self-employed farmer who establishes a qualified retirement plan, or is required to file excise, employment, alcohol, tobacco, or firearms returns, must have an EIN. **A partnership, corporation, REMIC (real estate mortgage investment conduit), nonprofit organization (church, club, etc.), or farmers' cooperative must use an EIN for any tax-related purpose even if the entity does not have employees.**

[2] However, **do not** apply for a new EIN if the existing entity only **(a)** changed its business name, **(b)** elected on Form 8832 to change the way it is taxed (or is covered by the default rules), or **(c)** terminated its partnership status because at least 50% of the total interests in partnership capital and profits were sold or exchanged within a 12-month period. (The EIN of the terminated partnership should continue to be used. See Regulations section 301.6109-1(d)(2)(iii).)

[3] Do not use the EIN of the prior business unless you became the "owner" of a corporation by acquiring its stock.

[4] However, IRA trusts that are required to file **Form 990-T,** Exempt Organization Business Income Tax Return, must have an EIN.

[5] A plan administrator is the person or group of persons specified as the administrator by the instrument under which the plan is operated.

[6] Entities applying to be a Qualified Intermediary (QI) need a QI-EIN even if they already have an EIN. **See Rev. Proc. 2000-12.**

[7] See also *Household employer* on page 4. (**Note:** State or local agencies may need an EIN for other reasons, e.g., hired employees.)

[8] Most LLCs **do not** need to file Form 8832. See **Limited liability company (LLC)** on page 4 for details on completing Form SS-4 for an LLC.

[9] An existing corporation that is electing or revoking S corporation status should use its previously-assigned EIN.

Instructions for Form SS-4

(Rev. September 2003)

Department of the Treasury
Internal Revenue Service

For use with Form SS-4 (Rev. December 2001)
Application for Employer Identification Number.

Section references are to the Internal Revenue Code unless otherwise noted.

General Instructions

Use these instructions to complete **Form SS-4,** Application for Employer Identification Number. Also see **Do I Need an EIN?** on page 2 of Form SS-4.

Purpose of Form

Use Form SS-4 to apply for an employer identification number (EIN). An EIN is a nine-digit number (for example, 12-3456789) assigned to sole proprietors, corporations, partnerships, estates, trusts, and other entities for tax filing and reporting purposes. The information you provide on this form will establish your business tax account.

*An EIN is for use in connection with your business activities only. Do **not** use your EIN in place of your social security number (SSN).*

Items To Note

Apply online. You can now apply for and receive an EIN online using the internet. See **How To Apply** below.

File only one Form SS-4. Generally, a sole proprietor should file only one Form SS-4 and needs only one EIN, regardless of the number of businesses operated as a sole proprietorship or trade names under which a business operates. However, if the proprietorship incorporates or enters into a partnership, a new EIN is required. Also, each corporation in an affiliated group must have its own EIN.

EIN applied for, but not received. If you do not have an EIN by the time a return is due, write "Applied For" and the date you applied in the space shown for the number. **Do not** show your SSN as an EIN on returns.

If you do not have an EIN by the time a tax deposit is due, send your payment to the Internal Revenue Service Center for your filing area as shown in the instructions for the form that you are filing. Make your check or money order payable to the "United States Treasury" and show your name (as shown on Form SS-4), address, type of tax, period covered, and date you applied for an EIN.

How To Apply

You can apply for an EIN online, by telephone, by fax, or by mail depending on how soon you need to use the EIN. Use only one method for each entity so you do not receive more than one EIN for an entity.

Online. You can receive your EIN by internet and use it immediately to file a return or make a payment. Go to the IRS website at **www.irs.gov/businesses** and click on **Employer ID Numbers** under **topics.**

Telephone. You can receive your EIN by telephone and use it immediately to file a return or make a payment. Call the IRS at **1-800-829-4933.** (International applicants must call 215-516-6999.) The hours of operation are 7:00 a.m. to 10:00 p.m. The person making the call must be authorized to sign the form or be an authorized designee. See **Signature** and **Third Party Designee** on page 6. Also see the **TIP** below.

If you are applying by telephone, it will be helpful to complete Form SS-4 before contacting the IRS. An IRS representative will use the information from the Form SS-4 to establish your account and assign you an EIN. Write the number you are given on the upper right corner of the form and sign and date it. Keep this copy for your records.

If requested by an IRS representative, mail or fax (facsimile) the signed Form SS-4 (including any Third Party Designee authorization) within 24 hours to the IRS address provided by the IRS representative.

*Taxpayer representatives can apply for an EIN on behalf of their client and request that the EIN be faxed to their **client** on the same day. **Note:** By using this procedure, you are authorizing the IRS to fax the EIN without a cover sheet.*

Fax. Under the Fax-TIN program, you can receive your EIN by fax within 4 business days. Complete and fax Form SS-4 to the IRS using the Fax-TIN number listed on page 2 for your state. A long-distance charge to callers outside of the local calling area will apply. Fax-TIN numbers can only be used to apply for an EIN. **The numbers may change without notice.** Fax-TIN is available 24 hours a day, 7 days a week.

Be sure to provide your fax number so the IRS can fax the EIN back to you. **Note:** By using this procedure, you are authorizing the IRS to fax the EIN without a cover sheet.

Mail. Complete Form SS-4 at least 4 to 5 weeks before you will need an EIN. Sign and date the application and mail it to the service center address for your state. You will receive your EIN in the mail in approximately 4 weeks. See also **Third Party Designee** on page 6.

Call 1-800-829-4933 to verify a number or to ask about the status of an application by mail.

If your principal business, office or agency, or legal residence in the case of an individual, is located in:	Call the Fax-TIN number shown or file with the "Internal Revenue Service Center" at:
Connecticut, Delaware, District of Columbia, Florida, Georgia, Maine, Maryland, Massachusetts, New Hampshire, New Jersey, New York, North Carolina, Ohio, Pennsylvania, Rhode Island, South Carolina, Vermont, Virginia, West Virginia	Attn: EIN Operation P. O. Box 9003 Holtsville, NY 11742-9003 Fax-TIN 631-447-8960
Illinois, Indiana, Kentucky, Michigan	Attn: EIN Operation Cincinnati, OH 45999 Fax-TIN 859-669-5760
Alabama, Alaska, Arizona, Arkansas, California, Colorado, Hawaii, Idaho, Iowa, Kansas, Louisiana, Minnesota, Mississippi, Missouri, Montana, Nebraska, Nevada, New Mexico, North Dakota, Oklahoma, Oregon, Puerto Rico, South Dakota, Tennessee, Texas, Utah, Washington, Wisconsin, Wyoming	Attn: EIN Operation Philadelphia, PA 19255 Fax-TIN 215-516-3990
If you have no legal residence, principal place of business, or principal office or agency in any state:	Attn: EIN Operation Philadelphia, PA 19255 Telephone 215-516-6999 Fax-TIN 215-516-3990

How To Get Forms and Publications

Phone. You can order forms, instructions, and publications by phone 24 hours a day, 7 days a week. Call 1-800-TAX-FORM (1-800-829-3676). You should receive your order or notification of its status within 10 workdays.

Personal computer. With your personal computer and modem, you can get the forms and information you need using the IRS website at **www.irs.gov** or File Transfer Protocol at **ftp.irs.gov.**

CD-ROM. For small businesses, return preparers, or others who may frequently need tax forms or publications, a CD-ROM containing over 2,000 tax products (including many prior year forms) can be purchased from the National Technical Information Service (NTIS).

To order **Pub. 1796,** Federal Tax Products on CD-ROM, call **1-877-CDFORMS (1-877-233-6767)** toll free or connect to **www.irs.gov/cdorders.**

Tax Help for Your Business

IRS-sponsored Small Business Workshops provide information about your Federal and state tax obligations.

For information about workshops in your area, call 1-800-829-4933.

Related Forms and Publications

The following **forms** and **instructions** may be useful to filers of Form SS-4:
- **Form 990-T,** Exempt Organization Business Income Tax Return
- **Instructions for Form 990-T**
- **Schedule C (Form 1040),** Profit or Loss From Business
- **Schedule F (Form 1040),** Profit or Loss From Farming
- **Instructions for Form 1041 and Schedules A, B, D, G, I, J, and K-1,** U.S. Income Tax Return for Estates and Trusts
- **Form 1042,** Annual Withholding Tax Return for U.S. Source Income of Foreign Persons
- **Instructions for Form 1065,** U.S. Return of Partnership Income
- **Instructions for Form 1066,** U.S. Real Estate Mortgage Investment Conduit (REMIC) Income Tax Return
- **Instructions for Forms 1120 and 1120-A**
- **Form 2553,** Election by a Small Business Corporation
- **Form 2848,** Power of Attorney and Declaration of Representative
- **Form 8821,** Tax Information Authorization
- **Form 8832,** Entity Classification Election
  For more **information** about filing Form SS-4 and related issues, see:
- **Circular A,** Agricultural Employer's Tax Guide (Pub. 51)
- **Circular E,** Employer's Tax Guide (Pub. 15)
- **Pub. 538,** Accounting Periods and Methods
- **Pub. 542,** Corporations
- **Pub. 557,** Exempt Status for Your Organization
- **Pub. 583,** Starting a Business and Keeping Records
- **Pub. 966,** Electronic Choices for Paying ALL Your Federal Taxes
- **Pub. 1635,** Understanding Your EIN
- **Package 1023,** Application for Recognition of Exemption Under Section 501(c)(3) of the Internal Revenue Code
- **Package 1024,** Application for Recognition of Exemption Under Section 501(a)

Specific Instructions

Print or type all entries on Form SS-4. Follow the instructions for each line to expedite processing and to avoid unnecessary IRS requests for additional information. Enter "N/A" (nonapplicable) on the lines that do not apply.

Line 1—Legal name of entity (or individual) for whom the EIN is being requested. Enter the legal name of the entity (or individual) applying for the EIN exactly as it appears on the social security card, charter, or other applicable legal document.

Individuals. Enter your first name, middle initial, and last name. If you are a sole proprietor, enter your individual name, not your business name. Enter your business name on line 2. Do not use abbreviations or nicknames on line 1.

Trusts. Enter the name of the trust.

Estate of a decedent. Enter the name of the estate.

Partnerships. Enter the legal name of the partnership as it appears in the partnership agreement.

Corporations. Enter the corporate name as it appears in the corporation charter or other legal document creating it.

Plan administrators. Enter the name of the plan administrator. A plan administrator who already has an EIN should use that number.

Line 2—Trade name of business. Enter the trade name of the business if different from the legal name. The trade name is the "doing business as " (DBA) name.

Use the full legal name shown on line 1 on all tax returns filed for the entity. (However, if you enter a trade name on line 2 and choose to use the trade name instead of the legal name, enter the trade name on all returns you file.) To prevent processing delays and errors, always use the legal name only (or the trade name only) on all tax returns.

Line 3—Executor, trustee, "care of" name. Trusts enter the name of the trustee. Estates enter the name of the executor, administrator, or other fiduciary. If the entity applying has a designated person to receive tax information, enter that person's name as the "care of" person. Enter the individual's first name, middle initial, and last name.

Lines 4a-b—Mailing address. Enter the mailing address for the entity's correspondence. If line 3 is completed, enter the address for the executor, trustee or "care of" person. Generally, this address will be used on all tax returns.

File Form 8822, Change of Address, to report any subsequent changes to the entity's mailing address.

Lines 5a-b—Street address. Provide the entity's physical address **only** if different from its mailing address shown in lines 4a-b. **Do not** enter a P.O. box number here.

Line 6—County and state where principal business is located. Enter the entity's primary **physical** location.

Lines 7a-b—Name of principal officer, general partner, grantor, owner, or trustor. Enter the first name, middle initial, last name, and SSN of **(a)** the principal officer if the business is a corporation, **(b)** a general partner if a partnership, **(c)** the owner of an entity that is disregarded as separate from its owner (disregarded entities owned by a corporation enter the corporation's name and EIN), or **(d)** a grantor, owner, or trustor if a trust.

If the person in question is an **alien individual** with a previously assigned individual taxpayer identification number (ITIN), enter the ITIN in the space provided and submit a copy of an official identifying document. If

necessary, complete **Form W-7,** Application for IRS Individual Taxpayer Identification Number, to obtain an ITIN.

You are **required** to enter an SSN, ITIN, or EIN unless the only reason you are applying for an EIN is to make an entity classification election (see Regulations sections 301.7701-1 through 301.7701-3) and you are a nonresident alien with no effectively connected income from sources within the United States.

Line 8a—Type of entity. Check the box that best describes the type of entity applying for the EIN. If you are an alien individual with an ITIN previously assigned to you, enter the ITIN in place of a requested SSN.

This is not an election for a tax classification of an entity. See Limited liability company (LLC) on page 4.

Other. If not specifically listed, check the "Other" box, enter the type of entity and the type of return, if any, that will be filed (for example, "Common Trust Fund, Form 1065" or "Created a Pension Plan"). Do not enter "N/A." If you are an alien individual applying for an EIN, see the **Lines 7a-b** instructions above.

• **Household employer.** If you are an individual, check the "Other" box and enter "Household Employer" and your SSN. If you are a state or local agency serving as a tax reporting agent for public assistance recipients who become household employers, check the "Other" box and enter "Household Employer Agent." If you are a trust that qualifies as a household employer, you do not need a separate EIN for reporting tax information relating to household employees; use the EIN of the trust.

• **QSub.** For a qualified subchapter S subsidiary (QSub) check the "Other" box and specify "QSub."

• **Withholding agent.** If you are a withholding agent required to file Form 1042, check the "Other" box and enter "Withholding Agent."

Sole proprietor. Check this box if you file Schedule C, C-EZ, or F (Form 1040) and have a qualified plan, or are required to file excise, employment, alcohol, tobacco, or firearms returns, or are a payer of gambling winnings. Enter your SSN (or ITIN) in the space provided. If you are a nonresident alien with no effectively connected income from sources within the United States, you do not need to enter an SSN or ITIN.

Corporation. This box is for any corporation **other than a personal service corporation.** If you check this box, enter the income tax form number to be filed by the entity in the space provided.

If you entered "1120S" after the "Corporation" checkbox, the corporation must file Form 2553 no later than the 15th day of the 3rd month of the tax year the election is to take effect. Until Form 2553 has been received and approved, you will be considered a Form 1120 filer. See the Instructions for Form 2553.

Personal service corp. Check this box if the entity is a personal service corporation. An entity is a personal service corporation for a tax year only if:

- The principal activity of the entity during the testing period (prior tax year) for the tax year is the performance of personal services substantially by employee-owners, and
- The employee-owners own at least 10% of the fair market value of the outstanding stock in the entity on the last day of the testing period.

Personal services include performance of services in such fields as health, law, accounting, or consulting. For more information about personal service corporations, see the Instructions for Forms 1120 and 1120-A and Pub. 542.

Other nonprofit organization. Check this box if the nonprofit organization is other than a church or church-controlled organization and specify the type of nonprofit organization (for example, an educational organization).

 *If the organization also seeks tax-exempt status, you **must** file either Package 1023 or Package 1024. See Pub. 557 for more information.*

If the organization is covered by a group exemption letter, enter the four-digit **group exemption number (GEN).** (Do not confuse the GEN with the nine-digit EIN.) If you do not know the GEN, contact the parent organization. Get Pub. 557 for more information about group exemption numbers.

Plan administrator. If the plan administrator is an individual, enter the plan administrator's SSN in the space provided.

REMIC. Check this box if the entity has elected to be treated as a real estate mortgage investment conduit (REMIC). See the Instructions for Form 1066 for more information.

Limited liability company (LLC). An LLC is an entity organized under the laws of a state or foreign country as a limited liability company. For Federal tax purposes, an LLC may be treated as a partnership or corporation or be disregarded as an entity separate from its owner.

By **default,** a domestic LLC with only one member is **disregarded** as an entity separate from its owner and must include all of its income and expenses on the owner's tax return (e.g., **Schedule C (Form 1040)).** Also by default, a domestic LLC with two or more members is treated as a partnership. A domestic LLC may file Form 8832 to avoid either default classification and elect to be classified as an association taxable as a corporation. For more information on entity classifications (including the rules for foreign entities), see the instructions for Form 8832.

 *Do not file Form 8832 if the LLC accepts the default classifications above. **However, if the LLC will be electing S Corporation status, it must timely file both Form 8832 and Form 2553.***

Complete Form SS-4 for LLCs as follows:
- A single-member domestic LLC that accepts the default classification (above) does not need an EIN and generally should not file Form SS-4. Generally, the LLC should use the name and EIN of its **owner** for all Federal tax purposes. However, the reporting and payment of employment taxes for employees of the LLC may be made using the name and EIN of **either** the owner or the LLC as explained in Notice 99-6. You can find Notice 99-6 on page 12 of Internal Revenue Bulletin 1999-3 at **www.irs.gov/pub/irs-irbs/irb99-03.pdf. (Note:** If the LLC applicant indicates in box 13 that it has employees or expects to have employees, the owner (whether an individual or other entity) of a single-member domestic LLC will also be assigned its own EIN (if it does not already have one) even if the LLC will be filing the employment tax returns.)
- A single-member, domestic LLC that accepts the default classification (above) and wants an EIN for filing employment tax returns (see above) or non-Federal purposes, such as a state requirement, must check the "Other" box and write "Disregarded Entity" or, when applicable, "Disregarded Entity—Sole Proprietorship" in the space provided.
- A multi-member, domestic LLC that accepts the default classification (above) must check the "Partnership" box.
- A domestic LLC that will be filing Form 8832 to elect corporate status must check the "Corporation" box and write in "Single-Member" or "Multi-Member" immediately below the "form number" entry line.

Line 9—Reason for applying. Check only **one** box. Do not enter "N/A."

Started new business. Check this box if you are starting a new business that requires an EIN. If you check this box, enter the type of business being started. **Do not** apply if you already have an EIN and are only adding another place of business.

Hired employees. Check this box if the existing business is requesting an EIN because it has hired or is hiring employees and is therefore required to file employment tax returns. **Do not** apply if you already have an EIN and are only hiring employees. For information on employment taxes (e.g., for family members), see Circular E.

 You may be required to make electronic deposits of all depository taxes (such as employment tax, excise tax, and corporate income tax) using the Electronic Federal Tax Payment System (EFTPS). See section 11, Depositing Taxes, of Circular E and Pub. 966.

Created a pension plan. Check this box if you have created a pension plan and need an EIN for reporting purposes. Also, enter the type of plan in the space provided.

 Check this box if you are applying for a trust EIN when a new pension plan is established. In addition, check the "Other" box in line 8a and write "Created a Pension Plan" in the space provided.

Banking purpose. Check this box if you are requesting an EIN for banking purposes only, and enter the banking purpose (for example, a bowling league for depositing dues or an investment club for dividend and interest reporting).

Changed type of organization. Check this box if the business is changing its type of organization. For example, the business was a sole proprietorship and has been incorporated or has become a partnership. If you check this box, specify in the space provided (including available space immediately below) the type of change made. For example, "From Sole Proprietorship to Partnership."

Purchased going business. Check this box if you purchased an existing business. **Do not** use the former owner's EIN unless you became the "owner" of a corporation by acquiring its stock.

Created a trust. Check this box if you created a trust, and enter the type of trust created. For example, indicate if the trust is a nonexempt charitable trust or a split-interest trust.

Exception. Do **not** file this form for certain grantor-type trusts. The trustee does not need an EIN for the trust if the trustee furnishes the name and TIN of the grantor/owner and the address of the trust to all payors. See the Instructions for Form 1041 for more information.

 Do not check this box if you are applying for a trust EIN when a new pension plan is established. Check "Created a pension plan."

Other. Check this box if you are requesting an EIN for any other reason; and enter the reason. For example, a newly-formed state government entity should enter "Newly-Formed State Government Entity" in the space provided.

Line 10—Date business started or acquired. If you are starting a new business, enter the starting date of the business. If the business you acquired is already operating, enter the date you acquired the business. If you are changing the form of ownership of your business, enter the date the new ownership entity began. Trusts should enter the date the trust was legally created. Estates should enter the date of death of the decedent whose name appears on line 1 or the date when the estate was legally funded.

Line 11—Closing month of accounting year. Enter the last month of your accounting year or tax year. An accounting or tax year is usually 12 consecutive months, either a calendar year or a fiscal year (including a period of 52 or 53 weeks). A calendar year is 12 consecutive months ending on December 31. A fiscal year is either 12 consecutive months ending on the last day of any month other than December or a 52-53 week year. For more information on accounting periods, see Pub. 538.

Individuals. Your tax year generally will be a calendar year.

Partnerships. Partnerships must adopt one of the following tax years:
• The tax year of the majority of its partners,
• The tax year common to all of its principal partners,
• The tax year that results in the least aggregate deferral of income, or
• In certain cases, some other tax year.

See the Instructions for Form 1065 for more information.

REMICs. REMICs must have a calendar year as their tax year.

Personal service corporations. A personal service corporation generally must adopt a calendar year unless:
• It can establish a business purpose for having a different tax year, or
• It elects under section 444 to have a tax year other than a calendar year.

Trusts. Generally, a trust must adopt a calendar year except for the following:
• Tax-exempt trusts,
• Charitable trusts, and
• Grantor-owned trusts.

Line 12—First date wages or annuities were paid or will be paid. If the business has or will have employees, enter the date on which the business began or will begin to pay wages. If the business does not plan to have employees, enter "N/A."

Withholding agent. Enter the date you began or will begin to pay income (including annuities) to a nonresident alien. This also applies to individuals who are required to file Form 1042 to report alimony paid to a nonresident alien.

Line 13—Highest number of employees expected in the next 12 months. Complete each box by entering the number (including zero ("-0-")) of "Agricultural," "Household," or "Other" employees expected by the applicant in the next 12 months. For a definition of agricultural labor (farmwork), see Circular A.

Lines 14 and 15. Check the **one** box in line 14 that best describes the principal activity of the applicant's business. Check the "Other" box (and specify the applicant's principal activity) if none of the listed boxes applies.

Use line 15 to describe the applicant's principal line of business in more detail. For example, if you checked the "Construction" box in line 14, enter additional detail such as "General contractor for residential buildings" in line 15.

Construction. Check this box if the applicant is engaged in erecting buildings or other structures, (e.g., streets, highways, bridges, tunnels). The term "Construction" also includes special trade contractors, (e.g., plumbing, HVAC, electrical, carpentry, concrete, excavation, etc. contractors).

Real estate. Check this box if the applicant is engaged in renting or leasing real estate to others; managing, selling, buying or renting real estate for others; or providing related real estate services (e.g., appraisal services).

Rental and leasing. Check this box if the applicant is engaged in providing tangible goods such as autos, computers, consumer goods, or industrial machinery and equipment to customers in return for a periodic rental or lease payment.

Manufacturing. Check this box if the applicant is engaged in the mechanical, physical, or chemical transformation of materials, substances, or components into new products. The assembling of component parts of manufactured products is also considered to be manufacturing.

Transportation & warehousing. Check this box if the applicant provides transportation of passengers or cargo; warehousing or storage of goods; scenic or sight-seeing transportation; or support activities related to these modes of transportation.

Finance & insurance. Check this box if the applicant is engaged in transactions involving the creation, liquidation, or change of ownership of financial assets and/or facilitating such financial transactions; underwriting annuities/insurance policies; facilitating such underwriting by selling insurance policies; or by providing other insurance or employee-benefit related services.

Health care and social assistance. Check this box if the applicant is engaged in providing physical, medical, or psychiatric care using licensed health care professionals or providing social assistance activities such as youth centers, adoption agencies, individual/family services, temporary shelters, etc.

Accommodation & food services. Check this box if the applicant is engaged in providing customers with lodging, meal preparation, snacks, or beverages for immediate consumption.

Wholesale–agent/broker. Check this box if the applicant is engaged in arranging for the purchase or sale of goods owned by others or purchasing goods on a commission basis for goods traded in the wholesale market, usually between businesses.

Wholesale–other. Check this box if the applicant is engaged in selling goods in the wholesale market generally to other businesses for resale on their own account.

Retail. Check this box if the applicant is engaged in selling merchandise to the general public from a fixed store; by direct, mail-order, or electronic sales; or by using vending machines.

Other. Check this box if the applicant is engaged in an activity not described above. Describe the applicant's principal business activity in the space provided.

Lines 16a-c. Check the applicable box in line 16a to indicate whether or not the entity (or individual) applying for an EIN was issued one previously. Complete lines 16b and 16c **only** if the "Yes" box in line 16a is checked. If the applicant previously applied for **more than one** EIN, write "See Attached" in the empty space in line 16a and attach a separate sheet providing the line 16b and 16c information for each EIN previously requested.

Third Party Designee. Complete this section **only** if you want to authorize the named individual to receive the entity's EIN and answer questions about the completion of Form SS-4. The designee's authority terminates at the time the EIN is assigned and released to the designee. **You must complete the signature area for the authorization to be valid.**

Signature. When required, the application must be signed by **(a)** the individual, if the applicant is an individual, **(b)** the president, vice president, or other

principal officer, if the applicant is a corporation, **(c)** a responsible and duly authorized member or officer having knowledge of its affairs, if the applicant is a partnership, government entity, or other unincorporated organization, or **(d)** the fiduciary, if the applicant is a trust or an estate. Foreign applicants may have any duly-authorized person, (e.g., division manager), sign Form SS-4.

Privacy Act and Paperwork Reduction Act Notice. We ask for the information on this form to carry out the Internal Revenue laws of the United States. We need it to comply with section 6109 and the regulations thereunder which generally require the inclusion of an employer identification number (EIN) on certain returns, statements, or other documents filed with the Internal Revenue Service. If your entity is required to obtain an EIN, you are required to provide all of the information requested on this form. Information on this form may be used to determine which Federal tax returns you are required to file and to provide you with related forms and publications.

We disclose this form to the Social Security Administration for their use in determining compliance with applicable laws. We may give this information to the Department of Justice for use in civil and criminal litigation, and to the cities, states, and the District of Columbia for use in administering their tax laws. We may also disclose this information to Federal and state agencies to enforce Federal nontax criminal laws and to combat terrorism.

We will be unable to issue an EIN to you unless you provide all of the requested information which applies to your entity. Providing false information could subject you to penalties.

You are not required to provide the information requested on a form that is subject to the Paperwork Reduction Act unless the form displays a valid OMB control number. Books or records relating to a form or its instructions must be retained as long as their contents may become material in the administration of any Internal Revenue law. Generally, tax returns and return information are confidential, as required by section 6103.

The time needed to complete and file this form will vary depending on individual circumstances. The estimated average time is:

Recordkeeping	6 min.
Learning about the law or the form	22 min.
Preparing the form	46 min.
Copying, assembling, and sending the form to the IRS	20 min.

If you have comments concerning the accuracy of these time estimates or suggestions for making this form simpler, we would be happy to hear from you. You can write to the Tax Products Coordinating Committee, Western Area Distribution Center, Rancho Cordova, CA 95743-0001. **Do not** send the form to this address. Instead, see **How To Apply** on page 1.

Printed on recycled paper

Form W-4 (2004)

Purpose. Complete Form W-4 so that your employer can withhold the correct Federal income tax from your pay. Because your tax situation may change, you may want to refigure your withholding each year.

Exemption from withholding. If you are exempt, complete only lines 1, 2, 3, 4, and 7 and sign the form to validate it. Your exemption for 2004 expires February 16, 2005. See **Pub. 505**, Tax Withholding and Estimated Tax.

Note: *You cannot claim exemption from withholding if:* **(a)** *your income exceeds $800 and includes more than $250 of unearned income (e.g., interest and dividends) and* **(b)** *another person can claim you as a dependent on their tax return.*

Basic instructions. If you are not exempt, complete the **Personal Allowances Worksheet** below. The worksheets on page 2 adjust your withholding allowances based on itemized

deductions, certain credits, adjustments to income, or two-earner/two-job situations. Complete all worksheets that apply. **However, you may claim fewer (or zero) allowances.**

Head of household. Generally, you may claim head of household filing status on your tax return only if you are unmarried and pay more than 50% of the costs of keeping up a home for yourself and your dependent(s) or other qualifying individuals. See line **E** below.

Tax credits. You can take projected tax credits into account in figuring your allowable number of withholding allowances. Credits for child or dependent care expenses and the child tax credit may be claimed using the **Personal Allowances Worksheet** below. See **Pub. 919**, How Do I Adjust My Tax Withholding? for information on converting your other credits into withholding allowances.

Nonwage income. If you have a large amount of nonwage income, such as interest or dividends, consider making estimated tax payments using

Form 1040-ES, Estimated Tax for Individuals. Otherwise, you may owe additional tax.

Two earners/two jobs. If you have a working spouse or more than one job, figure the total number of allowances you are entitled to claim on all jobs using worksheets from only one Form W-4. Your withholding usually will be most accurate when all allowances are claimed on the Form W-4 for the highest paying job and zero allowances are claimed on the others.

Nonresident alien. If you are a nonresident alien, see the **Instructions for Form 8233** before completing this Form W-4.

Check your withholding. After your Form W-4 takes effect, use Pub. 919 to see how the dollar amount you are having withheld compares to your projected total tax for 2004. See Pub. 919, especially if your earnings exceed $125,000 (Single) or $175,000 (Married).

Recent name change? If your name on line 1 differs from that shown on your social security card, call 1-800-772-1213 to initiate a name change and obtain a social security card showing your correct name.

Personal Allowances Worksheet (Keep for your records.)

A Enter "1" for **yourself** if no one else can claim you as a dependent . . . . **A** _____

B Enter "1" if:
- You are single and have only one job; or
- You are married, have only one job, and your spouse does not work; or
- Your wages from a second job or your spouse's wages (or the total of both) are $1,000 or less.

B _____

C Enter "1" for your **spouse**. But, you may choose to enter "-0-" if you are married and have either a working spouse or more than one job. (Entering "-0-" may help you avoid having too little tax withheld.) . . . . **C** _____

D Enter number of **dependents** (other than your spouse or yourself) you will claim on your tax return . . . . **D** _____

E Enter "1" if you will file as **head of household** on your tax return (see conditions under **Head of household** above) . . **E** _____

F Enter "1" if you have at least $1,500 of **child or dependent care expenses** for which you plan to claim a credit . . **F** _____
(**Note:** *Do not include child support payments. See* **Pub. 503**, *Child and Dependent Care Expenses, for details.*)

G **Child Tax Credit** (including additional child tax credit):
- If your total income will be less than $52,000 ($77,000 if married), enter "2" for each eligible child.
- If your total income will be between $52,000 and $84,000 ($77,000 and $119,000 if married), enter "1" for each eligible child plus "1" **additional** if you have four or more eligible children. **G** _____

H Add lines A through G and enter total here. **Note:** *This may be different from the number of exemptions you claim on your tax return.* ▶ **H** _____

For accuracy, complete all worksheets that apply.
- If you plan to **itemize or claim adjustments to income** and want to reduce your withholding, see the **Deductions and Adjustments Worksheet** on page 2.
- If you have **more than one job** or are **married and you and your spouse both work** and the combined earnings from all jobs exceed $35,000 ($25,000 if married) see the **Two-Earner/Two-Job Worksheet** on page 2 to avoid having too little tax withheld.
- If **neither** of the above situations applies, **stop here** and enter the number from line H on line 5 of Form W-4 below.

- **Cut here and give Form W-4 to your employer. Keep the top part for your records.** - - - - - - - - - -

Form **W-4**	**Employee's Withholding Allowance Certificate**	OMB No. 1545-0010
Department of the Treasury Internal Revenue Service	▶ Your employer must send a copy of this form to the IRS if: (a) you claim more than 10 allowances or (b) you claim "Exempt" and your wages are normally more than $200 per week.	**2004**

1 Type or print your first name and middle initial	Last name	**2** Your social security number

Home address (number and street or rural route)	**3** ☐ Single ☐ Married ☐ Married, but withhold at higher Single rate. **Note:** *If married, but legally separated, or spouse is a nonresident alien, check the "Single" box.*
City or town, state, and ZIP code	**4** If your last name differs from that shown on your social security card, check here. You must call 1-800-772-1213 for a new card. ▶ ☐

5 Total number of allowances you are claiming (from line **H** above **or** from the applicable worksheet on page 2) **5** _____

6 Additional amount, if any, you want withheld from each paycheck . . . . **6** $ _____

7 I claim exemption from withholding for 2004, and I certify that I meet **both** of the following conditions for exemption:
- Last year I had a right to a refund of **all** Federal income tax withheld because I had **no** tax liability **and**
- This year I expect a refund of **all** Federal income tax withheld because I expect to have **no** tax liability.
If you meet both conditions, write "Exempt" here . . . . ▶ **7** _____

Under penalties of perjury, I certify that I am entitled to the number of withholding allowances claimed on this certificate, or I am entitled to claim exempt status.

Employee's signature
(Form is not valid unless you sign it.) ▶ _____ Date ▶ _____

8 Employer's name and address (Employer: Complete lines 8 and 10 only if sending to the IRS.)	**9** Office code (optional)	**10** Employer identification number (EIN)

For Privacy Act and Paperwork Reduction Act Notice, see page 2. Cat. No. 10220Q Form **W-4** (2004)

Deductions and Adjustments Worksheet

Note: *Use this worksheet only if you plan to itemize deductions, claim certain credits, or claim adjustments to income on your 2004 tax return.*

1   Enter an estimate of your 2004 itemized deductions. These include qualifying home mortgage interest, charitable contributions, state and local taxes, medical expenses in excess of 7.5% of your income, and miscellaneous deductions. (For 2004, you may have to reduce your itemized deductions if your income is over $142,700 ($71,350 if married filing separately). See **Worksheet 3** in Pub. 919 for details.) . . .   **1** $ _____

2   Enter:
- $9,700 if married filing jointly or qualifying widow(er)
- $7,150 if head of household
- $4,850 if single
- $4,850 if married filing separately

. . . .   **2** $ _____

3   **Subtract** line 2 from line 1. If line 2 is greater than line 1, enter "-0-" . . . .   **3** $ _____

4   Enter an estimate of your 2004 adjustments to income, including alimony, deductible IRA contributions, and student loan interest   **4** $ _____

5   **Add** lines 3 and 4 and enter the total. (Include any amount for credits from **Worksheet 7** in Pub. 919) ..   **5** $ _____

6   Enter an estimate of your 2004 nonwage income (such as dividends or interest) . . . . .   **6** $ _____

7   **Subtract** line 6 from line 5. Enter the result, but not less than "-0-" . . . .   **7** $ _____

8   **Divide** the amount on line 7 by $3,000 and enter the result here. Drop any fraction . . . .   **8**   _____

9   Enter the number from the **Personal Allowances Worksheet,** line H, page 1 . . . .   **9**   _____

10   **Add** lines 8 and 9 and enter the total here. If you plan to use the **Two-Earner/Two-Job Worksheet,** also enter this total on line 1 below. Otherwise, **stop here** and enter this total on Form W-4, line 5, page 1 ..   **10**   _____

Two-Earner/Two-Job Worksheet (See **Two earners/two jobs** on page 1.)

Note: *Use this worksheet only if the instructions under line H on page 1 direct you here.*

1   Enter the number from line H, page 1 (or from line 10 above if you used the **Deductions and Adjustments Worksheet**)   **1**   _____

2   Find the number in **Table 1** below that applies to the **LOWEST** paying job and enter it here . . . .   **2**   _____

3   If line 1 is **more than or equal to** line 2, subtract line 2 from line 1. Enter the result here (if zero, enter "-0-") and on Form W-4, line 5, page 1. **Do not** use the rest of this worksheet . . . .   **3**   _____

Note: *If line 1 is **less than** line 2, enter "-0-" on Form W-4, line 5, page 1. Complete lines 4-9 below to calculate the additional withholding amount necessary to avoid a year-end tax bill.*

4   Enter the number from line 2 of this worksheet . . . .   **4**   _____

5   Enter the number from line 1 of this worksheet . . . .   **5**   _____

6   **Subtract** line 5 from line 4 . . . .   **6**   _____

7   Find the amount in **Table 2** below that applies to the **HIGHEST** paying job and enter it here . . . . ..   **7** $ _____

8   **Multiply** line 7 by line 6 and enter the result here. This is the additional annual withholding needed . ..   **8** $ _____

9   Divide line 8 by the number of pay periods remaining in 2004. For example, divide by 26 if you are paid every two weeks and you complete this form in December 2003. Enter the result here and on Form W-4, line 6, page 1. This is the additional amount to be withheld from each paycheck . . . .   **9** $ _____

Table 1: Two-Earner/Two-Job Worksheet

Married Filing Jointly			Married Filing Jointly			All Others	
If wages from **HIGHEST** paying job are-	AND, wages from **LOWEST** paying job are-	Enter on line 2 above	If wages from **HIGHEST** paying job are-	AND, wages from **LOWEST** paying job are-	Enter on line 2 above	If wages from **LOWEST** paying job are-	Enter on line 2 above
$0 - $40,000	$0 - $4,000	0	$40,001 and over	31,001 - 38,000	6	$0 - $6,000	0
	4,001 - 8,000	1		38,001 - 44,000	7	6,001 - 11,000	1
	8,001 - 17,000	2		44,001 - 50,000	8	11,001 - 18,000	2
	17,001 and over	3		50,001 - 55,000	9	18,001 - 25,000	3
				55,001 - 65,000	10	25,001 - 31,000	4
$40,001 and over	$0 - $4,000	0		65,001 - 75,000	11	31,001 - 44,000	5
	4,001 - 8,000	1		75,001 - 85,000	12	44,001 - 55,000	6
	8,001 - 15,000	2		85,001 - 100,000	13	55,001 - 70,000	7
	15,001 - 22,000	3		100,001 - 115,000	14	70,001 - 80,000	8
	22,001 - 25,000	4		115,001 and over	15	80,001 - 100,000	9
	25,001 - 31,000	5				100,001 and over	10

Table 2: Two-Earner/Two-Job Worksheet

Married Filing Jointly		All Others	
If wages from **HIGHEST** paying job are-	Enter on line 7 above	If wages from **HIGHEST** paying job are-	Enter on line 7 above
$0 - $60,000	$470	$0 - $30,000	$470
60,001 - 110,000	780	30,001 - 70,000	780
110,001 - 150,000	870	70,001 - 140,000	870
150,001 - 270,000	1,020	140,001 - 320,000	1,020
270,001 and over	1,090	320,001 and over	1,090

DTF-17 (8/00)

New York State Department of Taxation and Finance

Application for Registration as a Sales Tax Vendor

Department use only

Please print or type

1 Type of certificate you are applying for
(You must check one box; see instructions): ☐ Regular ☐ Temporary ☐ Show ☐ Entertainment

2 Legal name of vendor

3 Trade name or DBA (if different from item 2)

4 Federal employer identification number

5 Address of business location (show/entertainment or temporary vendors use home address)

Number and street	City	County	State	ZIP code	Country, if not U.S.

6 Business telephone number (include area code)
( )

7 Date you will begin business in New York State
(see instructions) / /

8 Temporary vendors: Enter the date you will end business in New York
/ /

9 Mailing address, if different from business address on line 5
c/o name

Number and street	City	State	ZIP code

10 Type of organization: ☐ Individual (sole proprietor) ☐ Partnership ☐ Trust ☐ Governmental ☐ Exempt organization
☐ Corporation ☐ Limited Liability Partnership ☐ Limited Liability Company ☐ Other *(specify)* _____

11 Reason for applying: ☐ Started new business ☐ Purchased existing business ☐ Adding a new location ☐ Change in organization ☐ Other *(specify)* _____

12 Regular vendors — Will you operate more than one place of business?

☐ Yes *(check appropriate box below)* ☐ No

A ☐ Separate sales tax return will be filed for each business location.

B ☐ One sales tax return will be filed for all business locations *(complete Form DTF-17-ATT and attach it to this application).*

13 List all owners/officers. Attach a separate sheet if necessary. All applicants must complete this section.

Name	Title	Social security number
Home address	City	State	ZIP code	Telephone number ( )

Name	Title	Social security number
Home address	City	State	ZIP code	Telephone number ( )

Name	Title	Social security number
Home address	City	State	ZIP code	Telephone number ( )

14 If your business currently files New York State returns for the following taxes, check the box for the appropriate tax type and enter the identification number used on the return:

☐ Corporation tax ID # _____

☐ Withholding tax ID # _____

☐ Other *(explain)* _____ ID # _____

15 If you have ever registered as a sales tax vendor with New York State, enter the information shown on the last sales tax return you filed:

Name _____ Identification number _____

16 Do you expect to **collect** any sales or use tax or **pay** any sales or use tax directly to the Department of Taxation and Finance? .... ☐ Yes ☐ No

17 Describe your major business activity and enter your six-digit NAICS code:

Describe your business activity in detail *(attach a separate sheet if necessary)*	North American Industry Classification System (NAICS)

18 Are you a sidewalk vendor? .... ☐ Yes ☐ No

If *Yes*, do you sell food? .... ☐ Yes ☐ No

19 Do you participate solely in flea markets, antique shows, or other "shows"? .... ☐ Yes ☐ No

20 Do you intend to make retail sales of cigarettes or other tobacco products? .... ☐ Yes ☐ No

21 If you withhold or will withhold New York State tax from employees, do you need withholding tax forms or information? .... ☐ Yes ☐ No

DTF-17 (8/00) (back)

22 If you acquired this business from a registered vendor, did you file Form AU-196.10, *Notification of Sale, Transfer or Assignment in Bulk,* with the Tax Department? ..... ☐ Yes ☐ No

Former owner's name _____ Address _____ ID # _____

23 Have you been notified that you owe any New York State tax? .... ☐ Yes   ☐ No

Type of tax	Amount due	Assessment number (if any)	Assessment date	Assessment currently being protested? ..... ☐ Yes ☐ No

24 Do any responsible officers, directors, partners, or employees owe New York State or local sales and use taxes on your behalf, on behalf of another person, or as a vendor of property or services? .... ☐ Yes   ☐ No

Individual's name		Street address	City	State	ZIP code

Social security number	Amount due	Assessment number (if any)	Assessment date	Assessment currently being protested? ..... ☐ Yes ☐ No

25 Have you been convicted of a crime under the Tax Law during the past year? .... ☐ Yes   ☐ No

Date of conviction	Court of conviction	Disposition *(fine, imprisonment, probation, etc.)*

26 During the past year, has any responsible officer, director, partner, or employee of the applicant been convicted of a crime under the Tax Law? .... ☐ Yes   ☐ No

Individual's name		Street address	City	State	ZIP code

Social security number	Date of conviction	Court of conviction	Disposition *(fine, imprisonment, probation, etc.)*

27 If previously registered as a New York State sales tax vendor, was your *Certificate of Authority* revoked or suspended during that past year? ☐ Yes   ☐ No   If *Yes*, please indicate why_____ .

_____

Questions 28, 29, and 30 apply to corporations only.

28 If any shareholder owns more than half of the shares of voting stock of the applicant, has this shareholder ever owned more than half of the shares of voting stock of another corporation? ☐ Yes   ☐ No **If *Yes*, complete questions 29 and 30.**

29 Did this shareholder own these shares of another corporation when the corporation had a tax liability that remains unpaid? .... ☐ Yes   ☐ No

Shareholder's name	Corporation name	Federal identification number

Street address	City	State	ZIP code

Type of tax	Amount due	Assessment number *(if any)*	Assessment date	Assessment currently being protested? ..... ☐ Yes ☐ No

30 Did this shareholder own these shares of another corporation at a time during the past year when the corporation was convicted of a crime under the Tax Law? .... ☐ Yes   ☐ No

Corporation name	Federal identification number

Street address	City	State	ZIP code

Date of conviction	Court of conviction	Disposition *(fine, imprisonment, probation, etc.)*

I certify that the information in this application is true and correct. Willfully filing a false application is a misdemeanor punishable under the Tax Law.

Signature	Title	Telephone number	Date

☐ Check this box if you want your sales tax returns mailed to a tax preparer rather than the address on the front of this application. Enter preparer information in the box below:

Name of preparer	Street Address	City	State	ZIP code

This application will be returned if it is not signed or if any other information is missing.
Mail your application to: NYS Tax Department, Sales Tax Registration Unit, W A Harriman Campus, Albany NY 12227, at least 20 days (but not more than 90 days) before you begin doing business in New York State.

New York State Department of Taxation and Finance

Instructions for Form DTF-17

DTF-17-I
(8/00)

Line 1 — There are four types of sales tax vendors, as defined below. Select the definition that best describes your business, then check the appropriate box on line 1.

A *regular vendor* is any individual, partnership, company, or organization who makes taxable sales within the state or who accepts or issues exemption certificates. Regular vendors always have permanent business locations. In addition, they may sell at craft fairs, flea markets, or similar enterprises.

A *temporary vendor* is anyone who expects to make sales of tangible personal property or taxable services in New York State for no more than two consecutive quarterly sales tax periods in any 12-month period. A vendor who attends shows or entertainment events on a continual basis, even for only short periods, should register as a show/entertainment vendor, not a temporary vendor.

A *show vendor* is anyone who displays for sale or sells taxable goods or services at a flea market, a craft fair, a coin show, an antique show, or any similar enterprise that occurs on either a regular or temporary basis. A show vendor does not have a permanent business location.

An *entertainment vendor* is anyone who makes taxable sales at a concert, an athletic contest or exhibition (other than amateur sports), or similar form of entertainment, in which performers do not appear on a regular, systematic, or recurring basis, held in a facility or site with capacity to accommodate more than 1,000 persons. An entertainment vendor does not have a permanent business location.

Line 2 — Enter the exact legal name of the business that you are registering. For a corporation, the legal name will be the name that appears on the *Certificate of Incorporation* filed with the New York State Department of State. For a business that is not incorporated, the legal name is the name in which the business owns property or acquires debt. If the business is a partnership, use the names of the individual partners. If the business is a sole proprietor, show or entertainment vendor, the legal name is the name of the individual owner of the business.

Line 3 — Enter the trade name, doing-business-as name, or assumed name if different from the legal name. For a corporation, enter the name that appears on the trade name certificate filed with the New York State Department of State. For a business that is not incorporated, enter the name filed with the county clerk's office under Section 130 of the General Business Law.

Line 4 — Enter your federal employer identification number (EIN). If you are not required by the IRS to have an EIN, or you do not yet have a required EIN, leave line 4 blank.

Line 5 — Regular vendors enter the actual street address of your business. Show/entertainment or temporary vendors use your home address. Do not enter a PO box on this line. This address **will** appear on your *Certificate of Authority*. It

will also be used for mailing unless you list a different mailing address on line 9 or a tax preparer's address on the back page of the form. If you have more than one location, see the instructions for line 12.

Line 7 — Enter the date you will begin making taxable sales or providing taxable services within New York State, or begin issuing or accepting New York State exemption certificates. Do not mail your application more than 90 days before this date.

Line 8 — If you are a temporary vendor, enter the date you will end business in New York State.

Line 10 — Indicate how your business is organized by checking the box that best describes it.

Governmental organizations include the federal government, New York State and any of its agencies, instrumentalities, public corporations, or political subdivisions (counties, towns, cities, villages, school districts, and fire districts).

An *exempt organization* is one that qualifies under Section 1116 of the Tax Law and has been issued an *Exempt Organization Certificate.*

Line 11 — Check the appropriate box to indicate why you are applying.

For a change in organizational structure, (for example, sole proprietor to corporation), you must register as a new business by completing Form DTF-17. You must file a final return and surrender your *Certificate of Authority* for the old business.

If you are going into business as, or changing your organizational structure to, a limited liability company (LLC) or a limited liability partnership (LLP), you must first contact the New York State Department of State. Once you have been granted your LLC or LLP status, you will be sent Form PR-570, *LLC/LLP Request for Information,* which contains instructions on how to register as a vendor for sales tax purposes.

For a change in business name or location, file Form DTF-95, *Business Tax Account Update.* We will send you a revised certificate.

Line 12 — If you will be operating from more than one business location, you must have a separate *Certificate of Authority* for each location. Check the appropriate box to indicate whether you will file one return for all locations or a separate return for each location.

If you check box A and will be filing separate returns for each location, you must file Form DTF-17 for each location.

If you check box B and will be filing one (consolidated) return, list all your business locations on Form DTF-17-ATT and attach it to your application.

Line 13 — Enter the required information for all owners or officers of the business who are responsible for the day-to-day operations of the business. This generally includes anyone who:

— signs checks on the company's bank account

— signs business tax returns

— pays creditors

— hires and fires employees

— determines which bills are to be paid

— attends to the general financial affairs of the business.

If a partnership, enter the required information for all general partners and for those limited partners who are active in running the business. Indicate whether the partner is a general partner or limited partner by entering **GP** or **LP** after the partner's name.

Include the social security number of all owners, partners, or officers listed. (The Tax Law requires you to disclose your social security number.) If your application is missing social security numbers, we will return it to you.

Line 16 — If you are a manufacturer or wholesaler whose activities are such that you are not required to collect any sales and use tax or pay any sales and use tax directly to the Department of Taxation and Finance, check *No*. Because you are registering only to accept or issue exemption certificates, you need only file an annual information return. There are other instances when you may file an annual return. Refer to Publication 750 for instructions on filing returns and for what constitutes a taxable sale. You will, of course, still have to collect sales or use tax and to pay sales or use tax on any taxable retail sale or purchase.

Line 17 — Business activity — Describe your business activity in the space provided. If you have more than one business activity, attach additional sheets.

North American Industry Classification System (NAICS) — Enter the six-digit code from Publication 910 that best describes your business. Show vendors and entertainment vendors use code **454390**.

Line 18 — You are a sidewalk vendor if you do **not** have a permanent business location, you operate in places other than or in addition to flea markets or other shows, and you make sales from a portable stand, pushcart, or other device in New York City.

Line 19 — Check *Yes* if you do not have a permanent place of business and you participate exclusively in flea markets or other shows.

Line 20 — If *Yes,* you must file Form DTF-716, *Application for Registration of Retail Dealers and Vending Machines for Sales of Cigarettes or Tobacco Products.* For forms, call us at the numbers listed in the **Need help?** section on this page.

Lines 22 through 30 — Answer *Yes* or *No* to each question. If you answer *Yes* to any question, enter the required information for that line. Attach additional sheets as necessary to fully answer all questions.

Responsible officers, directors, partners, and employees are those who act for the business in complying with the Tax Law.

Questions 28, 29, and 30 apply **only** to corporations.

Signature — This application must be signed by a person whose responsibility it is to act for the business in complying with the tax law. This person may be a member of a partnership, an officer or director of a corporation, the owner of a sole proprietorship, or an authorized employee of the business.

If the application is not signed or is incomplete, we will return it to you.

Mail your application to: NYS Tax Department, Sales Tax Registration Unit, W A Harriman Campus, Albany NY 12227, at least 20 days (but not more than 90 days) before you begin doing business in New York State.

☎ Need help?

Telephone assistance is available from 8:30 a.m. to 4:25 p.m. (eastern time), Monday through Friday.
Tax information: 1 800 225-5829
Forms and publications: 1 800 462-8100
Refund status: Access our website or call 1 800 443-3200;
    if electronically filed 1 800 353-0708; direct deposit refunds: 1 800 321-3213
    Automated service for refund status is available 24 hours a day, seven days a week.
From outside the U.S. and outside Canada: (518) 485-6800
Fax-on-demand forms (available 24 hours a day, seven days a week): 1 800 748-3676
Internet access: http://www.tax.state.ny.us
Hearing and speech impaired (telecommunications device for the
    deaf (TDD) callers only): 1 800 634-2110 (8:30 a.m. to 4:25 p.m., eastern time)

♿ **Persons with disabilities:** In compliance with the Americans with Disabilities Act, we will ensure that our lobbies, offices, meeting rooms, and other facilities are accessible to persons with disabilities. If you have questions about special accommodations for persons with disabilities, please call 1 800 225-5829.

✍ **If you need to write**, address your letter to: NYS Tax Department, Taxpayer Assistance Bureau, W A Harriman Campus, Albany NY 12227.

Privacy notification

The right of the Commissioner of Taxation and Finance and the Department of Taxation and Finance to collect and maintain personal information, including mandatory disclosure of social security numbers in the manner required by tax regulations, instructions, and forms, is found in Articles 8, 28, and 28-A of the Tax Law; and 42 USC 405(c)(2)(C)(i).

The Tax Department uses this information primarily to determine and administer sales and use taxes or liabilities under the Tax Law, and for any other purpose authorized by law.

Failure to provide the required information may subject you to civil or criminal penalties, or both, under the Tax Law.

This information is maintained by the Director of the Registration and Data Services Bureau, NYS Tax Department, Building 8 Room 338, W A Harriman Campus, Albany NY 12227; telephone 1 800 225-5829. From areas outside the U.S. and outside Canada, call (518) 485-6800.

Collection Charts for State and Local Sales and Use Tax

For amounts $10 or over, multiply by the applicable rate.

The following charts cover the state rates and the combined state and local rates currently in effect. You can get charts for local rates not shown by calling the numbers listed on the back cover.

4% Sales and use tax collection chart

Amount of sale	Tax to be collected	Amount of sale	Tax to be collected	Amount of sale	Tax to be collected
$0.01 to $0.12	$0.00	3.38 to 3.62	.14	6.88 to 7.12	.28
.13 to .33	.01	3.63 to 3.87	.15	7.13 to 7.37	.29
.34 to .58	.02	3.88 to 4.12	.16	7.38 to 7.62	.30
.59 to .83	.03	4.13 to 4.37	.17	7.63 to 7.87	.31
.84 to 1.12	.04	4.38 to 4.62	.18	7.88 to 8.12	.32
1.13 to 1.37	.05	4.63 to 4.87	.19	8.13 to 8.37	.33
1.38 to 1.62	.06	4.88 to 5.12	.20	8.38 to 8.62	.34
1.63 to 1.87	.07	5.13 to 5.37	.21	8.63 to 8.87	.35
1.88 to 2.12	.08	5.38 to 5.62	.22	8.88 to 9.12	.36
2.13 to 2.37	.09	5.63 to 5.87	.23	9.13 to 9.37	.37
2.38 to 2.62	.10	5.88 to 6.12	.24	9.38 to 9.62	.38
2.63 to 2.87	.11	6.13 to 6.37	.25	9.63 to 9.87	.39
2.88 to 3.12	.12	6.38 to 6.62	.26	9.88 to 9.99	.40
3.13 to 3.37	.13	6.63 to 6.87	.27		

4¼% Sales and use tax collection chart

Amount of sale	Tax to be collected	Amount of sale	Tax to be collected	Amount of sale	Tax to be collected
$0.01 to $0.11	$0.00	3.89 to 4.11	.17	7.89 to 8.11	.34
.12 to .33	.01	4.12 to 4.35	.18	8.12 to 8.35	.35
.34 to .57	.02	4.36 to 4.58	.19	8.36 to 8.58	.36
.58 to .81	.03	4.59 to 4.82	.20	8.59 to 8.82	.37
.82 to 1.05	.04	4.83 to 5.05	.21	8.83 to 9.05	.38
1.06 to 1.29	.05	5.06 to 5.29	.22	9.06 to 9.29	.39
1.30 to 1.52	.06	5.30 to 5.52	.23	9.30 to 9.52	.40
1.53 to 1.76	.07	5.53 to 5.76	.24	9.53 to 9.76	.41
1.77 to 1.99	.08	5.77 to 5.99	.25	9.77 to 9.99	.42
2.00 to 2.23	.09	6.00 to 6.23	.26		
2.24 to 2.47	.10	6.24 to 6.47	.27		
2.48 to 2.70	.11	6.48 to 6.70	.28		
2.71 to 2.94	.12	6.71 to 6.94	.29		
2.95 to 3.17	.13	6.95 to 7.17	.30		
3.18 to 3.41	.14	7.18 to 7.41	.31		
3.42 to 3.64	.15	7.42 to 7.64	.32		
3.65 to 3.88	.16	7.65 to 7.88	.33		

5½% Sales and use tax collection chart

Amount of sale	Tax to be collected	Amount of sale	Tax to be collected	Amount of sale	Tax to be collected
$0.01 to $0.09	$0.00	3.37 to 3.54	.19	6.82 to 6.99	.38
.10 to .27	.01	3.55 to 3.72	.20	7.00 to 7.18	.39
.28 to .45	.02	3.73 to 3.90	.21	7.19 to 7.36	.40
.46 to .63	.03	3.91 to 4.09	.22	7.37 to 7.54	.41
.64 to .81	.04	4.10 to 4.27	.23	7.55 to 7.72	.42
.82 to .99	.05	4.28 to 4.45	.24	7.73 to 7.90	.43
1.00 to 1.18	.06	4.46 to 4.63	.25	7.91 to 8.09	.44
1.19 to 1.36	.07	4.64 to 4.81	.26	8.10 to 8.27	.45
1.37 to 1.54	.08	4.82 to 4.99	.27	8.28 to 8.45	.46
1.55 to 1.72	.09	5.00 to 5.18	.28	8.46 to 8.63	.47
1.73 to 1.90	.10	5.19 to 5.36	.29	8.64 to 8.81	.48
1.91 to 2.09	.11	5.37 to 5.54	.30	8.82 to 8.99	.49
2.10 to 2.27	.12	5.55 to 5.72	.31	9.00 to 9.18	.50
2.28 to 2.45	.13	5.73 to 5.90	.32	9.19 to 9.36	.51
2.46 to 2.63	.14	5.91 to 6.09	.33	9.37 to 9.54	.52
2.64 to 2.81	.15	6.10 to 6.27	.34	9.55 to 9.72	.53
2.82 to 2.99	.16	6.28 to 6.45	.35	9.73 to 9.90	.54
3.00 to 3.18	.17	6.46 to 6.63	.36	9.91 to 9.99	.55
3.19 to 3.36	.18	6.64 to 6.81	.37		

6% Sales and use tax collection chart

Amount of sale	Tax to be collected	Amount of sale	Tax to be collected	Amount of sale	Tax to be collected
$0.01 to $0.10	$0.00	3.42 to 3.58	.21	6.92 to 7.08	.42
.11 to .22	.01	3.59 to 3.74	.22	7.09 to 7.24	.43
.23 to .38	.02	3.75 to 3.91	.23	7.25 to 7.41	.44
.39 to .56	.03	3.92 to 4.08	.24	7.42 to 7.58	.45
.57 to .72	.04	4.09 to 4.24	.25	7.59 to 7.74	.46
.73 to .88	.05	4.25 to 4.41	.26	7.75 to 7.91	.47
.89 to 1.08	.06	4.42 to 4.58	.27	7.92 to 8.08	.48
1.09 to 1.24	.07	4.59 to 4.74	.28	8.09 to 8.24	.49
1.25 to 1.41	.08	4.75 to 4.91	.29	8.25 to 8.41	.50
1.42 to 1.58	.09	4.92 to 5.08	.30	8.42 to 8.58	.51
1.59 to 1.74	.10	5.09 to 5.24	.31	8.59 to 8.74	.52
1.75 to 1.91	.11	5.25 to 5.41	.32	8.75 to 8.91	.53
1.92 to 2.08	.12	5.42 to 5.58	.33	8.92 to 9.08	.54
2.09 to 2.24	.13	5.59 to 5.74	.34	9.09 to 9.24	.55
2.25 to 2.41	.14	5.75 to 5.91	.35	9.25 to 9.41	.56
2.42 to 2.58	.15	5.92 to 6.08	.36	9.42 to 9.58	.57
2.59 to 2.74	.16	6.09 to 6.24	.37	9.59 to 9.74	.58
2.75 to 2.91	.17	6.25 to 6.41	.38	9.75 to 9.91	.59
2.92 to 3.08	.18	6.42 to 6.58	.39	9.92 to 9.99	.60
3.09 to 3.24	.19	6.59 to 6.74	.40		
3.25 to 3.41	.20	6.75 to 6.91	.41		

6¼% Sales and use tax collection chart

Amount of sale	Tax to be collected	Amount of sale	Tax to be collected	Amount of sale	Tax to be collected
$0.01 to $0.10	$0.00	3.28 to 3.43	.21	6.64 to 6.79	.42
.11 to .22	.01	3.44 to 3.59	.22	6.80 to 6.95	.43
.23 to .38	.02	3.60 to 3.75	.23	6.96 to 7.11	.44
.39 to .54	.03	3.76 to 3.91	.24	7.12 to 7.27	.45
.55 to .70	.04	3.92 to 4.07	.25	7.28 to 7.43	.46
.71 to .86	.05	4.08 to 4.23	.26	7.44 to 7.59	.47
.87 to 1.03	.06	4.24 to 4.39	.27	7.60 to 7.75	.48
1.04 to 1.19	.07	4.40 to 4.55	.28	7.76 to 7.91	.49
1.20 to 1.35	.08	4.56 to 4.71	.29	7.92 to 8.07	.50
1.36 to 1.51	.09	4.72 to 4.87	.30	8.08 to 8.23	.51
1.52 to 1.67	.10	4.88 to 5.03	.31	8.24 to 8.39	.52
1.68 to 1.83	.11	5.04 to 5.19	.32	8.40 to 8.55	.53
1.84 to 1.99	.12	5.20 to 5.35	.33	8.56 to 8.71	.54
2.00 to 2.15	.13	5.36 to 5.51	.34	8.72 to 8.87	.55
2.16 to 2.31	.14	5.52 to 5.67	.35	8.88 to 9.03	.56
2.32 to 2.47	.15	5.68 to 5.83	.36	9.04 to 9.19	.57
2.48 to 2.63	.16	5.84 to 5.99	.37	9.20 to 9.35	.58
2.64 to 2.79	.17	6.00 to 6.15	.38	9.36 to 9.51	.59
2.80 to 2.95	.18	6.16 to 6.31	.39	9.52 to 9.67	.60
2.96 to 3.11	.19	6.32 to 6.47	.40	9.68 to 9.83	.61
3.12 to 3.27	.20	6.48 to 6.63	.41	9.84 to 9.99	.62

6¾% Sales and use tax collection chart

Amount of sale	Tax to be collected	Amount of sale	Tax to be collected	Amount of sale	Tax to be collected
$0.01 to $0.10	$0.00	3.34 to 3.48	.23	6.75 to 6.88	.46
.11 to .21	.01	3.49 to 3.62	.24	6.89 to 7.03	.47
.22 to .35	.02	3.63 to 3.77	.25	7.04 to 7.18	.48
.36 to .49	.03	3.78 to 3.92	.26	7.19 to 7.33	.49
.50 to .64	.04	3.93 to 4.07	.27	7.34 to 7.48	.50
.65 to .79	.05	4.08 to 4.22	.28	7.49 to 7.62	.51
.80 to .95	.06	4.23 to 4.37	.29	7.63 to 7.77	.52
.96 to 1.11	.07	4.38 to 4.51	.30	7.78 to 7.92	.53
1.12 to 1.25	.08	4.52 to 4.66	.31	7.93 to 8.07	.54
1.26 to 1.40	.09	4.67 to 4.81	.32	8.08 to 8.22	.55
1.41 to 1.55	.10	4.82 to 4.96	.33	8.23 to 8.37	.56
1.56 to 1.70	.11	4.97 to 5.11	.34	8.38 to 8.51	.57
1.71 to 1.85	.12	5.12 to 5.25	.35	8.52 to 8.66	.58
1.86 to 1.99	.13	5.26 to 5.40	.36	8.67 to 8.81	.59
2.00 to 2.14	.14	5.41 to 5.55	.37	8.82 to 8.96	.60
2.15 to 2.29	.15	5.56 to 5.70	.38	8.97 to 9.11	.61
2.30 to 2.44	.16	5.71 to 5.85	.39	9.12 to 9.25	.62
2.45 to 2.59	.17	5.86 to 5.99	.40	9.26 to 9.40	.63
2.60 to 2.74	.18	6.00 to 6.14	.41	9.41 to 9.55	.64
2.75 to 2.88	.19	6.15 to 6.29	.42	9.56 to 9.70	.65
2.89 to 3.03	.20	6.30 to 6.44	.43	9.71 to 9.85	.66
3.04 to 3.18	.21	6.45 to 6.59	.44	9.86 to 9.99	.67
3.19 to 3.33	.22	6.60 to 6.74	.45		

Page 18 Publication 750 (12/98)

7% Sales and use tax collection chart

Amount of sale		Tax to be collected	Amount of sale		Tax to be collected	Amount of sale		Tax to be collected
$0.01 to $0.10		$0.00	3.36 to 3.49		.24	6.79 to 6.92		.48
.11 to .20		.01	3.50 to 3.64		.25	6.93 to 7.07		.49
.21 to .33		.02	3.65 to 3.78		.26	7.08 to 7.21		.50
.34 to .47		.03	3.79 to 3.92		.27	7.22 to 7.35		.51
.48 to .62		.04	3.93 to 4.07		.28	7.36 to 7.49		.52
.63 to .76		.05	4.08 to 4.21		29	7.50 to 7.64		.53
.77 to .91		.06	4.22 to 4.35		.30	7.65 to 7.78		.54
.92 to 1.07		.07	4.36 to 4.49		.31	7.79 to 7.92		.55
1.08 to 1.21		.08	4.50 to 4.64		.32	7.93 to 8.07		.56
1.22 to 1.35		.09	4.65 to 4.78		.33	8.08 to 8.21		.57
1.36 to 1.49		.10	4.79 to 4.92		.34	8.22 to 8.35		.58
1.50 to 1.64		.11	4.93 to 5.07		.35	8.36 to 8.49		.59
1.65 to 1.78		.12	5.08 to 5.21		.36	8.50 to 8.64		.60
1.79 to 1.92		.13	5.22 to 5.35		.37	8.65 to 8.78		.61
1.93 to 2.07		.14	5.36 to 5.49		.38	8.79 to 8.92		.62
2.08 to 2.21		.15	5.50 to 5.64		.39	8.93 to 9.07		.63
2.22 to 2.35		.16	5.65 to 5.78		.40	9.08 to 9.21		.64
2.36 to 2.49		.17	5.79 to 5.92		.41	9.22 to 9.35		.65
2.50 to 2.64		.18	5.93 to 6.07		.42	9.36 to 9.49		.66
2.65 to 2.78		.19	6.08 to 6.21		.43	9.50 to 9.64		.67
2.79 to 2.92		.20	6.22 to 6.35		.44	9.65 to 9.78		.68
2.93 to 3.07		.21	6.36 to 6.49		.45	9.79 to 9.92		.69
3.08 to 3.21		.22	6.50 to 6.64		.46	9.93 to 9.99		.70
3.22 to 3.35		.23	6.65 to 6.78		.47			

7¼% Sales and use tax collection chart

Amount of sale		Tax to be collected	Amount of sale		Tax to be collected	Amount of sale		Tax to be collected
$0.01 to $0.10		$0.00	3.38 to 3.51		.25	6.83 to 6.96		.50
.11 to .20		.01	3.52 to 3.65		.26	6.97 to 7.10		.51
.21 to .33		.02	3.66 to 3.79		.27	7.11 to 7.24		.52
.34 to .47		.03	3.80 to 3.93		.28	7.25 to 7.37		.53
.48 to .61		.04	3.94 to 4.06		.29	7.38 to 7.51		.54
.62 to .74		.05	4.07 to 4.20		.30	7.52 to 7.65		.55
.75 to .88		.06	4.21 to 4.34		.31	7.66 to 7.79		.56
.89 to 1.03		.07	4.35 to 4.48		.32	7.80 to 7.93		.57
1.04 to 1.17		.08	4.49 to 4.62		.33	7.94 to 8.06		.58
1.18 to 1.31		.09	4.63 to 4.75		.34	8.07 to 8.20		.59
1.32 to 1.44		.10	4.76 to 4.89		.35	8.21 to 8.34		.60
1.45 to 1.58		.11	4.90 to 5.03		.36	8.35 to 8.48		.61
1.59 to 1.72		.12	5.04 to 5.17		.37	8.49 to 8.62		.62
1.73 to 1.86		.13	5.18 to 5.31		.38	8.63 to 8.75		.63
1.87 to 1.99		.14	5.32 to 5.44		.39	8.76 to 8.89		.64
2.00 to 2.13		.15	5.45 to 5.58		.40	8.90 to 9.03		.65
2.14 to 2.27		.16	5.59 to 5.72		.41	9.04 to 9.17		.66
2.28 to 2.41		.17	5.73 to 5.86		.42	9.18 to 9.31		.67
2.42 to 2.55		.18	5.87 to 5.99		.43	9.32 to 9.44		.68
2.56 to 2.68		.19	6.00 to 6.13		.44	9.45 to 9.58		.69
2.69 to 2.82		.20	6.14 to 6.27		.45	9.59 to 9.72		.70
2.83 to 2.96		.21	6.28 to 6.41		.46	9.73 to 9.86		.71
2.97 to 3.10		.22	6.42 to 6.55		.47	9.87 to 9.99		.72
3.11 to 3.24		.23	6.55 to 6.68		.48			
3.25 to 3.37		.24	6.69 to 6.82		.49			

7½% Sales and use tax collection chart

Amount of sale			Tax to be collected	Amount of sale			Tax to be collected	Amount of sale			Tax to be collected
$0.01	to	$0.10	$0.00	3.40	to	3.53	.26	6.87	to	6.99	.52
.11	to	.18	.01	3.54	to	3.66	.27	7.00	to	7.13	.53
.19	to	.31	.02	3.67	to	3.79	.28	7.14	to	7.26	.54
.32	to	.45	.03	3.80	to	3.93	.29	7.27	to	7.39	.55
.46	to	.58	.04	3.94	to	4.06	.30	7.40	to	7.53	.56
.59	to	.71	.05	4.07	to	4.19	.31	7.54	to	7.66	.57
.72	to	.85	.06	4.20	to	4.33	.32	7.67	to	7.79	.58
.86	to	.99	.07	4.34	to	4.46	.33	7.80	to	7.93	.59
1.00	to	1.13	.08	4.47	to	4.59	.34	7.94	to	8.06	.60
1.14	to	1.26	.09	4.60	to	4.73	.35	8.07	to	8.19	.61
1.27	to	1.39	.10	4.74	to	4.86	.36	8.20	to	8.33	.62
1.40	to	1.53	.11	4.87	to	4.99	.37	8.34	to	8.46	.63
1.54	to	1.66	.12	5.00	to	5.13	.38	8.47	to	8.59	.64
1.67	to	1.79	.13	5.14	to	5.26	.39	8.60	to	8.73	.65
1.80	to	1.93	.14	5.27	to	5.39	.40	8.74	to	8.86	.66
1.94	to	2.06	.15	5.40	to	5.53	.41	8.87	to	8.99	.67
2.07	to	2.19	.16	5.54	to	5.66	.42	9.00	to	9.13	.68
2.20	to	2.33	.17	5.67	to	5.79	.43	9.14	to	9.26	.69
2.34	to	2.46	.18	5.80	to	5.93	.44	9.27	to	9.39	.70
2.47	to	2.59	.19	5.94	to	6.06	.45	9.40	to	9.53	.71
2.60	to	2.73	.20	6.07	to	6.19	.46	9.54	to	9.66	.72
2.74	to	2.86	.21	6.20	to	6.33	.47	9.67	to	9.79	.73
2.87	to	2.99	.22	6.34	to	6.46	.48	9.80	to	9.93	.74
3.00	to	3.13	.23	6.47	to	6.59	.49	9.94	to	9.99	.75
3.14	to	3.26	.24	6.60	to	6.73	.50				
3.27	to	3.39	.25	6.74	to	6.86	.51				

On sales of $10.00 or over, compute the tax by multiplying the amount of sale by the applicable tax rate and rounding the result to the nearest whole cent.

7¾% Sales and use tax collection chart

Amount of sale			Tax to be collected	Amount of sale			Tax to be collected	Amount of sale			Tax to be collected
$0.01	to	$0.10	$0.00	3.30	to	3.41	.26	6.65	to	6.77	.52
.11	to	.18	.01	3.42	to	3.54	.27	6.78	to	6.90	.53
.19	to	.31	.02	3.55	to	3.67	.28	6.91	to	7.03	.54
.32	to	.44	.03	3.68	to	3.80	29	7.04	to	7.16	.55
.45	to	.57	.04	3.81	to	3.93	.30	7.17	to	7.29	.56
.58	to	.69	.05	3.94	to	4.06	.31	7.30	to	7.41	.57
.70	to	.82	.06	4.07	to	4.19	.32	7.42	to	7.54	.58
.83	to	.95	.07	4.20	to	4.32	.33	7.55	to	7.67	.59
.96	to	1.09	.08	4.33	to	4.45	.34	7.68	to	7.80	.60
1.10	to	1.22	.09	4.46	to	4.58	.35	7.81	to	7.93	.61
1.23	to	1.35	.10	4.59	to	4.70	.36	7.94	to	8.06	.62
1.36	to	1.48	.11	4.71	to	4.83	.37	8.07	to	8.19	.63
1.49	to	1.61	.12	4.84	to	4.96	.38	8.20	to	8.32	.64
1.62	to	1.74	.13	4.97	to	5.09	.39	8.33	to	8.45	.65
1.75	to	1.87	.14	5.10	to	5.22	.40	8.46	to	8.58	.66
1.88	to	1.99	.15	5.23	to	5.35	.41	8.59	to	8.70	.67
2.00	to	2.12	.16	5.36	to	5.48	.42	8.71	to	8.83	.68
2.13	to	2.25	.17	5.49	to	5.61	.43	8.84	to	8.96	.69
2.26	to	2.38	.18	5.62	to	5.74	.44	8.97	to	9.09	.70
2.39	to	2.51	.19	5.75	to	5.87	.45	9.10	to	9.22	.71
2.52	to	2.64	.20	5.88	to	5.99	.46	9.23	to	9.35	.72
2.65	to	2.77	.21	6.00	to	6.12	.47	9.36	to	9.48	.73
2.78	to	2.90	.22	6.13	to	6.25	.48	9.49	to	9.61	.74
2.91	to	3.03	.23	6.26	to	6.38	.49	9.62	to	9.74	.75
3.04	to	3.16	.24	6.39	to	6.51	.50	9.75	to	9.87	.76
3.17	to	3.29	.25	6.52	to	6.64	.51	9.88	to	9.99	.77

Page 20 Publication 750 (12/98)

8% Sales and use tax collection chart

Amount of sale	Tax to be collected	Amount of sale	Tax to be collected	Amount of sale	Tax to be collected
$0.01 to $0.10	$0.00	3.32 to 3.43	.27	6.69 to 6.81	.54
.11 to .17	.01	3.44 to 3.56	.28	6.82 to 6.93	.55
.18 to .29	.02	3.57 to 3.68	.29	6.94 to 7.06	.56
.30 to .42	.03	3.69 to 3.81	.30	7.07 to 7.18	.57
.43 to .54	.04	3.82 to 3.93	.31	7.19 to 7.31	.58
.55 to .67	.05	3.94 to 4.06	.32	7.32 to 7.43	.59
.68 to .79	.06	4.07 to 4.18	.33	7.44 to 7.56	.60
.80 to .92	.07	4.19 to 4.31	.34	7.57 to 7.68	.61
.93 to 1.06	.08	4.32 to 4.43	.35	7.69 to 7.81	.62
1.07 to 1.18	.09	4.44 to 4.56	.36	7.82 to 7.93	.63
1.19 to 1.31	.10	4.57 to 4.68	.37	7.94 to 8.06	.64
1.32 to 1.43	.11	4.69 to 4.81	.38	8.07 to 8.18	.65
1.44 to 1.56	.12	4.82 to 4.93	.39	8.19 to 8.31	.66
1.57 to 1.68	.13	4.94 to 5.06	.40	8.32 to 8.43	.67
1.69 to 1.81	.14	5.07 to 5.18	.41	8.44 to 8.56	.68
1.82 to 1.93	.15	5.19 to 5.31	.42	8.57 to 8.68	.69
1.94 to 2.06	.16	5.32 to 5.43	.43	8.69 to 8.81	.70
2.07 to 2.18	.17	5.44 to 5.56	.44	8.82 to 8.93	.71
2.19 to 2.31	.18	5.57 to 5.68	.45	8.94 to 9.06	.72
2.32 to 2.43	.19	5.69 to 5.81	.46	9.07 to 9.18	.73
2.44 to 2.56	.20	5.82 to 5.93	.47	9.19 to 9.31	.74
2.57 to 2.68	.21	5.94 to 6.06	.48	9.32 to 9.43	.75
2.69 to 2.81	.22	6.07 to 6.18	.49	9.44 to 9.56	.76
2.82 to 2.93	.23	6.19 to 6.31	.50	9.57 to 9.68	.77
2.94 to 3.06	.24	6.32 to 6.43	.51	9.69 to 9.81	.78
3.07 to 3.18	.25	6.44 to 6.56	.52	9.82 to 9.93	.79
3.19 to 3.31	.26	6.57 to 6.68	.53	9.94 to 9.99	.80

8¼% Sales and use tax collection chart

Amount of sale	Tax to be collected	Amount of sale	Tax to be collected	Amount of sale	Tax to be collected
$0.01 to $0.10	$0.00	3.34 to 3.45	.28	6.73 to 6.84	.56
.11 to .17	.01	3.46 to 3.57	.29	6.85 to 6.96	.57
.18 to .29	.02	3.58 to 3.69	.30	6.97 to 7.09	.58
.30 to .42	.03	3.70 to 3.81	.31	7.10 to 7.21	.59
.43 to .54	.04	3.82 to 3.93	.32	7.22 to 7.33	.60
.55 to .66	.05	3.94 to 4.06	.33	7.34 to 7.45	.61
.67 to .78	.06	4.07 to 4.18	.34	7.46 to 7.57	.62
.79 to .90	.07	4.19 to 4.30	.35	7.58 to 7.69	.63
.91 to 1.03	.08	4.31 to 4.42	.36	7.70 to 7.81	.64
1.04 to 1.15	.09	4.43 to 4.54	.37	7.82 to 7.93	.65
1.16 to 1.27	.10	4.55 to 4.66	.38	7.94 to 8.06	.66
1.28 to 1.39	.11	4.67 to 4.78	.39	8.07 to 8.18	.67
1.40 to 1.51	.12	4.79 to 4.90	.40	8.19 to 8.30	.68
1.52 to 1.63	.13	4.91 to 5.03	.41	8.31 to 8.42	.69
1.64 to 1.75	.14	5.04 to 5.15	.42	8.43 to 8.54	.70
1.76 to 1.87	.15	5.16 to 5.27	.43	8.55 to 8.66	.71
1.88 to 1.99	.16	5.28 to 5.39	.44	8.67 to 8.78	.72
2.00 to 2.12	.17	5.40 to 5.51	.45	8.79 to 8.90	.73
2.13 to 2.24	.18	5.52 to 5.63	.46	8.91 to 9.03	.74
2.25 to 2.36	.19	5.64 to 5.75	.47	9.04 to 9.15	.75
2.37 to 2.48	.20	5.76 to 5.87	.48	9.16 to 9.27	.76
2.49 to 2.60	.21	5.88 to 5.99	.49	9.28 to 9.39	.77
2.61 to 2.72	.22	6.00 to 6.12	.50	9.40 to 9.51	.78
2.73 to 2.84	.23	6.13 to 6.24	.51	9.52 to 9.63	.79
2.85 to 2.96	.24	6.25 to 6.36	.52	9.64 to 9.75	.80
2.97 to 3.09	.25	6.37 to 6.48	.53	9.76 to 9.87	.81
3.10 to 3.21	.26	6.49 to 6.60	.54	9.88 to 9.99	.82
3.22 to 3.33	.27	6.61 to 6.72	.55		

8½% Sales and use tax collection chart

Amount of sale			Tax to be collected
$0.01	to	$0.10	$0.00
.11	to	.17	.01
.18	to	.29	.02
.30	to	.41	.03
.42	to	.52	.04
.53	to	.64	.05
.65	to	.76	.06
.77	to	.88	.07
.89	to	.99	.08
1.00	to	1.11	.09
1.12	to	1.23	.10
1.24	to	1.35	.11
1.36	to	1.47	.12
1.48	to	1.58	.13
1.59	to	1.70	.14
1.71	to	1.82	.15
1.83	to	1.94	.16
1.95	to	2.05	.17
2.06	to	2.17	.18
2.18	to	2.29	.19
2.30	to	2.41	.20
2.42	to	2.52	.21
2.53	to	2.64	.22
2.65	to	2.76	.23
2.77	to	2.88	.24
2.89	to	2.99	.25
3.00	to	3.11	.26
3.12	to	3.23	.27
3.24	to	3.35	.28
3.36	to	3.47	.29
3.48	to	3.58	.30
3.59	to	3.70	.31
3.71	to	3.82	.32
3.83	to	3.94	.33
3.95	to	4.05	.34
4.06	to	4.17	.35
4.18	to	4.29	.36
4.30	to	4.41	.37
4.42	to	4.52	.38
4.53	to	4.64	.39
4.65	to	4.76	.40
4.77	to	4.88	.41
4.89	to	4.99	.42
5.00	to	5.11	.43
5.12	to	5.23	.44
5.24	to	5.35	.45
5.36	to	5.47	.46
5.48	to	5.58	.47
5.59	to	5.70	.48
5.71	to	5.82	.49
5.83	to	5.94	.50
5.95	to	6.05	.51
6.06	to	6.17	.52
6.18	to	6.29	.53
6.30	to	6.41	.54
6.42	to	6.52	.55
6.53	to	6.64	.56
6.65	to	6.76	.57
6.77	to	6.88	.58
6.89	to	6.99	.59
7.00	to	7.11	.60
7.12	to	7.23	.61
7.24	to	7.35	.62
7.36	to	7.47	.63
7.48	to	7.58	.64
7.59	to	7.70	.65
7.71	to	7.82	.66
7.83	to	7.94	.67
7.95	to	8.05	.68
8.06	to	8.17	.69
8.18	to	8.29	.70
8.30	to	8.41	.71
8.42	to	8.52	.72
8.53	to	8.64	.73
8.65	to	8.76	.74
8.77	to	8.88	.75
8.89	to	8.99	.76
9.00	to	9.11	.77
9.12	to	9.23	.78
9.24	to	9.35	.79
9.36	to	9.47	.80
9.48	to	9.58	.81
9.59	to	9.70	.82
9.71	to	9.82	.83
9.83	to	9.94	.84
9.95	to	9.99	.85

10¼% Sales and use tax collection chart

Amount of sale			Tax to be collected
$0.01	to	$0.04	$0.00
.05	to	.14	.01
.15	to	.24	.02
.25	to	.34	.03
.35	to	.43	.04
.44	to	.53	.05
.54	to	.63	.06
.64	to	.73	.07
.74	to	.82	.08
.83	to	.92	.09
.93	to	1.02	.10
1.03	to	1.12	.11
1.13	to	1.21	.12
1.22	to	1.31	.13
1.32	to	1.41	.14
1.42	to	1.51	.15
1.52	to	1.60	.16
1.61	to	1.70	.17
1.71	to	1.80	.18
1.81	to	1.90	.19
1.91	to	1.99	.20
2.00	to	2.09	.21
2.10	to	2.19	.22
2.20	to	2.29	.23
2.30	to	2.39	.24
2.40	to	2.48	.25
2.49	to	2.58	.26
2.59	to	2.68	.27
2.69	to	2.78	.28
2.79	to	2.87	.29
2.88	to	2.97	.30
2.98	to	3.07	.31
3.08	to	3.17	.32
3.18	to	3.26	.33
3.27	to	3.36	.34
3.37	to	3.46	0.35
3.47	to	3.55	.36
3.56	to	3.65	.37
3.66	to	3.75	.38
3.76	to	3.85	.39
3.86	to	3.95	.40
3.96	to	4.04	.41
4.05	to	4.14	.42
4.15	to	4.24	.43
4.25	to	4.34	.44
4.35	to	4.43	.45
4.44	to	4.53	.46
4.54	to	4.63	.47
4.64	to	4.73	.48
4.74	to	4.82	.49
4.83	to	4.92	.50
4.93	to	5.02	.51
5.03	to	5.12	.52
5.13	to	5.21	.53
5.22	to	5.31	.54
5.32	to	5.41	.55
5.42	to	5.51	.56
5.52	to	5.60	.57
5.61	to	5.70	.58
5.71	to	5.80	.59
5.81	to	5.90	.60
5.91	to	5.99	.61
6.00	to	6.09	.62
6.10	to	6.19	.63
6.20	to	6.29	.64
6.30	to	6.39	.65
6.40	to	6.48	.66
6.49	to	6.58	.67
6.59	to	6.68	.68
6.69	to	6.78	.69
6.79	to	6.87	.70
6.88	to	6.97	.71
6.98	to	7.07	.72
7.08	to	7.17	.73
7.18	to	7.26	.74
7.27	to	7.36	.75
7.37	to	7.46	.76
7.47	to	7.56	.77
7.57	to	7.65	.78
7.66	to	7.75	.79
7.76	to	7.85	.80
7.86	to	7.95	.81
7.96	to	8.04	.82
8.05	to	8.14	.83
8.15	to	8.24	.84
8.25	to	8.34	.85
8.35	to	8.43	.86
8.44	to	8.53	.87
8.54	to	8.63	.88
8.64	to	8.73	.89
8.74	to	8.82	.90
8.83	to	8.92	.91
8.93	to	9.02	.92
9.03	to	9.12	.93
9.13	to	9.21	.94
9.22	to	9.31	.95
9.32	to	9.41	.96
9.42	to	9.51	.97
9.52	to	9.60	.98
9.61	to	9.70	.99
9.71	to	9.80	1.00
9.81	to	9.90	1.01
9.91	to	9.99	1.02

18¼% Sales and use tax collection chart

Amount of sale			Tax to be collected
$0.01	to	$0.02	$0.00
.03	to	.08	.01
.09	to	.13	.02
.14	to	.19	.03
.20	to	.24	.04
.25	to	.30	.05
.31	to	.35	.06
.36	to	.41	.07
.42	to	.46	.08
.47	to	.52	.09
.53	to	.57	.10
.58	to	.63	.11
.64	to	.68	.12
.69	to	.73	.13
.74	to	.79	.14
.80	to	.84	.15
.85	to	.90	.16
.91	to	.95	.17
.96	to	1.01	.18
1.02	to	1.06	.19
1.07	to	1.12	.20
1.13	to	1.17	.21
1.18	to	1.23	.22
1.24	to	1.28	.23
1.29	to	1.34	.24
1.35	to	1.39	.25
1.40	to	1.45	.26
1.46	to	1.50	.27
1.51	to	1.56	.28
1.57	to	1.61	.29
1.62	to	1.67	.30
1.68	to	1.72	.31
1.73	to	1.78	.32
1.79	to	1.83	.33
1.84	to	1.89	.34
1.90	to	1.94	.35
1.95	to	1.99	.36
2.00	to	2.05	.37
2.06	to	2.10	.38
2.11	to	2.16	.39
2.17	to	2.21	.40
2.22	to	2.27	.41
2.28	to	2.32	.42
2.33	to	2.38	.43
2.39	to	2.43	.44
2.44	to	2.49	.45
2.50	to	2.54	.46
2.55	to	2.60	.47
2.61	to	2.65	.48
2.66	to	2.71	.49
2.72	to	2.76	.50
2.77	to	2.82	.51
2.83	to	2.87	.52
2.88	to	2.93	.53
2.94	to	2.98	.54
2.99	to	3.04	.55
3.05	to	3.09	.56
3.10	to	3.15	.57
3.16	to	3.20	.58
3.21	to	3.26	.59
3.27	to	3.31	.60
3.32	to	3.36	.61
3.37	to	3.42	.62
3.43	to	3.47	.63
3.48	to	3.53	.64
3.54	to	3.58	.65
3.59	to	3.64	.66
3.65	to	3.69	.67
3.70	to	3.75	.68
3.76	to	3.80	.69
3.81	to	3.86	.70
3.87	to	3.91	.71
3.92	to	3.97	.72
3.98	to	4.02	.73
4.03	to	4.08	.74
4.09	to	4.13	.75
4.14	to	4.19	.76
4.20	to	4.24	.77
4.25	to	4.30	.78
4.31	to	4.35	.79
4.36	to	4.41	.80
4.42	to	4.46	.81
4.47	to	4.52	.82
4.53	to	4.57	.83
4.58	to	4.63	.84
4.64	to	4.68	.85
4.69	to	4.73	.86
4.74	to	4.79	.87
4.80	to	4.84	.88
4.85	to	4.90	.89
4.91	to	4.95	.90
4.96	to	5.01	.91
5.02	to	5.06	.92
5.07	to	5.12	.93
5.13	to	5.17	.94
5.18	to	5.23	.95
5.24	to	5.28	.96
5.29	to	5.34	.97
5.35	to	5.39	.98
5.40	to	5.45	.99
5.46	to	5.50	1.00
5.51	to	5.56	1.01
5.57	to	5.61	1.02
5.62	to	5.67	1.03
5.68	to	5.72	1.04
5.73	to	5.78	1.05
5.79	to	5.83	1.06
5.84	to	5.89	1.07
5.90	to	5.94	1.08
5.95	to	6.00	1.09
6.01	to	6.05	1.10
6.06	to	6.10	1.11
6.11	to	6.16	1.12
6.17	to	6.21	1.13
6.22	to	6.27	1.14
6.28	to	6.32	1.15
6.33	to	6.38	1.16
6.39	to	6.43	1.17
6.44	to	6.49	1.18
6.50	to	6.54	1.19
6.55	to	6.60	1.20
6.61	to	6.65	1.21
6.66	to	6.71	1.22
6.72	to	6.76	1.23
6.77	to	6.82	1.24
6.83	to	6.87	1.25
6.88	to	6.93	1.26
6.94	to	6.98	1.27
6.99	to	7.04	1.28
7.05	to	7.09	1.29
7.10	to	7.15	1.30
7.16	to	7.20	1.31
7.21	to	7.26	1.32
7.27	to	7.31	1.33
7.32	to	7.36	1.34
7.37	to	7.42	1.35
7.43	to	7.47	1.36
7.48	to	7.53	1.37
7.54	to	7.58	1.38
7.59	to	7.64	1.39
7.65	to	7.69	1.40
7.70	to	7.75	1.41
7.76	to	7.80	1.42
7.81	to	7.86	1.43
7.87	to	7.91	1.44
7.92	to	7.97	1.45
7.98	to	8.02	1.46
8.03	to	8.08	1.47
8.09	to	8.13	1.48
8.14	to	8.19	1.49
8.20	to	8.24	1.50
8.25	to	8.30	1.51
8.31	to	8.35	1.52
8.36	to	8.41	1.53
8.42	to	8.46	1.54
8.47	to	8.52	1.55
8.53	to	8.57	1.56
8.58	to	8.63	1.57
8.64	to	8.68	1.58
8.69	to	8.73	1.59
8.74	to	8.79	1.60
8.80	to	8.84	1.61
8.85	to	8.90	1.62
8.91	to	8.95	1.63
8.96	to	9.01	1.64
9.02	to	9.06	1.65
9.07	to	9.12	1.66
9.13	to	9.17	1.67
9.18	to	9.23	1.68
9.24	to	9.28	1.69
9.29	to	9.34	1.70
9.35	to	9.39	1.71
9.40	to	9.45	1.72
9.46	to	9.50	1.73
9.51	to	9.56	1.74
9.57	to	9.61	1.75
9.62	to	9.67	1.76
9.68	to	9.72	1.77
9.73	to	9.78	1.78
9.79	to	9.83	1.79
9.84	to	9.89	1.80
9.90	to	9.94	1.81
9.95	to	9.99	1.82

This page intentionally left blank.

Form **SS-8**
(Rev. June 2003)
Department of the Treasury
Internal Revenue Service

Determination of Worker Status
for Purposes of Federal Employment Taxes
and Income Tax Withholding

OMB No. 1545-0004

Name of firm (or person) for whom the worker performed services	Worker's name	
Firm's address (include street address, apt. or suite no., city, state, and ZIP code)	Worker's address (include street address, apt. or suite no., city, state, and ZIP code)	
Trade name	Telephone number (include area code) ( )	Worker's social security number
Telephone number (include area code) ( )	Firm's employer identification number	Worker's employer identification number (if any)

If the worker is paid by a firm other than the one listed on this form for these services, enter the name, address, and employer identification number of the payer.

Important Information Needed To Process Your Request

We must have your permission to disclose your name and the information on this form and any attachments to other parties involved with this request. **Do we have your permission to disclose this information?** . . . . ☐ Yes ☐ No
If you answered "No" or did not mark a box, we will not process your request and will not issue a determination.

You must answer ALL items OR mark them "Unknown" or "Does not apply." If you need more space, attach another sheet.

A This form is being completed by: ☐ Firm ☐ Worker; for services performed _____ to _____
(beginning date)   (ending date)

B Explain your reason(s) for filing this form (e.g., you received a bill from the IRS, you believe you received a Form 1099 or Form W-2 erroneously, you are unable to get worker's compensation benefits, you were audited or are being audited by the IRS). ----------------------

C Total number of workers who performed or are performing the same or similar services _____ .

D How did the worker obtain the job? ☐ Application ☐ Bid ☐ Employment Agency ☐ Other (specify) _____

E Attach copies of all supporting documentation (contracts, invoices, memos, Forms W-2, Forms 1099, IRS closing agreements, IRS rulings, etc.). In addition, please inform us of any current or past litigation concerning the worker's status. If no income reporting forms (Form 1099-MISC or W-2) were furnished to the worker, enter the amount of income earned for the year(s) at issue $ _____ .

F Describe the firm's business. ----------------------

G Describe the work done by the worker and provide the worker's job title. ----------------------

H Explain why you believe the worker is an employee or an independent contractor. ----------------------

I Did the worker perform services for the firm before getting this position? . . . . ☐ Yes ☐ No ☐ N/A
If "Yes," what were the dates of the prior service? ----------------------
If "Yes," explain the differences, if any, between the current and prior service. ----------------------

J If the work is done under a written agreement between the firm and the worker, attach a copy (preferably signed by both parties). Describe the terms and conditions of the work arrangement. ----------------------

Part I   Behavioral Control

1   What specific training and/or instruction is the worker given by the firm? ....

2   How does the worker receive work assignments? ....

3   Who determines the methods by which the assignments are performed? ....

4   Who is the worker required to contact if problems or complaints arise and who is responsible for their resolution? ....

5   What types of reports are required from the worker? Attach examples. ....

6   Describe the worker's daily routine (i.e., schedule, hours, etc.). ....

7   At what location(s) does the worker perform services (e.g., firm's premises, own shop or office, home, customer's location, etc.)? ....

8   Describe any meetings the worker is required to attend and any penalties for not attending (e.g., sales meetings, monthly meetings, staff meetings, etc.). ....

9   Is the worker required to provide the services personally? . . . . ☐ **Yes**   ☐ **No**

10 If substitutes or helpers are needed, who hires them? ....

11 If the worker hires the substitutes or helpers, is approval required? . . . . ☐ **Yes**   ☐ **No**
       If "Yes," by whom? ....

12 Who pays the substitutes or helpers? ....

13 Is the worker reimbursed if the worker pays the substitutes or helpers? . . . . ☐ **Yes**   ☐ **No**
       If "Yes," by whom?

Part II   Financial Control

1   List the supplies, equipment, materials, and property provided by each party:
       The firm ....
       The worker ....
       Other party ....

2   Does the worker lease equipment? . . . . ☐ **Yes**   ☐ **No**
       If "Yes," what are the terms of the lease? (Attach a copy or explanatory statement.) ....

3   What expenses are incurred by the worker in the performance of services for the firm? ....

4   Specify which, if any, expenses are reimbursed by:
       The firm ....
       Other party ....

5   Type of pay the worker receives: ☐ Salary   ☐ Commission   ☐ Hourly Wage   ☐ Piece Work
       ☐ Lump Sum   ☐ Other (specify) ....
       If type of pay is commission, and the firm guarantees a minimum amount of pay, specify amount $ _____ .

6   Is the worker allowed a drawing account for advances? . . . . ☐ **Yes**   ☐ **No**
       If "Yes," how often? ....
       Specify any restrictions. ....

7   Whom does the customer pay? . . . . ☐ Firm   ☐ Worker
       If worker, does the worker pay the total amount to the firm?   ☐ **Yes**   ☐ **No**   If "No," explain. ....

8   Does the firm carry worker's compensation insurance on the worker? . . . . ☐ **Yes**   ☐ **No**

9   What economic loss or financial risk, if any, can the worker incur beyond the normal loss of salary (e.g., loss or damage of equipment, material, etc.)? ....

Part III **Relationship of the Worker and Firm**

1   List the benefits available to the worker (e.g., paid vacations, sick pay, pensions, bonuses). ------------------------------------

----

2   Can the relationship be terminated by either party without incurring liability or penalty? . . . . ☐ **Yes**   ☐ **No**
    If "No," explain your answer. ---

----

3   Does the worker perform similar services for others? . . . . ☐ **Yes**   ☐ **No**
    If "Yes," is the worker required to get approval from the firm? . . . . ☐ **Yes**   ☐ **No**

4   Describe any agreements prohibiting competition between the worker and the firm while the worker is performing services or during any later
    period. Attach any available documentation. ---

----

5   Is the worker a member of a union? . . . . ☐ **Yes**   ☐ **No**

6   What type of advertising, if any, does the worker do (e.g., a business listing in a directory, business cards, etc.)? Provide copies, if applicable.

----

7   If the worker assembles or processes a product at home, who provides the materials and instructions or pattern? ----------------

----

8   What does the worker do with the finished product (e.g., return it to the firm, provide it to another party, or sell it)? ---------

----

9   How does the firm represent the worker to its customers (e.g., employee, partner, representative, or contractor)? --------------

----

10 If the worker no longer performs services for the firm, how did the relationship end? ---

----

Part IV   **For Service Providers or Salespersons-** Complete this part if the worker provided a service directly to
              customers or is a salesperson.

1   What are the worker's responsibilities in soliciting new customers? --

----

2   Who provides the worker with leads to prospective customers? --

3   Describe any reporting requirements pertaining to the leads. ---

----

4   What terms and conditions of sale, if any, are required by the firm? --

5   Are orders submitted to and subject to approval by the firm? . . . . ☐ **Yes**   ☐ **No**

6   Who determines the worker's territory? ---

7   Did the worker pay for the privilege of serving customers on the route or in the territory? . . . . ☐ **Yes**   ☐ **No**
    If "Yes," whom did the worker pay? ---
    If "Yes," how much did the worker pay? . . . . $ _____ .

8   Where does the worker sell the product (e.g., in a home, retail establishment, etc.)? ---

----

9   List the product and/or services distributed by the worker (e.g., meat, vegetables, fruit, bakery products, beverages, or laundry or dry cleaning
    services). If more than one type of product and/or service is distributed, specify the principal one. --------------------------------

10 Does the worker sell life insurance full time? . . . . ☐ **Yes**   ☐ **No**

11 Does the worker sell other types of insurance for the firm? . . . . ☐ **Yes**   ☐ **No**
    If "Yes," enter the percentage of the worker's total working time spent in selling other types of insurance. . . . _____ %

12 If the worker solicits orders from wholesalers, retailers, contractors, or operators of hotels, restaurants, or other similar
    establishments, enter the percentage of the worker's time spent in the solicitation. . . . . _____ %

13 Is the merchandise purchased by the customers for resale or use in their business operations? . . . . ☐ **Yes**   ☐ **No**
    Describe the merchandise and state whether it is equipment installed on the customers' premises. -------------------------------

----

Part V   **Signature** (see page 4)

Under penalties of perjury, I declare that I have examined this request, including accompanying documents, and to the best of my knowledge and belief, the facts
presented are true, correct, and complete.

Signature ▶ _____   Title ▶ _____   Date ▶ _____
                    (Type or print name below)

General Instructions

Section references are to the Internal Revenue Code unless otherwise noted.

Purpose

Firms and workers file Form SS-8 to request a determination of the status of a worker for purposes of Federal employment taxes and income tax withholding.

A Form SS-8 determination may be requested only in order to resolve Federal tax matters. If Form SS-8 is submitted for a tax year for which the statute of limitations on the tax return has expired, a determination letter will not be issued. The statute of limitations expires 3 years from the due date of the tax return or the date filed, whichever is later.

The IRS does not issue a determination letter for proposed transactions or on hypothetical situations. We may, however, issue an information letter when it is considered appropriate.

Definition

Firm. For the purposes of this form, the term "firm" means any individual, business enterprise, organization, state, or other entity for which a worker has performed services. The firm may or may not have paid the worker directly for these services. **If the firm was not responsible for payment for services, be sure to enter the name, address, and employer identification number of the payer on the first page of Form SS-8 below the identifying information for the firm and the worker.**

The SS-8 Determination Process

The IRS will acknowledge the receipt of your Form SS-8. Because there are usually two (or more) parties who could be affected by a determination of employment status, the IRS attempts to get information from all parties involved by sending those parties blank Forms SS-8 for completion. The case will be assigned to a technician who will review the facts, apply the law, and render a decision. The technician may ask for additional information from the requestor, from other involved parties, or from third parties that could help clarify the work relationship before rendering a decision. The IRS will generally issue a formal determination to the firm or payer (if that is a different entity), and will send a copy to the worker. A determination letter applies only to a worker (or a class of workers) requesting it, and the decision is binding on the IRS. In certain cases, a formal determination will not be issued. Instead, an information letter may be issued. Although an information letter is advisory only and is not binding on the IRS, it may be used to assist the worker to fulfill his or her Federal tax obligations.

Neither the SS-8 determination process nor the review of any records in connection with the determination constitutes an examination (audit) of any Federal tax return. If the periods under consideration have previously been examined, the SS-8 determination process will not constitute a reexamination under IRS reopening procedures. Because this is not an examination of any Federal tax return, the appeal rights available in connection with an examination do not apply to an SS-8 determination. However, if you disagree with a determination and you have additional information concerning the work relationship that you believe was not previously considered, you may request that the determining office reconsider the determination.

Completing Form SS-8

Answer all questions as completely as possible. Attach additional sheets if you need more space. Provide information for all years the worker provided services for the firm. Determinations are based on the entire relationship between the firm and the worker.

Additional copies of this form may be obtained by calling 1-800-829-4933 or from the IRS website at **www.irs.gov.**

Fee

There is no fee for requesting an SS-8 determination letter.

Signature

Form SS-8 must be signed and dated by the taxpayer. A stamped signature will not be accepted.

The person who signs for a corporation must be an officer of the corporation who has personal knowledge of the facts. If the corporation is a member of an affiliated group filing a consolidated return, it must be signed by an officer of the common parent of the group.

The person signing for a trust, partnership, or limited liability company must be, respectively, a trustee, general partner, or member-manager who has personal knowledge of the facts.

Where To File

Send the completed Form SS-8 to the address listed below for the firm's location. However, for cases involving Federal agencies, send Form SS-8 to the Internal Revenue Service, Attn: CC:CORP:T:C, Ben Franklin Station, P.O. Box 7604, Washington, DC 20044.

Firm's location:	Send to:
Alaska, Arizona, Arkansas, California, Colorado, Hawaii, Idaho, Illinois, Iowa, Kansas, Minnesota, Missouri, Montana, Nebraska, Nevada, New Mexico, North Dakota, Oklahoma, Oregon, South Dakota, Texas, Utah, Washington, Wisconsin, Wyoming, American Samoa, Guam, Puerto Rico, U.S. Virgin Islands	Internal Revenue Service SS-8 Determinations P.O. Box 630 Stop 631 Holtsville, NY 11742-0630
Alabama, Connecticut, Delaware, District of Columbia, Florida, Georgia, Indiana, Kentucky, Louisiana, Maine, Maryland, Massachusetts, Michigan, Mississippi, New Hampshire, New Jersey, New York, North Carolina, Ohio, Pennsylvania, Rhode Island, South Carolina, Tennessee, Vermont, Virginia, West Virginia, all other locations not listed	Internal Revenue Service SS-8 Determinations 40 Lakemont Road Newport, VT 05855-1555

Instructions for Workers

If you are requesting a determination for more than one firm, complete a separate Form SS-8 for each firm.

 Form SS-8 is not a claim for refund of social security and Medicare taxes or Federal income tax withholding.

If the IRS determines that you are an employee, you are responsible for filing an amended return for any corrections related to this decision. A determination that a worker is an employee does not necessarily reduce any current or prior tax liability. For more information, call 1-800-829-1040.

Time for filing a claim for refund. Generally, you must file your claim for a credit or refund within 3 years from the date your original return was filed or within 2 years from the date the tax was paid, whichever is later.

Filing Form SS-8 does not prevent the expiration of the time in which a claim for a refund must be filed. If you are concerned about a refund, and the statute of limitations for filing a claim for refund for the year(s) at issue has not yet expired, you should file **Form 1040X,** Amended U.S. Individual Income Tax Return, to protect your statute of limitations. File a separate Form 1040X for each year.

On the Form 1040X you file, do not complete lines 1 through 24 on the form. Write "Protective Claim" at the top of the form, sign and date it. In addition, you should enter the following statement in Part II, Explanation of Changes to Income, Deductions, and Credits: "Filed Form SS-8 with the Internal Revenue Service Office in (Holtsville, NY; Newport, VT; or Washington, DC; as appropriate). By filing this protective claim, I reserve the right to file a claim for any refund that may be due after a determination of my employment tax status has been completed."

Filing Form SS-8 does not alter the requirement to timely file an income tax return. Do not delay filing your tax return in anticipation of an answer to your SS-8 request. In addition, if applicable, do not delay in responding to a request for payment while waiting for a determination of your worker status.

Instructions for Firms

If a **worker** has requested a determination of his or her status while working for you, you will receive a request from the IRS to complete a Form SS-8. In cases of this type, the IRS usually gives each party an opportunity to present a statement of the facts because any decision will affect the employment tax status of the parties. Failure to respond to this request will not prevent the IRS from issuing a determination letter based on the information he or she has made available so that the worker may fulfill his or her Federal tax obligations. However, the information that you provide is extremely valuable in determining the status of the worker.

If **you** are requesting a determination for a particular class of worker, complete the form for **one** individual who is representative of the class of workers whose status is in question. If you want a written determination for more than one class of workers, complete a separate Form SS-8 for one worker from each class whose status is typical of that class. A written determination for any worker will apply to other workers of the same class if the facts are not materially different for these workers. Please provide a list of names and addresses of all workers potentially affected by this determination.

If you have a reasonable basis for not treating a worker as an employee, you may be relieved from having to pay employment taxes for that worker under section 530 of the 1978 Revenue Act. However, this relief provision cannot be considered in conjunction with a Form SS-8 determination because the determination does not constitute an examination of any tax return. For more information regarding section 530 of the 1978 Revenue Act and to determine if you qualify for relief under this section, you may visit the IRS website at **www.irs.gov.**

Privacy Act and Paperwork Reduction Act Notice. We ask for the information on this form to carry out the Internal Revenue laws of the United States. This information will be used to determine the employment status of the worker(s) described on the form. Subtitle C, Employment Taxes, of the Internal Revenue Code imposes employment taxes on wages. Sections 3121(d), 3306(a), and 3401(c) and (d) and the related regulations define employee and employer for purposes of employment taxes imposed under Subtitle C. Section 6001 authorizes the IRS to request information needed to determine if a worker(s) or firm is subject to these taxes. Section 6109 requires you to provide your taxpayer identification number. Neither workers nor firms are required to request a status determination, but if you choose to do so, you must provide the information requested on this form. Failure to provide the requested information may prevent us from making a status determination. If any worker or the firm has requested a status determination and you are being asked to provide information for use in that determination, you are not required to provide the requested information. However, failure to provide such information will prevent the IRS from considering it in making the status determination. Providing false or fraudulent information may subject you to penalties. Routine uses of this information include providing it to the Department of Justice for use in civil and criminal litigation, to the Social Security Administration for the administration of social security programs, and to cities, states, and the District of Columbia for the administration of their tax laws. We may also disclose this information to Federal and state agencies to enforce Federal nontax criminal laws and to combat terrorism. We may provide this information to the affected worker(s) or the firm as part of the status determination process.

You are not required to provide the information requested on a form that is subject to the Paperwork Reduction Act unless the form displays a valid OMB control number. Books or records relating to a form or its instructions must be retained as long as their contents may become material in the administration of any Internal Revenue law. Generally, tax returns and return information are confidential, as required by section 6103.

The time needed to complete and file this form will vary depending on individual circumstances. The estimated average time is: **Recordkeeping,** 22 hrs.; **Learning about the law or the form,** 47 min.; and **Preparing and sending the form to the IRS,** 1 hr., 11 min. If you have comments concerning the accuracy of these time estimates or suggestions for making this form simpler, we would be happy to hear from you. You can write to the Tax Products Coordinating Committee, Western Area Distribution Center, Rancho Cordova, CA 95743-0001. **Do not** send the tax form to this address. Instead, see **Where To File** on page 4.

This page intentionally left blank.

IRS Form 8300
(Rev. December 2001)

OMB No. 1545-0892
Department of the Treasury
Internal Revenue Service

Report of Cash Payments Over $10,000
Received in a Trade or Business
▶ See instructions for definition of cash.

▶ Use this form for transactions occurring after December 31, 2001. Do not use prior versions after this date.
For Privacy Act and Paperwork Reduction Act Notice, see page 4.

FinCEN Form 8300
(December 2001)

OMB No. 1506-0018
Department of the Treasury
Financial Crimes
Enforcement Network

---

1 Check appropriate box(es) if: **a** ☐ Amends prior report; **b** ☐ Suspicious transaction.

Part I   Identity of Individual From Whom the Cash Was Received

2 If more than one individual is involved, check here and see instructions . . . . ▶ ☐

3 Last name   **4** First name   **5** M.I.   **6** Taxpayer identification number

7 Address (number, street, and apt. or suite no.)   **8** Date of birth . ▶   M M D D Y Y Y Y
(see instructions)

9 City   **10** State   **11** ZIP code   **12** Country (if not U.S.)   **13** Occupation, profession, or business

14 Document used to verify identity: **a** Describe identification ▶
   b Issued by   **c** Number

Part II   Person on Whose Behalf This Transaction Was Conducted

15 If this transaction was conducted on behalf of more than one person, check here and see instructions . . . . ▶ ☐

16 Individual's last name or Organization's name   **17** First name   **18** M.I.   **19** Taxpayer identification number

20 Doing business as (DBA) name (see instructions)   Employer identification number

21 Address (number, street, and apt. or suite no.)   **22** Occupation, profession, or business

23 City   **24** State   **25** ZIP code   **26** Country (if not U.S.)

27 Alien identification: **a** Describe identification ▶
   b Issued by   **c** Number

Part III   Description of Transaction and Method of Payment

28 Date cash received
M M D D Y Y Y Y

29 Total cash received
$ .00

30 If cash was received in more than one payment, check here . . . . ▶ ☐

31 Total price if different from item 29
$ .00

32 Amount of cash received (in U.S. dollar equivalent) (must equal item 29) (see instructions):

a U.S. currency $ _____ .00   (Amount in $100 bills or higher $ _____ .00)

b Foreign currency $ _____ .00   (Country ▶ _____)

c Cashier's check(s) $ _____ .00 ⎫ Issuer's name(s) and serial number(s) of the monetary instrument(s) ▶

d Money order(s) $ _____ .00 ⎪

e Bank draft(s) $ _____ .00 ⎬

f Traveler's check(s) $ _____ .00 ⎭

33 Type of transaction

a ☐ Personal property purchased
b ☐ Real property purchased
c ☐ Personal services provided
d ☐ Business services provided
e ☐ Intangible property purchased
f ☐ Debt obligations paid
g ☐ Exchange of cash
h ☐ Escrow or trust funds
i ☐ Bail received by court clerks
j ☐ Other (specify) ▶

34 Specific description of property or service shown in 33. (Give serial or registration number, address, docket number, etc.) ▶

Part IV   Business That Received Cash

35 Name of business that received cash   **36** Employer identification number

37 Address (number, street, and apt. or suite no.)   Social security number

38 City   **39** State   **40** ZIP code   **41** Nature of your business

42 Under penalties of perjury, I declare that to the best of my knowledge the information I have furnished above is true, correct, and complete.

Signature ▶ _____ Title ▶ _____
Authorized official

43 Date of signature   M M D D Y Y Y Y   **44** Type or print name of contact person   **45** Contact telephone number ( )

IRS Form 8300 (Rev. 12-2001)   Cat. No. 62133S   **FinCEN Form 8300** (12-2001)

IRS Form 8300 (Rev. 12-2001) Page **2** **FinCEN Form 8300** (12-2001)

Multiple Parties
(Complete applicable parts below if box 2 or 15 on page 1 is checked)

Part I Continued- Complete if box 2 on page 1 is checked

3 Last name | **4** First name | **5** M.I. | **6** Taxpayer identification number

7 Address (number, street, and apt. or suite no.) | **8** Date of birth ▶ M M D D Y Y Y Y (see instructions)

9 City | **10** State | **11** ZIP code | **12** Country (if not U.S.) | **13** Occupation, profession, or business

14 Document used to verify identity: **a** Describe identification ▶
b Issued by   **c** Number

---

3 Last name | **4** First name | **5** M.I. | **6** Taxpayer identification number

7 Address (number, street, and apt. or suite no.) | **8** Date of birth ▶ M M D D Y Y Y Y (see instructions)

9 City | **10** State | **11** ZIP code | **12** Country (if not U.S.) | **13** Occupation, profession, or business

14 Document used to verify identity: **a** Describe identification ▶
b Issued by   **c** Number

Part II Continued- Complete if box 15 on page 1 is checked

16 Individual's last name or Organization's name | **17** First name | **18** M.I. | **19** Taxpayer identification number

20 Doing business as (DBA) name (see instructions)   Employer identification number

21 Address (number, street, and apt. or suite no.) | **22** Occupation, profession, or business

23 City | **24** State | **25** ZIP code | **26** Country (if not U.S.)

27 Alien identification: **a** Describe identification ▶
b Issued by   **c** Number

---

16 Individual's last name or Organization's name | **17** First name | **18** M.I. | **19** Taxpayer identification number

20 Doing business as (DBA) name (see instructions)   Employer identification number

21 Address (number, street, and apt. or suite no.) | **22** Occupation, profession, or business

23 City | **24** State | **25** ZIP code | **26** Country (if not U.S.)

27 Alien identification: **a** Describe identification ▶
b Issued by   **c** Number

IRS Form 8300 (Rev. 12-2001)   **FinCEN Form 8300** (12-2001)

Section references are to the Internal Revenue Code unless otherwise noted.

Changes To Note

- Section 6050I (26 United States Code (U.S.C.) 6050I) and 31 U.S.C. 5331 require that certain information be reported to the IRS and the Financial Crimes Enforcement Network (FinCEN). This information must be reported on **IRS/FinCEN Form 8300.**
- Item 33 box **i** is to be checked **only** by clerks of the court; box **d** is to be checked by bail bondsmen. See the instructions on page 4.
- For purposes of section 6050I and 31 U.S.C. 5331, the word "cash" and "currency" have the same meaning. See **Cash** under **Definitions** below.

General Instructions

Who must file. Each person engaged in a trade or business who, in the course of that trade or business, receives more than $10,000 in cash in one transaction or in two or more related transactions, must file Form 8300. Any transactions conducted between a payer (or its agent) and the recipient in a 24-hour period are related transactions. Transactions are considered related even if they occur over a period of more than 24 hours if the recipient knows, or has reason to know, that each transaction is one of a series of connected transactions.

Keep a copy of each Form 8300 for 5 years from the date you file it.

Clerks of Federal or State courts must file Form 8300 if more than $10,000 in cash is received as bail for an individual(s) charged with certain criminal offenses. For these purposes, a clerk includes the clerk's office or any other office, department, division, branch, or unit of the court that is authorized to receive bail. If a person receives bail on behalf of a clerk, the clerk is treated as receiving the bail. See the instructions for **Item 33** on page 4.

If multiple payments are made in cash to satisfy bail and the initial payment does not exceed $10,000, the initial payment and subsequent payments must be aggregated and the information return must be filed by the 15th day after receipt of the payment that causes the aggregate amount to exceed $10,000 in cash. In such cases, the reporting requirement can be satisfied either by sending a single written statement with an aggregate amount listed or by furnishing a copy of each Form 8300 relating to that payer. Payments made to satisfy separate bail requirements are not required to be aggregated. See Treasury Regulations section 1.6050I-2.

Casinos must file Form 8300 for nongaming activities (restaurants, shops, etc.).

Voluntary use of Form 8300. Form 8300 may be filed voluntarily for any suspicious transaction (see **Definitions**) for use by FinCEN and the IRS, even if the total amount does not exceed $10,000.

Exceptions. Cash is not required to be reported if it is received:

- By a financial institution required to file **Form 4789,** Currency Transaction Report.
- By a casino required to file (or exempt from filing) **Form 8362,** Currency Transaction Report by Casinos, if the cash is received as part of its gaming business.
- By an agent who receives the cash from a principal, if the agent uses all of the cash within 15 days in a second transaction that is reportable on Form 8300 or on Form 4789, and discloses all the information necessary to complete Part II of Form 8300 or Form 4789 to the recipient of the cash in the second transaction.

- In a transaction occurring entirely outside the United States. See **Pub. 1544,** Reporting Cash Payments Over $10,000 (Received in a Trade or Business), regarding transactions occurring in Puerto Rico, the Virgin Islands, and territories and possessions of the United States.
- In a transaction that is not in the course of a person's trade or business.

When to file. File Form 8300 by the 15th day after the date the cash was received. If that date falls on a Saturday, Sunday, or legal holiday, file the form on the next business day.

Where to file. File the form with the Internal Revenue Service, Detroit Computing Center, P.O. Box 32621, Detroit, MI 48232.

Statement to be provided. You must give a written statement to each person named on a required Form 8300 on or before January 31 of the year following the calendar year in which the cash is received. The statement must show the name, telephone number, and address of the information contact for the business, the aggregate amount of reportable cash received, and that the information was furnished to the IRS. Keep a copy of the statement for your records.

Multiple payments. If you receive more than one cash payment for a single transaction or for related transactions, you must report the multiple payments any time you receive a total amount that exceeds $10,000 within any 12-month period. Submit the report within 15 days of the date you receive the payment that causes the total amount to exceed $10,000. If more than one report is required within 15 days, you may file a combined report. File the combined report no later than the date the earliest report, if filed separately, would have to be filed.

Taxpayer identification number (TIN). You must furnish the correct TIN of the person or persons from whom you receive the cash and, if applicable, the person or persons on whose behalf the transaction is being conducted. **You may be subject to penalties for an incorrect or missing TIN.**

The TIN for an individual (including a sole proprietorship) is the individual's social security number (SSN). For certain resident aliens who are not eligible to get an SSN and nonresident aliens who are required to file tax returns, it is an IRS Individual Taxpayer Identification Number (ITIN). For other persons, including corporations, partnerships, and estates, it is the employer identification number (EIN).

If you have requested but are not able to get a TIN for one or more of the parties to a transaction within 15 days following the transaction, file the report and attach a statement explaining why the TIN is not included.

Exception: *You are not required to provide the TIN of a person who is a nonresident alien individual or a foreign organization **if** that person does not have income effectively connected with the conduct of a U.S. trade or business **and** does not have an office or place of business, or fiscal or paying agent, in the United States. See Pub. 1544 for more information.*

Penalties. You may be subject to penalties if you fail to file a correct and complete Form 8300 on time and you cannot show that the failure was due to reasonable cause. You may also be subject to penalties if you fail to furnish timely a correct and complete statement to each person named in a required report. A minimum penalty of $25,000 may be imposed if the failure is due to an intentional or willful disregard of the cash reporting requirements.

Penalties may also be imposed for causing, or attempting to cause, a trade or business to fail to file a required report; for causing, or

attempting to cause, a trade or business to file a required report containing a material omission or misstatement of fact; or for structuring, or attempting to structure, transactions to avoid the reporting requirements. These violations may also be subject to criminal prosecution which, upon conviction, may result in imprisonment of up to 5 years or fines of up to $250,000 for individuals and $500,000 for corporations or both.

Definitions

Cash. The term "cash" means the following:

- U.S. and foreign coin and currency received in any transaction.
- A cashier's check, money order, bank draft, or traveler's check having a face amount of $10,000 or less that is received in a **designated reporting transaction** (defined below), or that is received in any transaction in which the recipient knows that the instrument is being used in an attempt to avoid the reporting of the transaction under either section 6050I or 31 U.S.C. 5331.

Note: *Cash does not include a check drawn on the payer's own account, such as a personal check, regardless of the amount.*

Designated reporting transaction. A retail sale (or the receipt of funds by a broker or other intermediary in connection with a retail sale) of a consumer durable, a collectible, or a travel or entertainment activity.

Retail sale. Any sale (whether or not the sale is for resale or for any other purpose) made in the course of a trade or business if that trade or business principally consists of making sales to ultimate consumers.

Consumer durable. An item of tangible personal property of a type that, under ordinary usage, can reasonably be expected to remain useful for at least 1 year, and that has a sales price of more than $10,000.

Collectible. Any work of art, rug, antique, metal, gem, stamp, coin, etc.

Travel or entertainment activity. An item of travel or entertainment that pertains to a single trip or event if the combined sales price of the item and all other items relating to the same trip or event that are sold in the same transaction (or related transactions) exceeds $10,000.

Exceptions. A cashier's check, money order, bank draft, or traveler's check is not considered received in a designated reporting transaction if it constitutes the proceeds of a bank loan or if it is received as a payment on certain promissory notes, installment sales contracts, or down payment plans. See Pub. 1544 for more information.

Person. An individual, corporation, partnership, trust, estate, association, or company.

Recipient. The person receiving the cash. Each branch or other unit of a person's trade or business is considered a separate recipient unless the branch receiving the cash (or a central office linking the branches), knows or has reason to know the identity of payers making cash payments to other branches.

Transaction. Includes the purchase of property or services, the payment of debt, the exchange of a negotiable instrument for cash, and the receipt of cash to be held in escrow or trust. A single transaction may not be broken into multiple transactions to avoid reporting.

Suspicious transaction. A transaction in which it appears that a person is attempting to cause Form 8300 not to be filed, or to file a false or incomplete form. The term also includes any transaction in which there is an indication of possible illegal activity.

Specific Instructions

You must complete all parts. However, you may skip Part II if the individual named in Part I is conducting the transaction on his or her behalf only. **For voluntary reporting of suspicious transactions, see Item 1 below.**

Item 1. If you are amending a prior report, check box 1a. Complete the appropriate items with the correct or amended information only. Complete all of Part IV. Staple a copy of the original report to the amended report.

To voluntarily report a suspicious transaction (see **Definitions**), check box 1b. You may also telephone your local IRS Criminal Investigation Division or call 1-800-800-2877.

Part I

Item 2. If two or more individuals conducted the transaction you are reporting, check the box and complete Part I for any one of the individuals. Provide the same information for the other individual(s) on the back of the form. If more than three individuals are involved, provide the same information on additional sheets of paper and attach them to this form.

Item 6. Enter the taxpayer identification number (TIN) of the individual named. See **Taxpayer identification number (TIN)** on page 3 for more information.

Item 8. Enter eight numerals for the date of birth of the individual named. For example, if the individual's birth date is July 6, 1960, enter 07 06 1960.

Item 13. Fully describe the nature of the occupation, profession, or business (for example, "plumber," "attorney," or "automobile dealer"). Do not use general or nondescriptive terms such as "businessman" or "self-employed."

Item 14. You must verify the name and address of the named individual(s). Verification must be made by examination of a document normally accepted as a means of identification when cashing checks (for example, a driver's license, passport, alien registration card, or other official document). In item 14a, enter the type of document examined. In item 14b, identify the issuer of the document. In item 14c, enter the document's number. For example, if the individual has a Utah driver's license, enter "driver's license" in item 14a, "Utah" in item 14b, and the number appearing on the license in item 14c.

Part II

Item 15. If the transaction is being conducted on behalf of more than one person (including husband and wife or parent and child), check the box and complete Part II for any one of the persons. Provide the same information for the other person(s) on the back of the form. If more than three persons are involved, provide the same information on additional sheets of paper and attach them to this form.

Items 16 through 19. If the person on whose behalf the transaction is being conducted is an individual, complete items 16, 17, and 18. Enter his or her TIN in item 19. If the individual is a sole proprietor and has an employer identification number (EIN), you must enter both the SSN and EIN in item 19. If the person is an organization, put its name as shown on required tax filings in item 16 and its EIN in item 19.

Item 20. If a sole proprietor or organization named in items 16 through 18 is doing business under a name other than that entered in item 16 (e.g., a "trade" or "doing business as (DBA)" name), enter it here.

Item 27. If the person is not required to furnish a TIN, complete this item. See **Taxpayer Identification Number (TIN)** on page 3. Enter a

description of the type of official document issued to that person in item 27a (for example, "passport"), the country that issued the document in item 27b, and the document's number in item 27c.

Part III

Item 28. Enter the date you received the cash. If you received the cash in more than one payment, enter the date you received the payment that caused the combined amount to exceed $10,000. See **Multiple payments** under **General Instructions** for more information.

Item 30. Check this box if the amount shown in item 29 was received in more than one payment (for example, as installment payments or payments on related transactions).

Item 31. Enter the total price of the property, services, amount of cash exchanged, etc. (for example, the total cost of a vehicle purchased, cost of catering service, exchange of currency) if different from the amount shown in item 29.

Item 32. Enter the dollar amount of each form of cash received. Show foreign currency amounts in U.S. dollar equivalent at a fair market rate of exchange available to the public. **The sum of the amounts must equal item 29.** For cashier's check, money order, bank draft, or traveler's check, provide the name of the issuer and the serial number of each instrument. Names of all issuers and all serial numbers involved must be provided. If necessary, provide this information on additional sheets of paper and attach them to this form.

Item 33. Check the appropriate box(es) that describe the transaction. If the transaction is not specified in boxes a-i, check box j and briefly describe the transaction (for example, "car lease," "boat lease," "house lease," or "aircraft rental"). If the transaction relates to the receipt of bail by a court clerk, check box **i**, "Bail received by court clerks." This box is **only** for use by court clerks. If the transaction relates to cash received by a bail bondsman, check box **d,** "Business services provided."

Part IV

Item 36. If you are a sole proprietorship, you must enter your SSN. If your business also has an EIN, you must provide the EIN as well. All other business entities must enter an EIN.

Item 41. Fully describe the nature of your business, for example, "attorney" or "jewelry dealer." Do not use general or nondescriptive terms such as "business" or "store."

Item 42. This form must be signed by an individual who has been authorized to do so for the business that received the cash.

Privacy Act and Paperwork Reduction Act Notice. Except as otherwise noted, the information solicited on this form is required by the Internal Revenue Service (IRS) and the Financial Crimes Enforcement Network (FinCEN) in order to carry out the laws and regulations of the United States Department of the Treasury. Trades or businesses, except for clerks of criminal courts, are required to provide the information to the IRS and FinCEN under both section 6050I and 31 U.S.C. 5331. Clerks of criminal courts are required to provide the information to the IRS under section 6050I. Section 6109 and 31 U.S.C. 5331 require that you provide your social security number in order to adequately identify you and process your return and other papers. The principal purpose for collecting the information on this form is to maintain reports or records where such reports or records have a high degree of usefulness in criminal, tax, or regulatory investigations or proceedings, or in the conduct of intelligence or

counterintelligence activities, by directing the Federal Government's attention to unusual or questionable transactions.

While such information is invaluable with regards to the purpose of this form, you are not required to provide information as to whether the reported transaction is deemed suspicious. No penalties or fines will be assessed for failure to provide such information, even if you determine that the reported transaction is indeed suspicious in nature. Failure to provide all other requested information, or the provision of fraudulent information, may result in criminal prosecution and other penalties under Title 26 and Title 31 of the United States Code.

Generally, tax returns and return information are confidential, as stated in section 6103. However, section 6103 allows or requires the IRS to disclose or give the information requested on this form to others as described in the Code. For example, we may disclose your tax information to the Department of Justice, to enforce the tax laws, both civil and criminal, and to cities, states, the District of Columbia, U.S. commonwealths or possessions, and certain foreign governments to carry out their tax laws. We may disclose your tax information to the Department of Treasury and contractors for tax administration purposes; and to other persons as necessary to obtain information which we cannot get in any other way in order to determine the amount of or to collect the tax you owe. We may disclose your tax information to the Comptroller General of the United States to permit the Comptroller General to review the IRS. We may disclose your tax information to Committees of Congress; Federal, state, and local child support agencies; and to other Federal agencies for the purposes of determining entitlement for benefits or the eligibility for and the repayment of loans. We may also disclose this information to Federal agencies that investigate or respond to acts or threats of terrorism or participate in intelligence or counterintelligence activities concerning terrorism.

FinCEN may provide the information collected through this form to those officers and employees of the Department of the Treasury who have a need for the records in the performance of their duties. FinCEN may also refer the records to any other department or agency of the Federal Government upon the request of the head of such department or agency and may also provide the records to appropriate state, local, and foreign criminal law enforcement and regulatory personnel in the performance of their official duties.

You are not required to provide the information requested on a form that is subject to the Paperwork Reduction Act unless the form displays a valid OMB control number. Books or records relating to a form or its instructions must be retained as long as their contents may become material in the administration of any law under Title 26 or Title 31.

The time needed to complete this form will vary depending on individual circumstances. The estimated average time is 21 minutes. If you have comments concerning the accuracy of this time estimate or suggestions for making this form simpler, you can write to the Tax Forms Committee, Western Area Distribution Center, Rancho Cordova, CA 95743-0001. **Do not** send this form to this office. Instead, see **Where To File** on page 3.

Form 8850
(Rev. October 2002)
Department of the Treasury
Internal Revenue Service

Pre-Screening Notice and Certification Request for the Work Opportunity and Welfare-to-Work Credits

▶ See separate instructions.

OMB No. 1545-1500

Job applicant: Fill in the lines below and check any boxes that apply. Complete only this side.

Your name _____   Social security number ▶ _____

Street address where you live _____

City or town, state, and ZIP code _____

Telephone number ( ) - _____

If you are under age 25, enter your date of birth (month, day, year) ___/___/___

Work Opportunity Credit

1 ☐ Check here if you received a conditional certification from the state employment security agency (SESA) or a participating local agency for the work opportunity credit.

2 ☐ Check here if **any** of the following statements apply to you.

- I am a member of a family that has received assistance from Temporary Assistance for Needy Families (TANF) for any 9 months during the last 18 months.

- I am a veteran and a member of a family that received food stamps for at least a 3-month period within the last 15 months.

- I was referred here by a rehabilitation agency approved by the state or the Department of Veterans Affairs.

- I am at least age 18 but **not** age 25 or older and I am a member of a family that:

  a Received food stamps for the last 6 months **or**

  b Received food stamps for at least 3 of the last 5 months, **but** is no longer eligible to receive them.

- Within the past year, I was convicted of a felony or released from prison for a felony **and** during the last 6 months I was a member of a low-income family.

- I received supplemental security income (SSI) benefits for any month ending within the last 60 days.

Welfare-to-Work Credit

3 ☐ Check here if you received a conditional certification from the SESA or a participating local agency for the welfare-to-work credit.

4 ☐ Check here if you are a member of a family that:
- Received TANF payments for at least the last 18 months, **or**
- Received TANF payments for any 18 months beginning after August 5, 1997, **and** the earliest 18-month period beginning after August 5, 1997, ended within the last 2 years, **or**
- Stopped being eligible for TANF payments within the last 2 years because Federal or state law limited the maximum time those payments could be made.

All Applicants

Under penalties of perjury, I declare that I gave the above information to the employer on or before the day I was offered a job, and it is, to the best of my knowledge, true, correct, and complete.

Job applicant's signature ▶   Date ___/___/___

For Privacy Act and Paperwork Reduction Act Notice, see page 2.   Cat. No. 22851L   Form **8850** (Rev. 10-02)

Form 8850 (Rev. 10-02)

For Employer's Use Only

Employer's name _____ Telephone no. ( ) - _____ EIN ▶ _____

Street address _____

City or town, state, and ZIP code _____

Person to contact, if different from above _____ Telephone no. ( ) -

Street address _____

City or town, state, and ZIP code _____

If, based on the individual's age and home address, he or she is a member of group 4 or 6 (as described under **Members of Targeted Groups** in the separate instructions), enter that group number (4 or 6) . . . . ▶ _____

Date applicant: Gave information / /   Was offered job / /   Was hired / /   Started job / /

Under penalties of perjury, I declare that I completed this form on or before the day a job was offered to the applicant and that the information I have furnished is, to the best of my knowledge, true, correct, and complete. Based on the information the job applicant furnished on page 1, I believe the individual is a member of a targeted group or a long-term family assistance recipient. I hereby request a certification that the individual is a member of a targeted group or a long-term family assistance recipient.

Employer's signature ▶ _____ **Title** _____ **Date** / /

Privacy Act and Paperwork Reduction Act Notice

Section references are to the Internal Revenue Code.

Section 51(d)(12) permits a prospective employer to request the applicant to complete this form and give it to the prospective employer. The information will be used by the employer to complete the employer's Federal tax return. Completion of this form is voluntary and may assist members of targeted groups and long-term family assistance recipients in securing employment. Routine uses of this form include giving it to the state employment security agency (SESA), which will contact appropriate sources to confirm that the applicant is a member of a targeted group or a long-term family assistance recipient. This form may also be given to the Internal Revenue Service

for administration of the Internal Revenue laws, to the Department of Justice for civil and criminal litigation, to the Department of Labor for oversight of the certifications performed by the SESA, and to cities, states, and the District of Columbia for use in administering their tax laws. In addition, we may disclose this information to Federal, state, or local agencies that investigate or respond to acts or threats of terrorism or participate in intelligence or counterintelligence activities concerning terrorism.

You are not required to provide the information requested on a form that is subject to the Paperwork Reduction Act unless the form displays a valid OMB control number. Books or records relating to a form or its instructions must be retained as long as their contents may become material in the administration of any Internal Revenue law. Generally, tax returns and return information are confidential, as required by section 6103.

The time needed to complete and file this form will vary depending on individual circumstances. The estimated average time is:

Recordkeeping . . . . 2 hr., 46 min.
Learning about the law or the form . . . . 36 min.
Preparing and sending this form to the SESA . . . . 36 min.

If you have comments concerning the accuracy of these time estimates or suggestions for making this form simpler, we would be happy to hear from you. You can write to the Tax Forms Committee, Western Area Distribution Center, Rancho Cordova, CA 95743-0001.

Do not send this form to this address. Instead, see **When and Where To File** in the separate instructions.

Instructions for Form 8850

(Rev. October 2002)

Department of the Treasury
Internal Revenue Service

Pre-Screening Notice and Certification Request for the Work Opportunity and Welfare-to-Work Credits

Section references are to the Internal Revenue Code unless otherwise noted.

General Instructions

Changes To Note

- The categories of high-risk youth and summer youth employees now include qualified individuals who live in renewal communities and begin work for you after December 31, 2001.
- The work opportunity credit and the welfare-to-work credit are now allowed for qualified individuals who begin work for you before January 1, 2004.

Purpose of Form

Employers use Form 8850 to pre-screen and to make a written request to a state employment security agency (SESA) to certify an individual as:

- A member of a targeted group for purposes of qualifying for the work opportunity credit or
- A long-term family assistance recipient for purposes of qualifying for the welfare-to-work credit.

Submitting Form 8850 to the SESA is but one step in the process of qualifying for the work opportunity credit or the welfare-to-work credit. The SESA must certify the job applicant is a member of a targeted group or is a long-term family assistance recipient. After starting work, the employee must meet the minimum number-of-hours-worked requirement for the work opportunity credit or the minimum number-of-hours, number-of-days requirement for the welfare-to-work credit. The employer may elect to take the applicable credit by filing **Form 5884**, Work Opportunity Credit, or **Form 8861**, Welfare-to-Work Credit.

Note: *Do not use Form 8850 with respect to New York Liberty Zone business employees. Certification is not required for these employees. See **Form 8884,** New York Liberty Zone Business Employee Credit, for details.*

Who Should Complete and Sign the Form

The job applicant gives information to the employer on or before the day a job offer is made. This information is entered on Form 8850. Based on the applicant's information, the employer determines whether or not he or she believes the applicant is a member of a targeted group (as defined under **Members of Targeted Groups** on page 2) or a long-term family assistance recipient (as defined under **Welfare-to-Work Job Applicants** on page 2). If the employer believes the applicant is a member of a targeted group or a long-term family assistance recipient, the employer completes the rest of the form no later than the day the job offer is made. Both the job applicant and the employer must sign Form 8850 no later than the date for submitting the form to the SESA.

Instructions for Employer

When and Where To File

Do not file Form 8850 with the Internal Revenue Service. Instead, file it with the work opportunity tax credit (WOTC) coordinator for your SESA no later than the 21st day after the job applicant begins work for you. You may be able to file Form 8850 electronically. See Announcement 2002-44 for details. You can find Announcement 2002-44 on page 809 of Internal Revenue Bulletin 2002-17 at **www.irs.gov/pub/irs-irbs/ irb02-17.pdf**.

To get the name, address, phone and fax numbers, and e-mail address of the WOTC coordinator for your SESA, visit the Department of Labor Employment and Training Administration (ETA) web site at **www.ows.doleta.gov/employ/tax.asp**.

Additional Requirements for Certification

In addition to filing Form 8850, you must complete and send to your state's WOTC coordinator **either**:

- **ETA Form 9062,** Conditional Certification Form, if the job applicant received this form from a participating agency (e.g., the Jobs Corps) **or**
- **ETA Form 9061,** Individual Characteristics Form, if the job applicant did not receive a conditional certification.

You can get ETA Form 9061 from your local public employment service office, or you can download it from the ETA web site at **www.ows.doleta.gov**.

Recordkeeping

Keep copies of Forms 8850, along with any transmittal letters that you submit to your SESA, as long as they may be needed for the administration of the Internal Revenue Code provisions relating to the work opportunity credit and the welfare-to-work credit. Records that support these credits usually must be kept for 3 years from the date any income tax return claiming the credits is due or filed, whichever is later.

Cat. No. 24833J

Members of Targeted Groups

A job applicant may be certified as a member of a targeted group if he or she is described in one of the following groups.

1. Qualified IV-A recipient. A member of a family receiving assistance under a state plan approved under part A of title IV of the Social Security Act relating to Temporary Assistance for Needy Families (TANF). The assistance must be received for any 9 months during the 18-month period that ends on the hiring date.

2. Qualified veteran. A veteran who is a member of a family receiving assistance under the Food Stamp program for generally at least a 3-month period during the 15-month period ending on the hiring date. See section 51(d)(3). To be considered a **veteran**, the applicant must:

● Have served on active duty (not including training) in the Armed Forces of the United States for more than 180 days or have been discharged for a service-connected disability and

● Not have a period of active duty (not including training) of more than 90 days that ended during the 60-day period ending on the hiring date.

3. Qualified ex-felon. An ex-felon who:

● Has been convicted of a felony under any Federal or state law,

● Is hired not more than 1 year after the conviction or release from prison for that felony, and

● Is a member of a family that had income on an annual basis of 70% or less of the Bureau of Labor Statistics lower living standard during the 6 months preceding the earlier of the month the income determination occurs or the month in which the hiring date occurs.

4. High-risk youth. An individual who is at least 18 but not yet 25 on the hiring date and lives in an empowerment zone, enterprise community, or renewal community.

5. Vocational rehabilitation referral. An individual who has a physical or mental disability resulting in a substantial handicap to employment and who was referred to the employer upon completion of (or while receiving) rehabilitation services under a state plan of employment or a program approved by the Department of Veterans Affairs.

6. Summer youth employee. An individual who:

● Performs services for the employer between May 1 and September 15,

● Is age 16 but not yet age 18 on the hiring date (or if later, on May 1),

● Has never worked for the employer before, and

● Lives in an empowerment zone, enterprise community, or renewal community.

7. Food stamp recipient. An individual who:

● Is at least age 18 but not yet age 25 and

● Is a member of a family that—

a. Has received food stamps for the 6-month period ending on the hiring date or

b. Is no longer eligible for such assistance under section 6(o) of the Food Stamp Act of 1977, but the family received food stamps for at least 3 months of the 5-month period ending on the hiring date.

8. SSI recipient. An individual who is receiving supplemental security income benefits under title XVI of the Social Security Act (including benefits of the type described in section 1616 of the Social Security Act or section 212 of Public Law 93-66) for any month ending within the 60-day period ending on the hiring date.

Empowerment zones, enterprise communities, and renewal communities. For details about rural empowerment zone and enterprise communities, you can access **www.ezec.gov**, call 1-800-645-4712, or contact your SESA. For details on all empowerment zones, enterprise communities, and renewal communities, you can access **http://hud.esri.com/locateservices/ezec**. You can also call HUD at 1-800-998-9999 for details on renewal communities, urban empowerment zones, and urban enterprise communities.

Note: *Parts of Washington, DC, are treated as an empowerment zone. For details, see section 1400 and Notice 98-57, 1998-2 C.B. 671 (you can find Notice 98-57 on page 9 of Internal Revenue Bulletin 1998-47 at www.irs.gov/pub/irs-irbs/irb98-47.pdf). Also, there are no areas designated in Puerto Rico, Guam, or any U.S. possession.*

Welfare-to-Work Job Applicants

An individual may be certified as a long-term family assistance recipient if he or she is a member of a family that:

● Has received TANF payments for at least 18 consecutive months ending on the hiring date, **or**

● Receives TANF payments for any 18 months (whether or not consecutive) beginning after August 5, 1997, **and** the earliest 18-month period beginning after August 5, 1997, ended within the last 2 years, **or**

● Stopped being eligible for TANF payments because Federal or state law limits the maximum period such assistance is payable **and** the individual is hired not more than 2 years after such eligibility ended.

Department of Taxation and Finance and
Department of Labor-Unemployment Insurance Div Reg Sec
W A Harriman State Campus Bldg 12
Albany NY 12240-0339

NYS-100
(12/99)

New York State Employer Registration for Unemployment Insurance, Withholding, and Wage Reporting

For office use only: U.I.
Employer Registration No.

Return completed form (*type or print in ink*) to the address above, **or** fax to **(518) 485-8010**

Need Help? Call (518) 485-8057

PART A - Employer Information

1. Type (*check one*):
   ☐ Business (*complete parts A, B, D, and E*)
   ☐ Household Employer of Domestic Services (*complete parts A, C, D, and E-1*)

   ∗ If nonprofit IRC 501 (C) (3), agricultural, or governmental employer, **do not** complete this form. Phone (518) 485-8589 or write to the above address to request the applicable form.

2. Legal entity (*check one - do not complete if household employer*):
   ☐ Corporation (*includes Sub-Chapter S*)   ☐ Limited liability company
   ☐ Sole proprietorship   ☐ Limited liability partnership
   ☐ Partnership
   ☐ Other (please describe) _____

3. FEIN (*Fed. Id. no.*) ☐☐☐–☐☐☐☐☐☐☐

4. Telephone no. ( )

5. Fax no. ( )

6. Legal name _____

7. Trade name (*doing business as*), if any _____

PART B - Business Employer

1. Enter date of first operations in New York State..................... ☐☐☐☐☐☐ (*mmddyy*)

2. Enter the date of the first payroll from which you withheld or will withhold NYS Income Tax from your employees' pay......... ☐☐☐☐☐☐ (*mmddyy*)

3. Indicate the first calendar quarter and enter the year you paid (*or expect to pay*) total remuneration of **$300** or more. (*Remuneration is every form of compensation, including payments to employees or to corporate and Sub-Chapter S officers for services*) ....
   ☐ Jan 1 - Mar 31 **1**   ☐ Apr 1 - Jun 30 **2**   ☐ Jul 1 - Sep 30 **3**   ☐ Oct 1 - Dec 31 **4**   Tax Year ☐☐ Y Y

4. Total number of employees _____

5. Do persons work for you whom you do not consider employees? ☐ Yes ☐ No If *Yes*, explain the services performed and the reason you do not consider these persons employees. _____

6. Have you acquired the business of another employer liable for NYS Unemployment Insurance? ☐ Yes ☐ No If *Yes*, did you acquire ☐ All or ☐ Part? Date of acquisition ☐☐☐☐☐☐ (*mmddyy*) Enter previous owner information below:

   Business name and address _____

   Employer Registration No. _____   FEIN _____ ☐☐☐☐☐☐ (*mmddyy*)

7. Have you changed legal entity? ☐ Yes ☐ No. If *Yes*, enter the date of legal entity change...................
   Previous Employer Registration Number _____   Previous FEIN _____

PART C - Household Employer of Domestic Services

1. Indicate the first calendar quarter and enter the year you paid (*or expect to pay*) total cash wages of **$500** or more.
   ☐ Jan 1 - Mar 31 **1**   ☐ Apr 1 - Jun 30 **2**   ☐ Jul 1 - Sep 30 **3**   ☐ Oct 1 - Dec 31 **4**   Tax Year ☐☐ Y Y

2. Enter the total number of persons employed in your home _____

3. Will you withhold New York State income tax from these employees? ☐ Yes ☐ No

PART D - Address/Telephone Information

Please enter your mailing and/or physical location address, as well as the physical location of your books/records. If you wish to provide us with **ADDITIONAL** addresses to direct specific forms, please indicate below.

1. **MAILING ADDRESS:** This is **YOUR** business mailing address (*NOT your agent or paid preparer*) where all your Unemployment Insurance/Withholding Tax mail will be directed unless otherwise indicated.
   *If all your Unemployment Insurance/Withholding Tax mail (*including Forms NYS-45 and NYS-1*) is to be received at this mailing address, **do not** complete sections 4 through 6.

Street or PO Box		
City	State	ZIP Code

2. **PHYSICAL ADDRESS:** This is the **ACTUAL** location of your business if different from the mailing address, or if your mailing address is a P.O. Box. If you have more than one location, list your primary location.

Street		
City	State	ZIP Code

3. **BOOKS/RECORDS ADDRESS:** This is the physical location where your **BOOKS/RECORDS** can be found.

   ☐ Same as no. 1   ☐ Same as no. 2

   ☐ Other - please complete

c/o		
Street		
City	State	ZIP Code

ADDITIONAL ADDRESSES

4. **AGENT ADDRESS (*C/O*):** This is the address of your **AGENT,** where all your Unemployment Insurance mail will be directed unless other addresses have been provided for the mailing of specific forms in sections 5 and/or 6.
   Note: All withholding tax mail (*except quarterly return NYS-45 and Return of Tax Withheld coupon NYS-1*) must be sent to your mailing address (*no. 1*). However, the quarterly return NYS-45 and coupon NYS-1 may be directed to a separate address if no. 5 below is completed.

c/o		
Street or PO Box		
City	State	ZIP Code
Telephone ( )		

5. **QUARTERLY COMBINED WITHHOLDING, WAGE REPORTING AND UNEMPLOYMENT INSURANCE RETURN (*Form NYS-45*) AND RETURN OF TAX WITHHELD (*Form NYS-1*) ADDRESS:** If completed, this is the address to which your NYS-45 and NYS-1 will be directed.

   ☐ Same as no. 4   ☐ Other - please complete

c/o		
Street or PO Box		
City	State	ZIP Code

6. **NOTICE OF ENTITLEMENT AND POTENTIAL CHARGES ADDRESS:** If completed, this is the address to which the Notice of Entitlement and Potential Charges will be mailed. This form is mailed each time a former employee files a claim for Unemployment Insurance benefits. Please attach a separate sheet if you need to indicate different Notice of Entitlement and Potential Charges addresses for more than one physical location.

c/o		
Street or PO Box		
City	State	ZIP Code

PART E - Business Information

1. Complete the following for **sole proprietor, household employer of domestic services, all partners** (*including partners of LLP or RLLP*), all **members** (*of LLC or PLLC*), and all **corporate officers**, whether or not remuneration is received or services are performed in New York State.

Name	Social Security no.	Title	Residence Address

Enter legal name

For office
use only

PART E- Business Information (*Continued*)

2. For **each** of your establishments in New York State, answer A-E below. Use a separate sheet for each establishment.

A. Location _____
   No. and Street   City or Town   County   ZIP Code

B. Approximately how many persons do you employ there?_____

C. Check the principal activity at the above location

☐ Manufacturing   ☐ Transportation   ☐ Scientific/professional & technical services
☐ Wholesale trade   ☐ Computer services   ☐ Finance and insurance
☐ Retail trade   ☐ Educational services   ☐ Arts, entertainment, & recreation
☐ Construction   ☐ Health & social assistance   ☐ Food service, drinking, & accommodations
☐ Warehousing   ☐ Real estate   ☐ Corporate, subsidiary managing office
☐ Other (*Please specify*) _____

D. If you are primarily engaged in manufacturing, complete the following:

Principal Products Produced   Percent of Total Sales Value   Principal Raw Materials Used

_____   _____   _____

E. If your principal activity is not manufacturing, indicate products sold or services rendered:

Type of Establishment   Principal Product Sold or   Percent of Total Revenue
                               Service Rendered

_____   _____   _____

I affirm that I have read the above questions and that the answers provided are true to the best of my knowledge and belief.

_____   Official Position   Date
Signature of Officer, Partner,
Proprietor, Member or Individual

Instructions

General Information:
- If you are a business employer or a household employer of domestic services, complete and return Form NYS-100.
- If you are a nonprofit, agricultural, or governmental employer, **do not** complete Form NYS-100. Phone (518) 485-8589 or write to the address on page one of this form to request information and necessary forms.
- Voluntary Coverage for U.I. purposes - if you are not liable for UI tax but want to provide voluntary coverage for employees, phone (518) 457-2635.

Part - A

Item 3   Enter your nine digit Federal Identification Number. This number is used to certify your payments to the IRS under the Federal Unemployment Tax Act.

Item 6-7 Enter the legal name of the employer and the trade name, firm name, registered name, etc., if any, used for business purposes. If the employer is a partnership, enter the full name of each partner. If the employer is a corporation, enter the corporate name shown in its Certificate of Incorporation or other official document. In the case of an estate of a decedent, insolvent, incompetent, etc., enter the name of the estate, and the name of the administrator or other fiduciary.

Part - B

Item 2   Any person or organization qualifying as an employer on the basis of instructions contained in federal Circular E that maintains an office or transacts business in New York State is an employer for New York State withholding tax purposes and must withhold from compensation paid to its employees.

Item 3   Enter the first calendar quarter in which you paid (*or expect to pay*) total remuneration of $300 or more. Do not go back beyond 3 years from January of the current year. Remuneration includes compensation such as: salary, cash wages, commissions, bonuses, payments to corporate officers for services rendered regardless of their stock ownership and without regard to how such payments are treated under Sub-Chapter S of the IRS Code or any other tax law, reasonable money value of board, rent, housing, lodging, or any similar advantage received, and the value of tips or other gratuities received from persons other than the employer. Note: **do not** include compensation paid to: daytime elementary or secondary students working after school or during vacation periods; the spouse or child (*under 21*) of an individual owner; children under age 14; employees who perform no services in New York State; or employees whose services are considered agricultural employment. If you have employees who work both within and outside NY State, please request a ruling from the Liability and Determination Section of the Department of Labor. Phone (518) 457-2635 for information.

Item 5   Answer *Yes*, if there are persons working for you whom you do not consider to be your employees. Do not include those described in Part B instructions for Item 3 which follow the Note. Attach a separate sheet if additional lines are required to accommodate your explanation.

Item 6   Answer *Yes*, if one or more of the following are true: you employed substantially the same employees as the previous owner; you continued or resumed the business of the previous owner at the same or another location; you assumed the previous owner's obligations; and/or you acquired the previous owner's good will.

Instructions (*Continued*)

Item 7   Answer *Yes,* if legal entity has changed. Types of legal entity appear in Part A, Item 2 of this form. A New York State Employer Registration Number is assigned to an employer who is liable to pay Unemployment Insurance tax. It is used to identify an individual account for recording tax payments due and Unemployment Insurance benefits paid.

Part C

Item 1   Enter the first calendar quarter and year in which you paid (*or expect to pay*) total cash wages of $500 or more to your household employees. Do not go back beyond 3 years from January of the current year. **Do not** include as cash wages payments to: household employees for carfare or other travel expenses; your spouse or your child under 21 years of age; elementary or secondary school students who attend school in the daytime; children under 14 years of age; babysitters under age 18, or casual laborers under age 21.

Item 3   Withholding of New York State, New York City or Yonkers income tax from household employees performing domestic services is voluntary. Answer *Yes* to this question only if there is a voluntary agreement in effect between you and the domestic employee to withhold New York State, New York City, or Yonkers income tax.

Part E

Item 2   Describe (1) principal activity or (2) product which produces greatest gross sales value. Examples:
(C - E)

Manufacturing	State type of establishment (*e.g., sawmill, vegetable cannery, printing and publishing*). Show principal products, percent of total sales value, and principal raw materials used. Specify principal products (*e.g., upholstered household furniture, ladies' sweaters hand knit from yarn*).
Trade	State principal product distributed. If sold to businesses (*wholesale*) or general public (*retail*), indicate which is primary.
Construction	Specify general or special trade contractor and show usual type of work (*e.g., general contractor-apartment houses or trade contractor-plumbing*).
Warehousing	State type of storage (*e.g., refrigerated, general, self-storage units for the public*).
Transportation	Includes establishments in railroading; local and suburban transit; interurban highway passenger transportation; motor freight transportation; water transportation (*deep sea foreign transportation, lighterage, etc.*); transportation by air, etc. Be specific.
Computer services	State primary activity (*e.g., computer analysis and design, custom programming, Internet access or data processing, etc.*).
Educational services	Includes all schools (*e.g., elementary, colleges, universities, vocational schools*). Be specific in Section E.
Health & social services	Includes health referral agencies, operation of clinics, hospital or homes. Be specific.
Real estate	Include owners/operators of real estate and agents. If owner/operator, specify type of property (*e.g., commercial or residential building*).
Scientific/professional & technical services	Includes lawyers, accountants, business consultants (*contractors*), architects, engineers, doctors, surveyors, etc. Be specific in Section E.
Finance & insurance	Includes bank and trust companies, credit agencies other than banks, insurance carriers. State if national or commercial banks, charter, and if accepting deposits from the general public. Insurance underwriters are classified by type of insurance (*e.g., life, accident and health, etc*).
Arts, entertainment & recreation	Includes theater operation, entertainers, commercial parks, casinos, professional athletes, sports recreational facilities, etc. Be specific.
Food service, drinking & accommodations	State type of service rendered (*e.g., operation of hotel, sports camp, restaurant [full or limited service], taverns or catering service*). Be specific.
Corporate, subsidiary managing office	Includes administrative, management consultant, and human resource consultants. Be specific.
Other activities	Indicate type of activity not covered by above paragraphs (*e.g., agriculture, forestry, fisheries, mining, motion picture or television production, etc*).

INDEX